Small Business Made Simple

Small
Business
Accounting
Simplified

Small Business Made Simple

Small Business Accounting Simplified

DANIEL SITARZ, ATTORNEY-AT-LAW

Nova Publishing Company
Small Business and Consumer Legal Books
Carbondale Illinois

ISBN 978-1-892949-50-9   Book ($29.95)

Cataloging-in-Publication Data
  Sitarz, Dan, 1948-
    Small Business Accounting Simplified / by Daniel Sitarz. -- 5th ed.
    p. cm. -- (Small business made simple). Includes index.
    ISBN 978-1-892949-50-9   Book ($29.95).
   1. Small business--Accounting. I. Title. II. Series.
   HF5371.S58 2010   651'.29   QBI01-201307
   Originally titled *Simplified Small Business Accounting*

Nova Publishing Company is dedicated to providing up-to-date and accurate legal and business information to the public. All Nova publications are periodically revised to contain the latest available legal and business information.

5th Edition, 1st Printing	February, 2010	2nd Edition; 3rd Printing	December, 2000
4th Edition, 3rd Printing	January, 2008	2nd Edition; 2nd Printing	December, 1999
4th Edition, 2nd Printing	June, 2007	2nd Edition; 1st Printing	December, 1998
4th Edition, 1st Printing	October, 2006	1st Edition; 3rd Printing	May, 1997
3rd Edition; 3rd Printing	July, 2004	1st Edition; 2nd Printing	February, 1996
3rd Edition; 2nd Printing	April, 2003	1st Edition; 1st Printing	October, 1995
3rd Edition; 1st Printing	October, 2002		

This publication is designed to provide accurate and authoritative information in regard to the subject matter covered. It is sold with the understanding that the publisher and author are not engaged in rendering legal, accounting, or other professional services. If legal advice or other expert assistance is required, the services of a competent professional person should be sought.
                 —From a Declaration of Principles jointly adopted by a Committee of
                      the American Bar Association and a Committee of Publishers

DISCLAIMER

Because of possible unanticipated changes in governing statutes and case law relating to the application of any information contained in this book, the author, publisher, and any and all persons or entities involved in any way in the preparation, publication, sale, or distribution of this book disclaim all responsibility for the legal effects or consequences of any document prepared or action taken in reliance upon information contained in this book. No representations, either express or implied, are made or given regarding the legal consequences of the use of any information contained in this book. Purchasers and persons intending to use this book for the preparation of any legal documents are advised to check specifically on the current applicable laws in any jurisdiction in which they intend the documents to be effective.

Nova Publishing Company Green Business Policies

Nova Publishing Company takes seriously the impact of book publishing on the Earth and its resources. Nova Publishing Company is committed to protecting the environment and to the responsible use of natural resources. As a book publisher, with paper as a core part of our business, we are very concerned about the future of the world's remaining endangered forests and the environmental impacts of paper production. We are committed to implementing policies that will support the preservation of endangered forests globally and to advancing 'best practices' within the book and paper industries. Nova Publishing Company is committed to preserving ancient forests and natural resources. Our company's policy is to print all of our books on Forest Stewardship Council certified 100%- recycled paper, with 100% post-consumer waste content, de-inked in a chlorine-free process. In addition, all Nova Publishing Company books are printed using soy-based inks. As a result of these environmental policies, Nova Publishing has saved hundreds of thousands of gallons of water, hundreds of thousands of kilowatts of electricity, thousand of pounds of pollution and carbon dioxide, and thousands of trees that would otherwise have been used in the traditional manner of publishing its books. Nova Publishing Company is very proud to be one of the first members of the Green Press Initiative, a nonprofit program dedicated to supporting publishers in their efforts to reduce their use of fiber obtained from endangered forests. Nova Publishing Company is also proud to be an initial signatory on the Book Industry Treatise on Responsible Paper Use (see: www.greenpressinitiative.org). In addition, Nova Publishing Company uses all compact fluorescent lighting; recycles all office paper products, aluminum and plastic beverage containers, and printer cartridges; uses 100% post-consumer fiber, process-chlorine-free, acid-free paper for 95% of in-house paper use; and, when possible, uses electronic equipment that is EPA Energy Star-certified. Nova's freight shipments are coordinated to minimize energy use whenever possible. Finally, all carbon emissions from Nova Publishing Company office energy use are offset by the purchase of wind-energy credits that are used to subsidize the building of wind turbines on the Rosebud Sioux Reservation in South Dakota (see www.nativeenergy.com). We strongly encourage other publishers and all partners in publishing supply chains to adopt similar policies.

Nova Publishing Company
Small Business and Consumer Legal Books and Software
1103 West College Street
Carbondale, IL 62901
Tech support: (800) 748-1175
www.novapublishing.com

Distributed by:
National Book Network
4501 Forbes Blvd., #200
Lanham, MD 20706
Orders: (800) 462-6420

Table of Contents

List of Forms

The following forms are all included in this book. In addition, all forms are provided on the CD as computer-fillable PDF forms with the exception of the various checklists. Please also note that the IRS forms are **not** included on the CD.

CHAPTER 3: Simplified Accounting System
  Financial Recordkeeping Checklist
CHAPTER 4: Business Chart of Accounts
  Income Chart of Accounts
  Expense Chart of Accounts
  Balance Sheet Chart of Accounts
  Chart of Accounts
CHAPTER 5: Business Bank Accounts and Petty Cash Fund
  Check Register
  Monthly Bank Statement Reconciliation
  Petty Cash Register
  Bank Account Checklist
  Petty Cash Fund Checklist
CHAPTER 6: Tracking Business Assets
  Current Asset Account Record
  Physical Inventory Record
  Periodic Inventory Record
  Perpetual Inventory Record
  Cost of Goods Sold Report
  Fixed Asset Account Record
  Business Assets Checklist
CHAPTER 7: Tracking Business Debts
  Accounts Payable Record
  Individual Accounts Payable Record
  Long-Term Debt Record
  Business Debts Checklist
CHAPTER 8: Tracking Business Expenses
  Daily Expense Record
  Weekly Expense Record
  Monthly Expense Summary
  Annual Expense Summary
  Weekly Travel Expense Record
  Monthly Travel Expense Record
  Annual Travel Expense Summary
  Weekly Auto Expense Record
  Monthly Auto Expense Record
  Annual Auto Expense Summary
  Weekly Meals and Entertainment Expense Record

U.S. Self-Employment Tax Return: IRS Form 1040-SS

Expenses for Business Use of Your Home: IRS Form 8829

U.S. Return of Partnership Income: IRS Form 1065

Partner's Share of Income, Credits, Deductions, etc.: IRS Form 1065 (Schedule K-1)

U.S. Corporation Income Tax Return: IRS Form 1120

U.S. Income Tax Return for an S-Corporation: IRS Form 1120-S

Shareholder's Share of Income, Credits, Deductions, etc.: IRS Form 1120-S (Schedule K-1)

Estimated Tax for Corporations: IRS Form 1120-W (Worksheet)

Election by a Small Business Corporation: IRS Form 2553

Entity Classification Election: IRS Form 8832

Employer's Annual Federal Unemployment (FUTA) Tax Return: IRS Form 940

State Unemployment Tax Agencies

Employer's Quarterly Federal Tax Return: IRS Form 941

Annual Summary and Transmittal of U.S. Information Returns: IRS Form 1096

Miscellaneous Income: IRS Form 1099

Wage and Tax Statement: IRS Form W-2

Transmittal of Wage and Tax Statements: IRS Form W-3

Employee's Withholding Allowance Certificate: IRS Form W-4

Employee's Withholding Allowance Certificate: IRS Form W-4 (Worksheet)

Federal Tax Deposit Coupon: IRS Form 8109-B

IMPORTANT NOTE:

The U.S. IRS Tax Forms included in this book on pages 211–261 are provided for informational purposes only and should not be reproduced or photocopied for filing purposes by taxpayers. Additionally, tax forms are subject to change at any time to comply with everchanging tax laws. For filing purposes, taxpayers should use the most current forms available. Any of the IRS tax forms included in this book may be obtained, free of charge, by calling 1-800-TAXFORM (1-800-829-3676). Be sure to order using the IRS publication number. You can also access forms and instructions on the web at www.irs.gov and go to the Forms and Publications page. Note that some downloaded forms are not acceptable for filing and must be ordered via mail. Check the FAQ's on the IRS publications website for current IRS restrictions. Please also see page 211 of this book for more information.

Chapter 1

Using Small Business Accounting Simplified

Keeping accurate and clear business financial records can, for many business owners, be the most difficult part of running a business. For most business owners, understanding those records is, at best, a struggle. And yet maintaining a set of clear and understandable financial records is perhaps the single most important factor that separates successful businesses from those that fail. The purpose of this book is to provide the small business owner with a clear, concise, and easily-understood system for setting up a financial recordkeeping system, keeping the books for a business, and, perhaps most importantly, actually understanding those records.

Modern business practices have tended to complicate many areas of business when, in many cases, simplification is what most business owners need. In law, management, and accounting, many important business functions have been obscured from their owners by intricate systems and complex terminology. Business owners must then turn the handling of these affairs over to specialized professionals in a particular field. The result, in many cases, is that business owners lose crucial understanding of those portions of their business. With this loss of understanding comes the eventual and almost inevitable loss of control.

This is particularly true for small business owners and their financial records. It is absolutely vital that small emerging business owners intimately understand their financial position. Daily decisions must be made that can make or break a fledgling business. If the financial records of a small business are delegated to an outside accountant or bookkeeper, it is often difficult, if not impossible, for a novice business owner to understand the current financial position of the business on a day-to-day basis. Critical business decisions are then made on the basis of incomplete or often unknown financial information.

The financial recordkeeping system presented here seeks to remedy this situation. The basic aspects of the accounting system outlined in this book have been used successfully by millions of businesses in the past. The recordkeeping forms in this book have been developed to make accuracy, clarity, and ease-of-use the primary objectives. The system presented in this book is designed to be set up and initially used by the business owners themselves. This will insure that the system is both thoroughly understood by the owner and provides the type of information that the owner actually wants. As a business grows and becomes more complex, and a business owner becomes more comfortable with financial recordkeeping, other more sophisticated and complex accounting systems may become appropriate.

Chapter 2 outlines the basic fundamentals of business financial recordkeeping and presents some basic terminology. Chapter 3 outlines how the financial recordkeeping system in this book operates. Chapter 4 discusses setting up a chart of accounts for your business. Setting up the business bank account and petty cash fund is the topic of Chapter 5. Chapter 6 shows how to track business assets. Chapter 7 does the same for business debts. Chapter 8 explains business expense records in detail. Chapter 9 does the same for income records. The details of payroll are explained and clarified in Chapter 10. Chapter 11 shows how to prepare profit and loss statements with the information relating to income and expenses. Chapter 12 explains how to prepare a balance sheet for your business. Chapter 13 explains how to analyze these two basic financial statements. Chapter 14 presents schedules of financial recordkeeping and the mechanics of how to actually use the forms and records in practice. Finally, Chapter 15 explains which tax forms are necessary for businesses, presents tax filing schedules, and provides a sample of each appropriate form. Throughout each chapter, the actual recordkeeping forms are presented, along with clear instructions on how to fill them in. A Glossary of Accounting Terms is provided at the end of this book to explain any unfamiliar accounting terms you might encounter.

Although there are dozens of financial record forms provided, not all of them are appropriate for all businesses. As each chapter is read, the reader is prompted to assess the needs of their individual business and decide which of the forms would be most appropriate for their needs. Checklists are provided for most chapters for quick review of the essential elements. Finally, if, after reading through this book, you are unable to understand how to set up the books for your company, you are urged to seek the assistance of a competent accounting professional. Although the majority of small businesses can successfully use the system that is outlined in this book, a few types of business finances are not appropriate to being handled by this system. Other types of more complex accounting systems may be more appropriate if the proposed business is extremely complex, is involved at all in securities or other interstate financial transactions, or expects to handle very large amounts of daily transactions. If there is any question that the system outlined will not be appropriate, please consult an accounting professional. Please note that the forms in this book are not designed to be torn out of this book (particularly if you are reading a library copy of this book!)

The purpose of this book is to allow small business owners to have the tools they will need to set up a clear recordkeeping system and understand their financial situation. As with any tools, there are dangers if they are misused. Please read all of the instructions carefully and be certain that you understand the concepts before using the financial recordkeeping system that is presented.

Installation Instructions for the Forms-on-CD

Quick-Start Installation for PCs

1. Insert the enclosed CD in your computer.
2. The installation program will start automatically. Follow the onscreen dialogue and make your appropriate choices.
3. If the CD installation does not start automatically, click on START, then RUN, then BROWSE, and select your CD drive, and then select the file "Install.exe." Finally, click OK to run the installation program.
4. During the installation program, you will be prompted as to whether or not you wish to install the Adobe Acrobat Reader® program. If you do not already have the Adobe Acrobat Reader® program installed on your hard drive, you will need to select the full installation that will install this program to your computer.

Installation Instructions for MACs®

1. Insert the enclosed CD in your computer.
2. Copy the folder "Forms for Macs" to your hard drive. All of the PDF forms are included in this folder.
3. If you do not already have the Adobe Acrobat Reader® program installed on your hard drive, you will need to download the version of this software that is appropriate for you particular MAC operating system from www.adobe.com. Note: The latest versions of the MAC operating system (OS-X) has PDF capabilities built into it.

Instructions for Using Forms-on-CD

All of the forms which are included in this book have been provided on the Forms-on-CD for your use if you have access to a computer. If you have completed the Forms-on-CD installation program, all of the forms will have been copied to your computer's hard drive. By default, these files are installed in the C:\Small Business Accounting Simplified\Forms folder which is created by the installation program. (Note for MAC users: see instructions above). Opening the Forms folder will provide you with access to folders for each of the topics corresponding to chapters in the book.

PDF forms may be filled in on your computer screen and printed out on any printer. This particular format provides the most widely-used cross-platform format for accessing computer files. Files in this format may be opened as images on your computer and printed out on any printer. The files in Adobe PDF format all have the file extension: .pdf. Although this format provides the easiest method for completing the forms, the forms in this format can not be altered (other than to fill in the information required on the blanks provided). To access the PDF forms, please see below.

To Access Adobe PDF Forms

1. You must have already installed the Adobe Acrobat Reader® program to your computer's hard drive. This program is installed automatically by the installation program. (MAC users will need to install this program via www.adobe.com).

2. On your computer's desktop, you will find a shortcut icon labeled "Acrobat Reader®" Using your mouse, left double click on this icon. This will open the Acrobat Reader® program. When the Acrobat Reader® program is opened for the first time, you will need to accept the Licensing Agreement from Adobe in order to use this program. Click "Accept" when given the option to accept or decline the Agreement.

3. Once the Acrobat Reader® program is open on your computer, click on FILE (in the upper left-hand corner of the upper taskbar). Then click on OPEN in the drop down menu. Depending on which version of Windows or other operating system you are using, a box will open which will allow you to access files on your computer's hard drive. The files for Small Business Accounting are located on your computer's "C" drive, under the folder "Small Business Accounting Simplified." In this folder, you will find a subfolder "Forms." (Note: if you installed the forms folder on a different drive, access the forms on that particular drive).

4. If you desire to work with one of the forms, you should then left double-click your mouse on the sub-folder: "Forms." Left double click your mouse on the PDF forms folder and a list of the PDF forms for that topic should appear. Left double click your mouse on the form of your choice. This will open the appropriate form within the Adobe Acrobat Reader® program.

To Fill in Forms in the Adobe Acrobat Reader® Program

1. Once you have opened the appropriate form in the Acrobat Reader® program, filling in the form is a simple process. A 'hand tool' icon will be your cursor in the Acrobat Reader® program. Move the 'hand tool' cursor to the first blank space that will need to be completed on the form. A vertical line or "I-beam" should appear at the beginning of the first space on a form that you will need to fill in. You may then begin to type the necessary information in the space provided. When you have filled in the first blank space, hit the TAB key on your keyboard. This will move the 'hand' cursor to the next space which must be filled in. Please note that some of the spaces in the forms must be completed by hand, specifically the signature blanks. NOTE: On some computers and with some versions of Adobe Reader®, you may need to make a change to the Preferences in order for the 'tabbing' feature to work correctly with the forms. If the TAB key does not move the cursor to the next logical box on the forms, you should click on EDIT, then PREFERENCES, then select ACCESSIBILITY in the list to the left. On this screen, in the box titles "Tab Order", uncheck the box that states: "Use Document Structure for Tab order when no explicit Tab order is specified." Then click OK, and return to the form. The tab order should now work correctly, moving the cursor to the next logical box.

2. Move through the form, completing each required space, and hitting TAB to move to the next space to be filled in. For information on the information required for each blank on the forms, please read the instructions in this book. When you have completed all of the fill-ins, you may print out the form on your computer's printer. (Please note: hitting TAB after the last fill-in will return you to the first page of the form.)

3. When the form is complete, you may print out the completed form and you may save the completed form. If you wish to save the completed form, you should rename the form so that your hard drive will retain an unaltered original version of the form.

Technical Support

Nova Publishing will provide technical support for installing the provided software. Please also note that Nova Publishing Company cannot provide legal advice regarding the effect or use of the forms on this software. For questions about installing the Forms-on-CD, you may call Nova Technical Support at 1-800-748-1175.

In addition, Nova cannot provide technical support for the use of the Adobe Acrobat Reader®. For any questions relating to Adobe Acrobat Reader®, please access Adobe Technical Support at www.adobe.com/support/main.html or you may search for assistance in the HELP area of Adobe Acrobat Reader® (located in approximately the center of the top line of the program's desktop).

Chapter 2

Understanding Business Financial Recordkeeping

Each year, thousands of small businesses fail because their owners have lost control of their finances. Many of these failures are brought on by the inability of the business owners to understand the complex accounting processes and systems that have become relatively standard in modern business. Accounting and bookkeeping have, in most businesses, been removed from the direct control and, therefore, understanding of the business owners themselves. If business owners cannot understand the financial situation of their own businesses, they have little chance of succeeding. The purpose of this book is to present a simplified system of business recordkeeping that small business owners themselves can use to track their company's financial situation.

The purpose of any business financial recordkeeping system is to provide a clear vision of the relative health of the business, both on a day-to-day basis and periodically. Business owners themselves need to know whether they are making a profit, why they are making a profit, which parts of the business are profitable and which are not. This information is only available if the business owner has a clear and straightforward recordkeeping system. Business owners also need to be able to produce accurate financial statements for income tax purposes, for loan proposals, and for the purpose of selling the business. Clear, understandable, and accurate business records are vital to the success of any small business. In order to design a good recordkeeping system for a particular business, an understanding of certain fundamental ideas of accounting is necessary. For those unfamiliar with the terms and concepts of accounting, grasping these basic ideas may be the most difficult part of accounting, even simplified accounting.

Recordkeeping Terminology

First, let's get some of the terminology clarified. *Accounting* is the design of the recordkeeping system that a business uses and the preparation and interpretation of reports based on the information that is gathered and put into the system. *Bookkeeping* is the actual input of the financial information into the recordkeeping system. In this book, these two activities will be combined to allow the small business owner to understand how the records are organized, how to keep the records, and how to prepare and interpret summarized reports of the records.

The purpose of any business recordkeeping system is to allow the business owner to easily understand and use the information gathered. Certain accounting principles and terms have been adopted as standard over the years to make it easier to understand a wide range of business transactions. In order to understand what a recordkeeping system is trying to accomplish, it is necessary to define some of the standard ways of looking at a business. There are two standard reports which are the main sources of business financial information and which will be the focus of this book: the *balance sheet* and the *profit and loss statement.*

The Balance Sheet

The purpose of the balance sheet is to look at what the business owns and owes on a specific date. By seeing what a business owns and owes, anyone looking at a balance sheet can tell the relative financial position of the business at that point in time. If the business owns more than it owes, it is in good shape financially. On the other hand, if it owes more than it owns, the business may be in trouble. The balance sheet is the universal financial document used to view this aspect of a business. It provides this information by laying out the value of the assets and the liabilities of a business. One of the most critical financial tasks that a small business owner must confront is keeping track of what the business owns and owes. Before the business buys or sells anything or makes a profit or loss, the business must have some assets.

The *assets* of a business are anything that the business owns. These can be cash, on hand or in a bank account; they can be personal property, like office equipment, vehicles, tools, or supplies; they can be inventory, or material which will be sold to customers; they can be real estate, buildings and land; and they can be money that is owed to the business. Money that is owed to a business is called its *accounts receivable*, basically the money that the business hopes to eventually receive. The total of all of these things which a business owns are the business's assets.

The *liabilities* of a business are anything that the business owes to others. These consist of long-term debts, such as a mortgage on real estate or a long-term loan. It also consists of any short-term debts, such as money owed for supplies or taxes. Money that a business owes to others is called its *accounts payable*, basically the money which the business hopes to eventually pay. In addition to money owed to others, the *equity* of a business is also considered a liability. The equity of a business is the value of the ownership of the business. It is the value that would be left over if all of the debts of the business were paid off. If it is a partnership or a sole proprietorship, the business equity is referred to a the *net worth* of the business. If the business is a corporation, the owner's equity is called the *capital surplus* or *retained capital*. All of the debts of a business and its equity are together referred to as the business's liabilities.

The basic relationship between the assets and liabilities can be shown in a simple equation:

Assets = Liabilities

This simple equation is the basis of business accounting. When the books of a business are said to *balance*, it is this equation which is in balance: the assets of a business must equal the liabilities of a business. Since the liabilities of a business consists of both equity and debts, the equation can be expanded to read:

Assets = Debts + Equity

Rearranging the equation can provide a simple explanation of how to arrive at the value of a business to the owner, or its equity:

Equity = Assets – Debts

A basic tenet of recordkeeping is that both sides of this financial equation must always be equal. The formal statement of the assets and liabilities of a specific business on a specific date is called a *balance sheet*. A balance sheet is usually prepared on the last day of a month, quarter, or year. A balance sheet simply lists the amounts of the business assets and liabilities in a standardized format.

On a balance sheet, the assets of a business are generally broken down into two groups: *current assets* and *fixed assets*. Current assets consist of cash, accounts receivable (remember, money which the business intends to receive; basically, bills owed to the business); and inventory. Current assets are generally considered anything that could be converted into cash within one year. Fixed assets are more permanent-type assets and include vehicles, equipment, machinery, land, and buildings owned by the business.

The liabilities of a business are broken down into three groups: *current liabilities, long-term liabilities*, and *owner's equity*. Current liabilities are short-term debts, generally those that a business must pay off within one year. This includes accounts payable (remember, money that the business intends to pay; basically, bills the business owes), and taxes that are due. Long-term liabilities are long-term debts such as mortgages or long-term business loans. Owner's equity is whatever is left after debts are deducted from assets. Thus the owner's equity is what the owner would have left after all of the debts of the business are paid off. Owner's equity is the figure that is adjusted to make the equation of assets and liabilities balance.

Let's look at a simple example. Later on in the following chapters, we'll look at a more complicated example. But for now let's look at a basic sales business.

Smith's Gourmet Foods has the following assets: Smith has $500.00 in a bank account, is owed $70.00 by customers who pay for their food monthly, has $200.00 worth of food supplies, and owns food preparation equipment worth $1,300.00.

These are the assets of Smith's Gourmet Foods and they are shown on a balance sheet as follows:

Cash	*$ 500.00*
+ Accounts owed to it	*$ 70.00*
+ Inventory	*$ 200.00*
+ Equipment	*$ 1,300.00*
= Total Assets	*$ 2,070.00*

Smith also has owes the following debts: $100.00 owed to the supplier of the food, $200.00 owed to the person from whom she bought the food equipment, and $100.00 owed to the state for sales taxes that have been collected on food sales. Thus, the debts of Smith's Gourmet Foods are shown as follows:

Accounts it owes	*$ 100.00*
+ Loans it owes	*$ 200.00*
+ Taxes it owes	*$ 100.00*
= Total Debts	*$ 400.00*

To find what Smith's equity in this business is, we need to subtract the amount of the debts from the amount of the assets. Remember: Assets – debts = equity. Thus, the owner's equity in Smith's Gourmet Foods is as follows:

Total Assets	*$ 2,070.00*
– Total Debts	*$ 400.00*
= Owner's Equity	*$ 1,670.00*

That's it. The business of Smith's Gourmet Foods has a net worth of $1,670.00. If Smith paid off all of the debts of the business, there would be $1,670.00 left. This basic method is used to determine the net worth of businesses worldwide, from the smallest to the largest. Assets = debts + equity or Assets – debts = equity. Remember, both sides of the equation always have to be equal. We'll get into more detail regarding balance sheets in Chapter 12.

The Profit and Loss Statement

The other main business report is called the *profit and loss statement*. This report is a summary of the income and expenses of the business during a certain period. Profit and loss statements are generally prepared monthly, quarterly, or annually, depending on the type of business. Profit and loss statements are sometimes referred to as *income statements* or as *operating statements*.

Generally, *income* for a business is any money that it has received or will receive during a certain period. *Expenses* are any money that the business has paid or will pay out during a certain period. Simply put, if it has more income than expenses during a certain period, it has made a profit. If it has more expenses than income, then the business has a loss for that period of time.

Income can be broken down into two basic types: service income and sales income. The difference between the two types of income lies in the need to consider inventory costs. Service income is income derived from performing a service for someone (cutting hair, for example). Sales income is revenue derived from selling a product of some type. With service income, the profit can be determined simply by deducting the expenses that are associated with making the income. With sales income, however, in addition to deducting the expenses of making the income, the cost of the product that was sold must also be taken into account. This is done through inventory costs. Thus, for sales income, the actual income from selling a product is actually the sales income minus the cost of the product to the seller. This inventory cost is referred to as the *cost of goods sold*.

A profit and loss statement begins with a sale. Back to the food business. Smith had the following transactions during the month of July: $250.00 worth of food was sold, the wholesale cost of the food that was sold was $50.00, the cost of napkins, condiments, other supplies, and rent amounted to $100.00, and interest payments on the equipment loan were $50.00. Thus, Smith's profit and loss statement would be prepared as follows:

Gross sales income	**$ 250.00**
– Cost of food	**$ 50.00**
= Net sales income	**$ 200.00**
Operating Expenses	**$ 100.00**
+ Interest payments	**$ 50.00**
= Net expenses	**$ 150.00**

Thus, for the month of July, Smith's business performed as follows:

Net sales income	**$ 200.00**
– Net expenses	**$ 150.00**
= Net profit	**$ 50.00**

Again, this simple set-up reflects the basics of profit and loss statements for all types of businesses, no matter their size. For a pure service business, with no inventory of any type sold to customers: Income – expenses = net profit. For a sales-type business or a sales/service-combined business: Income – cost of goods sold – expenses = profit.

These two types of summary reports, the balance sheet and the profit and loss statement are the basic tools for understanding the financial health of any business. The figures on them can be used for many purposes to understand the operations of a business. The balance sheet shows what proportion of a business's assets are actually owned by the business owner and what proportion is owned by or owed to someone else.

Looking at Smith's balance sheet, we can see that the owner's equity is $1,670.00 of assets of $2,070.00. Thus, we can see that the owner has over 80 percent ownership of the business, a very healthy situation. There are numerous ways to analyze the figures on these two financial statements. Understanding what these figures mean and how they represent the health of a business are keys to keeping control of a business's finances. Chapter 13 explains how to analyze these statements in further detail.

Accounting Methods

There are a few more items that must be understood regarding financial recordkeeping. First is the method for recording the records. There are two basic methods for measuring transactions: the *cash method* and the *accrual method*. Cash method accounting is a system that records income when it is received and records expenses when they are paid. Beginning in 2000, IRS regulations allow the cash method of accounting for a business with a gross annual revenue of less than $1 million for the previous three tax years (or less if the business has been operating for fewer years). (If you have been an "accrual" taxpayer, you must file IRS Form 3115: *Application for Change in Accounting Period* to change your accounting method.) Thus the IRS now allows the cash method of accounting for most small businesses. However, if your business has inventory, it is still wise to use the accrual method in order to accurately track your inventory.

The accrual method of accounting counts income and expenses when they are due to the business. Income is recorded when the business has a right to receive the income. In other words, accounts receivable (bills owed to the business) are considered as income that has already been received by the business. Expenses are considered and recorded when they are due, even if they are not yet paid. In other words, accounts payable (bills owed by the business) are considered expenses to the business when they are received, not when they are actually paid. The recordkeeping system in this book provides a simplified method of keeping accrual-method books. There is, however, a clear explanation provided in Chapter 11 on how to easily convert the records to the cash method. A business must choose to keep its records either on the accrual basis or on the cash basis. Once this decision is made, approval from the Internal Revenue Service must be obtained before the method can be changed.

Accounting Systems

In addition, there are two basic types of recordkeeping systems: *single-entry* or *double-entry*. Both types can be used to keep accurate records, although the double-entry system has more ways available to double-check calculations. Double-entry recordkeeping is, however, much more difficult to master, in that each and every transaction must be entered in two separate places in the records. The system that is used in this book is a modified form of single-entry accounting. The benefits of ease of use of a single-entry system far outweigh the disadvantages of this system. The Internal Revenue Service recommends single-entry records for beginning small businesses, and states that this type of system can be "relatively simple…used effectively…and is adequate for income tax purposes." Many accountants will disagree with this and insist that only double-entry accounting is acceptable. For the small business owner who wishes to understand his or her own company's finances, the advantages of single-entry accounting far outweigh the disadvantages.

Accounting Periods

A final item to consider is the accounting period for your business. A business is allowed to choose between a *fiscal year* accounting period and a *calendar year* period. A fiscal year consists of 12 consecutive months that *do not* end on December 31st. A calendar year consists of 12 consecutive months that *do* end on December 31st. There are complex rules relating to the choice of fiscal year accounting. If a sole-proprietorship reports income on a fiscal year, then all non-business income must also be reported on the same fiscal year. This most often unnecessarily complicates tax reporting and should generally be avoided. Partnerships and S-corporations may generally only choose to report on a fiscal year basis if there is a valid business purpose that supports the use of a fiscal year. This, again, generally, complicates the reporting of income and should be avoided unless there is an important reason to choose a fiscal year accounting period. If a fiscal year period is considered necessary, please consult a tax or accounting professional as there are complicated rules to comply with.

For the majority of small businesses, the choice of a calendar year period is perfectly adequate and, in most cases, will simplify the tax reporting and accounting recordkeeping. In the year in which a business is either started or ended, the business year for reporting may not be a full year. Thus, even for those who choose to use a calendar year, the first year may actually start on a date other than January 1st.

Recordkeeping Review

The purpose of a business financial recordkeeping system is to provide a method for the owner to keep track of the ongoing health of the business. This is done primarily by providing the owner with information on two basic financial statements. The balance sheet provides the business owner with a quick look at the assets and debts of the business and at the equity or ownership value of the business. The profit and loss statement furnishes the owner with an immediate view of the current flow of income and expenses of the business.

The business recordkeeping system that is provided in this book will detail how to set up the books for a small business. The method of reporting for this system is the accrual method. The type of system used is a single-entry system of accounting. The time period used for the system is a calendar year.

Accounting Software

The CD which accompanies this book contains computer-fillable PDF-format versions of the forms that are included in this book. They can be filled in on any computer or they may be printed out and filled in by hand. These forms do *not* comprise an integrated accounting software program. They are meant to be used by small business owners that have little or no knowledge of accounting practices. There are many fine accounting software programs on the market that may be used for small business accounting when you have acquired sufficient knowledge to use them. *Quickbooks* is the most widely-used accounting software and is a full-featured fully-integrated accounting software program. As such, it does take a working knowledge of small business accounting to set up and use correctly. *Peachtree Accounting* also produces a fine full-featured accounting software program. Microsoft recently discontinued its production of its small business accounting software. There are also dozens of other accounting software programs on the market that range from very simple glorified checkbook registers to very high-level advanced accounting software.

In using any of these software products, however, an good understanding of the fundamentals of bookkeeping and accounting are necessary for their use. This book is designed to provide its readers with a working understanding of an accrual single-entry accounting system, one of the simplest small business accounting methods available to the novice business owner. Once you feel comfortable with the terms and methods that are used in this system of accounting, and if you are relatively comfortable navigating complex computer programs, you may wish to move on to a full-featured integrated accounting software program.

Chapter 3

Simplified Accounting System

The simplified small business accounting system that is provided in this book is a modi-fied single-entry accounting system. It is presented as a system for accrual-basis accounting for small businesses. The records are designed to be used on a calendar-year basis. Within these basic parameters, the system can be individually tailored to meet the needs of most small businesses.

The backbone of the recordkeeping system is the *chart of accounts* for your business. A chart of accounts will list each of the income, expense, asset, or debt categories that you wish to keep track of. Every business transaction that you make and every financial record that you create will fit into one of these four main categories. Your transactions will either be money coming in (income) or money going out (expenses). Your records will also track either things the business owns (assets) or things the business owes (debts). The chart of accounts which you create in the next chapter will allow you to itemize and track each of these four broad categories in detail.

After you have set up a basic chart of accounts for your business, you will proceed with your first financial transaction: setting up a business bank account and a petty cash fund. Every business must have at least one business checking account to be used to keep a record of payments for expenses and to record income deposits. How to use a check register and the reconciliation of bank accounts will be explained. Additionally, every business should set up a petty cash fund in order to simplify the recording of cash transactions. Some businesses will have few and some may have many such cash transactions. Regardless of the number of transactions, a clear and understandable system to keep track of such transactions is necessary. The use of petty cash reports will be explained.

After the bank account and petty cash fund are set up, the first of the recordkeeping accounts that you set up will be the asset accounts. Each of the assets of a business within a single category will be assigned a separate asset account. Any real estate owned by the business will have an account; any vehicles will have an account; any inventory will have an account. Using these asset accounts, you will be able to track the ongoing value of your business possessions. Double-entry accounting provides that every income and expense transaction also alters various asset and liability account balances. While this is true, for most business purposes it is unnecessary and overburdening to keep a day-to-day balance in most asset and liability accounts. Thus, these accounts will be updated only periodically; either monthly, quarterly, or annually, depending on your particular business needs.

When you set up asset accounts, you will also set up inventory accounts. This particular form of asset has its own rules which govern how the accounts should be arranged in order to provide you with a clear picture of your inventory and to comply with tax regulations. You will be shown how to record additions and reductions to your inventory.

You will also be setting up debt accounts for any debts of your business. Each debt will be assigned a separate account so that the principal and interest of each debt can be clearly recorded and tracked. As with the asset accounts, you will be updating these accounts only on a periodic basic, depending on your business needs.

Expense accounts will most likely be the most complex and numerous of the type of accounts which you will set up. You will be setting up an account for each type of expense that you may encounter in your business. Most of these accounts will be arranged to correspond to the information that you will need to supply for tax purposes. The various expense accounts that you set up will allow you to substantiate all of the business deductions that you take at tax time. Expense accounts may also, of course, need to be set up to allow you to track expenses for particular projects, particular properties, or particular portions of your business. The purpose of setting up your expense accounts is to allow you to categorize and itemize the amounts which you spend on each particular aspect of your business. This will then allow you to see what your costs are per category at a glance. In order to do this you will be shown how to keep daily or weekly track of your expenses and how to total your expenses periodically to summarize your spending. The use and tracking of purchase orders will also be explained.

As you set up expense accounts, you will also be setting up a system of recordkeeping to keep track of certain expenses for which the Internal Revenue Service requires more detailed records. Automobile expenses and expenses associated with travel, entertainment, meals, and lodging are some of these types of expenses.

Income accounts will be set up for each type and category of income that you will be dealing with. This will allow you to track the sources and amounts of revenue that your business takes in. The use of invoices and statements as well as the details of credit sales will be coordinated with the recordkeeping requirements of income accounts.

Payroll is a subset of business expenses that is one of the most difficult for most business owners to understand. How to set up a simple system to deal with payroll will be clearly explained. The payment and recordkeeping necessary for payroll taxes will also be explained.

You will be shown how to summarize the information from your income and expense account records and prepare periodic profit and loss statements. Depending on your type of business, these statements may be prepared monthly, quarterly, or only annually. Clear forms for their easy preparation will be presented and explained. The analysis of the information on your profit and loss statement will also be detailed.

Summaries of the information from your asset and liability accounts will be used to prepare balance sheets on a periodic basis. This will allow you to monitor the relative health of your business. Numerous methods for analyzing the figures on your balance sheet will be explained.

How to actually set up and operate the financial recordkeeping system will be explained. Clear schedules of tasks will be outlined for your use as you work with the forms.

The preparation of your tax returns will be covered in the final chapter. We'll take a look at federal tax forms for sole proprietorships, partnerships, and corporations and see which forms will be necessary for each. Note, however, that this book is in no way a substitute for detailed information on taxes or for competent tax preparation assistance if needed.

Following is a checklist for setting up your business financial recordkeeping using this book:

Financial Recordkeeping Checklist

❏ Set up your business chart of accounts

❏ Open a business checking account

❏ Prepare a check register

❏ Set up a business petty cash fund

❏ Prepare a petty cash register

❏ Set up asset accounts

❏ Prepare current asset account records

❏ Prepare fixed asset account records

❏ Set up expense account records

❏ Set up income account records

❏ Set up payroll system

❏ Prepare payroll time sheets

❏ Prepare payroll depository records

❏ Determine proper tax forms for use in business

Chapter 4

Business Chart of Accounts

The financial recordkeeping system that you will set up using this book is designed to be adaptable to any type of business. Whether your business is a service business, a manufacturing business, a retail business, a wholesale distributorship, or combination of any of these, you will be able to easily adapt this simplified system to work with your particular situation. A key to designing the most useful recordkeeping system for your particular needs is to examine your type of business in depth. After a close examination of the particular needs and operations of your type of business, you will need to set up an array of specific accounts to handle your financial records. This set of general accounts is called a chart of accounts.

A chart of accounts will list all of the various categories of financial transactions which you will need to track. There will be an account for each general type of expense which you want to keep track of. You will also have separate accounts for each type of income your business will receive. Accounts will also be set up for your business assets and liabilities. Setting up an account for each of these categories consists of the simple task of deciding which items you will need to categorize, selecting a name for the account, and assigning a number for the account.

Before you can set up your accounts, you need to understand the reason for setting up these separate accounts. It is possible, although definitely not recommended, to run a business and merely keep track of your income and expenses without any itemization at all. However, you would be unable to analyze how the business is performing beyond a simple check to see if you have any money left after paying the expenses. You would also be unable to properly fill in the necessary information for business income tax returns.

A major reason for setting up separate accounts for many business's expense and income transactions is to separate and itemize the amounts spent in each category so that this information is available at tax time. This insures that a business is taking all of its allowable business deductions. The main reason, however, to set up individual accounts is to allow the business owner to have a clear view of the financial health of the business. With separate accounts for each type of transaction, a business owner can analyze the proportional costs and revenues of each aspect of the business. Is advertising costing more than labor expenses? Is the income derived from sales items worth the discounts of the sale? Only by using the figures obtained from separate itemized accounts can these questions be answered.

In the following sections, you will select and number the various accounts for use in your business chart of accounts. You will select various income accounts, expense accounts, asset accounts, and liability accounts. For each account, you will also assign it a number. For ease of use, you should assign a particular number value to all accounts of one type. For example, all income accounts may be assigned numbers 10–29. Sales income may be account number 11; service income may be assigned account number 12, interest income may be account number 13. Similarly, expenses may be assigned numbers 30–79. Balance sheet accounts for assets and liabilities may be numbers 80–99. Be sure to leave enough numbers for future expansion of your list of accounts. There will normally be far more expense accounts than any other type of account.

If you have income or expenses from many sources, you may wish to use three-digit numbers to identify each separate category. For example, if your business consists of renting out residential houses and you have 10 properties, you may wish to set up a separate income and expense account for each property. You may wish to assign accounts numbers 110–119 to income from all properties. Thus, for example, you could then assign rental income from property number 1 to account number 111, rental income from property number 2 to account number 112, rental income from property number 3 to account number 113 and so on. Similarly, expenses can be broken down into separate accounts for individual properties. Advertising expenses might all be account numbers 510–519, thus advertising expenses for property number 1 might then be assigned number 511, advertising expenses for property number 2 would be assigned account number 512, etc.

How your individual chart of accounts will be organized will be specific to your particular business. If you have a simple business with all income coming from one source, you will probably desire a two-digit number from, perhaps, 10–29 assigned to that income account. On the other hand a more complex business with many sources of income and many different types of expenses may wish to use a system of three-digit numbers. Take some time to analyze your specific business to decide how you wish to set up your accounts. Ask yourself what type of information will you want to extract from your financial records. Do you need more details of your income sources? Then you should set up several income accounts for each type and possibly even each source of your income. Would you like more specific information on your expenses? Then you would most likely wish to set up clear and detailed expense accounts for each type of expense that you must pay.

Be aware that you may wish to alter your chart of accounts as your business grows. You may find that you have set up too many accounts and unnecessarily complicated your recordkeeping tasks. You may wish to set up more accounts once you see how your balance sheets and profit and loss statements look. You may change, add, or delete accounts at any time. Remember, however, that any transactions that have been recorded in an account must be transferred to any new account or accounts that take the place of the old account.

Income Accounts

These are accounts that are used to track the various sources of your company's income. There may be only a few sources of income for your business, or you may wish to track your income in more detail. The information which you collect in your income accounts will be used to prepare your profit and loss statements periodically. Recall that a profit and loss statement is also referred to as an income and expense statement.

On the chart of accounts that is used in this book, income is separated into several categories. You can choose the income account categories which best suit your type of business. If your business is a service business, you may wish to set up accounts for labor income and for materials income. Or you may wish to set up income accounts in more detail, for example: sales income, markup income, income from separate properties, or income from separate sources in your business, etc. Non-sales income such as bank account interest income or income on the sale of business equipment should be placed in separate individual income accounts. You may also wish to set up separate income accounts for income from different ongoing projects or income from separate portions of your business.

Following is a list of various general income accounts. Decide how much detail you will want in your financial records regarding income and then choose the appropriate accounts. You may wish to name and create different accounts than are listed here. After you have chosen your income accounts, assign a number to each account.

Income Chart of Accounts

Account #	Account Name and Description
	Income from sale of goods
	Income from services
	Income from labor charges
	Income from sales discounts
	Income from interest revenue
	Income from consulting
	Miscellaneous income

Expense Accounts

These are the accounts that you will use to keep track of your expenses. Each separate category of expense should have its own account. Many of the types of accounts are dictated by the types of expenses which should be itemized for tax purposes. You will generally have separate accounts for advertising costs, utility expenses, rent, phone costs, etc. One or more separate accounts should also be set up to keep track of inventory expenses. These should be kept separate from other expense accounts as they must be itemized for tax purposes.

Following is a list of various general expense accounts. Please analyze your business and determine which accounts would be best suited to select for your particular situation. You will then number these accounts, as you did the income accounts. The categories presented are general categories which match most IRS forms. You may, of course, set up separate accounts which are not listed to suit your particular needs. Try not to set up too many accounts or you will have a hard time trying to remember all of them. Also note that you may add or delete accounts as you need them. If you delete an account, however, you must shift any transactions that you have recorded in that account to the new account.

Expense Chart of Accounts

Account #	Account Name and Description
	Advertising expenses
	Auto expenses
	Cleaning and maintenance expenses
	Charitable contributions
	Dues and publications
	Office equipment expenses
	Freight and shipping expenses
	Business insurance expenses
	Business interest expenses
	Legal expenses
	Business meals and lodging
	Miscellaneous expenses
	Postage expenses
	Office rent expenses
	Repair expenses
	Office supplies
	Sales taxes paid
	Federal unemployment taxes paid
	State unemployment taxes paid
	Telephone expenses
	Utility expenses
	Wages and commissions

Asset and Liability Accounts

Asset and liability accounts are collectively referred to as *balance sheet accounts*. This is because the information collected on them is used to prepare your business balance sheets. You will set up current and fixed asset accounts and current and long-term liability accounts. Types of current asset accounts are cash, short-term notes receivable, accounts receivable, inventory, and pre-paid expenses. Fixed assets may include equipment, vehicles, buildings, land, long-term notes receivable, and long-term loans receivable.

Types of current liability accounts are short-term notes payable (money due within one year), short-term loans payable (money due on loan within one year), unpaid taxes, and unpaid wages. Long-term liability accounts may be long-term notes payable (money due over one year) or long-term loans payable (money due over one year). Finally, you will need an owner's equity account to tally the ownership value of your business.

Choose the asset and liability accounts which best suit your business and assign appropriate numbers to each account.

Balance Sheet Chart of Accounts

Account #	Account Name and Description
	Accounts receivable (current asset)
	Bank checking account (current asset)
	Bank savings account (current asset)
	Cash on hand (current asset)
	Notes receivable (current asset, if short-term)
	Loans receivable (current asset, if short-term)
	Inventory (current asset)
	Land (fixed asset)
	Buildings (fixed asset)
	Vehicles (fixed asset)
	Equipment (fixed asset)
	Machinery (fixed asset)
	Accounts payable (current debt)
	Notes payable (current, if due within 1 year)
	Loans payable (current, if due within 1 year)
	Notes payable (long-term debt, if over 1 year)
	Loans payable (long-term debt, if over 1 year)
	Mortgage payable (long-term debt, if over 1 year)
	Retained capital

Sample Chart of Accounts

After you have selected and numbered each of your accounts, you should prepare your chart of accounts. Simply type the number and name of each account in a numerical list. You will refer to this chart often as you prepare your financial records. Following is a sample completed chart of accounts.

This sample chart is set up to reflect the business operations of our sample company: Smith's Gourmet Foods. This is a sole proprietorship company which prepares and packages food products and delivers the products directly to consumers in their homes.

The chart reflects that the income will primarily come from one source: direct customer payments for the products which are sold. The expense accounts are chosen to cover most of the standard types of business expenses which a small business will encounter. The balance sheet accounts reflect that the business will only have as assets a bank account, some accounts receivable, inventory, and some equipment. The only liabilities that this business will have, at least initially, will be a loan for equipment and accounts payable.

Although this sample chart of accounts is fairly brief, it covers all of the basic accounts which the business will need as it begins. There is sufficient room in the numbering system chosen to add additional accounts as the business expands.

Sample Chart of Accounts

Account #	Account Name and Description
11	Income from sale of goods
12	Miscellaneous income
31	Advertising expenses
32	Auto expenses
33	Cleaning and maintenance expenses
34	Office equipment expenses
35	Business insurance expenses
36	Business meals and lodging
37	Miscellaneous expenses
38	Postage expenses
39	Repair expenses
40	Office supplies
41	Sales taxes paid
42	Telephone expenses
43	Office rent expense
51	Cash on hand (current asset)
52	Accounts receivable (current asset)
53	Bank checking account (current asset)
54	Inventory (current asset)
61	Equipment (fixed asset)
71	Accounts payable (current debt)
81	Loans payable (long-term debt)
91	Retained capital

Chapter 5

Business Bank Accounts and Petty Cash Fund

The first financial action which a new small business should take is to set up a business bank account. A bank account is necessary to provide the business owner with a clear written record of all initial transactions. There are numerous types of business bank accounts available: some pay interest, some charge for each check written or deposited, some return your cancelled checks each month, and some provide other benefits. Check with various local banking institutions to see which types are available and then choose the bank account which is best suited to your needs.

The business bank account will be the first record of many of your business's financial transactions. All of the income received by a business and all of the expenses which a business pays should be recorded in the check register for the business banking account. Your business bank account should always be a separate checking account. However, there may be instances when certain items will need to be paid for with cash. For this purpose, a *petty cash fund* will need to be set up. This is explained at the end of this chapter.

Bank Account Procedures

There are certain guidelines which should be adhered to regarding the use of the business bank account.

① Every transaction should be recorded in the check register. The details of each transaction will be important as you prepare your financial records. What you need to record is explained later in this chapter.

② All of your business expenses and bills should be paid by check. If it is necessary to pay by cash, carefully record the payment in the Petty Cash Register which follows. Don't write checks to "Cash."

③ Balance your checking account every month. This is vital in keeping close track of your finances. If the bank's statement does not match your records, contact the bank to determine where the discrepancy is. Bouncing a check because you have insufficient funds in the bank will leave a blemish on the reputation of your business.

④ Never use your business bank account to pay for personal expenses. Keep all of your business finances scrupulously separate from your personal affairs. If some expenses are part personal and part business, make a careful record of the amount of each portion of the expense.

⑤ Retain your cancelled checks and bank statements for at least three years. If your business is ever audited by the Internal Revenue Service, you will need to produce these records to substantiate your business income and deductions.

In many respects, your business bank account is the main financial corridor for your business. In dealings with banks, suppliers, employees, and other businesses, your business account is the primary conduit for conducting your financial transactions. It is vital to your success that you are able to keep the records for this main financial account straight. On the next few pages, the following forms are provided to help you in this task: Check Register, Monthly Bank Statement Reconciliation, and Petty Cash Register.

For each of these forms, instructions for their use are provided, as well as a filled-in sample check register based on information provided for our fictitious company, Smith's Gourmet Foods.

Check Register Instructions

Although most people have handled money in a bank account by the time they open a business, many people have difficulty with the method by which transactions are recorded in a bank account. By following a specific set of recording rules, a business bank account can provide a detailed and clear record of the financial flow of a business.

① The first transaction in the account will be the initial deposit. Put this on the first line in the register. Fill in the amount in the Deposit column. Carry this amount over into the Balance column.

② If you desire, each transaction may take up two lines in the Register. The first line may be used to record the details of the transaction. The second line may be used to figure the balance. By using two lines, you will leave yourself enough room to allow for easy reading of the transactions.

③ For each check that is written, record the following information:
   ◆ The date the check was written
   ◆ The number of the check

✦ The name of person or company to whom the check was written

✦ A description of the reason for the check (ie., what was purchased, what was paid for, etc.)

✦ What expense account the check should be listed under. In the previous chapter, you set up expense account numbers for each type of expense. The appropriate account number should be entered in this column

✦ The amount of the check

④ For each deposit, record the following information:

✦ The date of the deposit

✦ A description of the deposit. This should include information regarding what specific checks were deposited or if the deposit was cash

✦ To what income account number the deposit should be credited

✦ The amount of the deposit

⑤ For each transaction, the current balance of the checkbook should be calculated. This should be done at the time that you write the check or make the deposit. Don't let the balance go un-calculated for any length of time. Errors are more likely if you do not keep an accurate running balance.

Check Register

Date	Check #	Description	Acct #	Clear	Payment	Deposit	Balance

Sample Check Register

Let's look at the finances of our fictitious company: Smith's Gourmet Foods. Sandy Smith has decided to open a business which delivers gourmet food directly to the consumer. She will start the business with $10,000.00, which she has managed to save over a period of several years and an additional $10,000.00 which she has borrowed from her local bank. Her very first financial transaction as a business is to open a business bank account and deposit the $20,000.00 into the account. Ms. Smith has decided to operate as a sole proprietorship.

Once the bank account is open, Ms. Smith's first transaction is to buy inventory for $5,000.00. The next day, she makes her first sale for $150.00. She then withdraws $50.00 to set up a petty cash fund. The procedures for this are detailed later in this chapter. Ms. Smith's next transaction is the rental of an office for the cost of $300.00 per month. She writes a separate check for a security deposit for the office, amounting to another $300.00.

Her next transactions are the purchase of various supplies and services. She purchases the following items:

- $2,200.00 worth of office supplies from Office Mart
- $3,000.00 worth of cooking equipment from Restaurant Supply Company
- $500.00 worth of office furniture from Furniture Mart
- $300.00 worth of advertising from the Local Newspaper Company
- She also hires a freelance artist to design a logo for the company and brochure for the company. This costs her $400.00
- She has the flyers printed for $200.00 by Printing-Is-Us Company

On the following page, all of these transactions are recorded on the sample Check Register. Note that the account's numbers are listed for each transaction. Also note that there are two account numbers for the equipment purchases. This is because the transactions will be listed as both an equipment purchase (expense) and as a fixed asset. Please see Chapter 6 for more details about fixed assets.

Sample Check Register

Date	Check #	Description	Acct #	Clear	Payment		Deposit		Balance	
2/13		initial deposit					10,000	00	10,000	00
2/13		deposit loan proceeds	81				10,000	00	20,000	00
2/13	101	food wholesalers	54		5,000	00			15,000	00
2/14		Joanne Smith (sale)	11				150	00	15,150	00
2/14		petty cash fund	51		50	00			15,100	00
2/15	102	Harry Jones (office rent)	43		300	00			14,800	00
2/15	103	Harry Jones (security deposit)	43		300	00			14,500	00
2/16	104	office mart	40		2,200	00			12,300	00
2/17	105	restaurant supply co.	34/61		3,000	00			9,300	00
2/20	106	furniture mart	34/61		500	00			8,800	00
2/21	107	local newspaper (ad)	31		300	00			8,500	00
2/22	108	Freddy Harris (logo design)	31		400	00			8,100	00
2/22	109	printing-is-us	31		200	00			7,900	00

Reconciling Your Monthly Bank Statement

Perhaps the most difficult part of handling money through a bank account is getting the account to balance each month. Every month you will get a statement from the bank which will detail all of the transactions which occurred during the previous month. The bank statement will normally list all of the checks by number and amount. It will also list all of the deposits by date and amount. Any service charges or charges for bank checks will be shown. Finally, any returned checks, other charges, or interest paid will be listed.

The bank statement will normally also state your balance at the beginning of the month and your balance at the end of the month. Neither of these balances will generally ever match the balance shown in your check register. This is because the bank only records the transactions when the checks you write are actually paid by the bank. This may be weeks or even months after you write the check. The following procedure should help you to reconcile your bank statement with your check register each month:

① Carefully review the bank statement when you receive it each month. Make a note of any extra items such as service charges or interest paid. Sort all of the cancelled checks into numerical order. Some banks no longer supply cancelled checks back to the account holder. In this case, refer to your bank statement for cancelled check details.

② Using either the sorted cancelled checks or the statement, match the checks which the bank has processed with your own check register. Put a checkmark in the Clear column of the check register for each check that has cleared the bank and been returned to you (or been noted on the statement). There will be some checks which you have written which have not cleared. We will deal with these later.

③ Do the same for your deposits. If the bank has supplied your deposit slips, sort them by date. If not, use your bank statement. Match each deposit slip or statement entry against your record in your check register. For each match, check it off in the Clear column of the register.

④ If there are additional items such as service charges or interest paid to you, enter an appropriate entry in your register and then check it off as "Clear."

⑤ Finally, take one of the Monthly Bank Statement Reconciliation sheets out and follow the directions on the next page to fully complete your monthly reconciliation.

Monthly Bank Statement Reconciliation

On the next page you will find a Monthly Bank Statement Reconciliation sheet. Every month, on this form, you will compare your bank statement with the balance in your Check Register. Using the method outlined will give you a clear picture of any discrepancies between the bank's records and your own. To fill in this form, follow these instructions:

① Fill in the month and year on the form. Fill in your account balance from your *bank statement* where shown. Fill in your account balance from your *check register* on the last line where shown.

② Using your check register, under "Checks Outstanding" on this form, fill in the amounts for each check that you have written that has not be checked off as "Clear." Total this amount and *subtract* it from the Bank Statement Balance where shown.

③ Again using your check register, under "Deposits Outstanding" on this form, fill in the amounts for any deposits which you have made that have not been checked off as "Clear." Total these deposits and *add* this amount to your Bank Statement Balance where shown.

④ If there are any service charges or other fees on your Bank Statement, total these and *subtract* them from the Bank Statement Balance where shown. If your account has earned any interest, *add* this to your Bank Statement Balance where shown.

⑤ Finish all of the calculations. The final Check Register Balance shown on this sheet should match the balance shown on your Check Register. If it doesn't, go back over all of your calculations and try again. If it still doesn't match, carefully check your cancelled checks and deposits to make certain that you have checked off as "Clear" all of the appropriate items. If this does not rectify the error, you will need to check all of the amounts on all of the checks and deposits. This is often where the error was made. Check and recheck all of your calculations and entries. If you still cannot find the discrepancy, take your bank statement, check register, cancelled checks, and deposit slips to your bank and ask them to check the balances. Most banks are more than willing to help their customers.

⑥ When you have finally reconciled your monthly statement with your check register, file the cancelled checks and bank statement. You will need to keep these bank records for at least three years.

Monthly Bank Statement Reconciliation

Checks

Check Number	Amount
TOTAL	**0.00**

Deposits

Date	Amount
TOTAL	**0.00**

Bank Statement Balance	
+ ADD Outstanding Deposits	
+ADD Interest Earned	
= SUBTOTAL	
- SUBTRACT Outstanding Checks	
- SUBTRACT Service Charge/Fees	
= TOTAL	

(this should agree with your check register balance)

Petty Cash Fund

The handling of cash often poses problems for small businesses. Unless you have a simple system to keep track of your petty cash in place, it is often difficult to keep accurate and current records of the use of cash in your business. The use of a petty cash fund is to provide you with a clear record of the payment of expenses with small amounts of cash; amounts which are too small to be handled by the use of a check. Petty cash is different from the cash which you might use in a cash register to take in payments for merchandise or services. That use of cash is discussed in Chapter 9. For a petty cash fund, you generally will not need to set aside more than $50.00. Following is how to handle your petty cash:

①   Get a small cashbox or something similar, with a lock and key.

②   Write a check from your business bank account made out to "Petty Cash" for the amount that you will begin your fund with. In your check register, record the account number as the account listed for your current asset account for cash on hand. Put the cash in the cashbox.

③   Using the Petty Cash Register on the next page, record the starting amount as "Cash In," just like you would record a deposit in a checkbook register. Record cash which you pay out as "Cash Out," similar to how you would record a payment in a check register.

④   Record each transaction that you make using your petty cash fund just as you would in a check register. Record the date, description of the use of the money or of money taken in, the account which it should be listed under, and the amount of the transaction.

⑤   When your petty cash fund gets low, note what the balance is and write another check to "Petty Cash" which will cause your balance to equal the amount which you have chosen as a total for your petty cash fund. For example, you have decided to have a $50.00 petty cash fund. In two months, you have used up $46.00 of the cash (and recorded each transaction). You should have $4.00 in cash left in your box and as a written balance on your Petty Cash Register. Simply write a check to "Petty Cash" for $46.00, cash the check, and put the cash in the box to replenish the petty cash fund.

⑥   At the time that you replenish your petty cash fund, you will need to record all of your transactions on your main income and expense records. You will simply transfer all of the amounts to the main sheets and check the box on the petty cash ledger marking them as cleared transactions. The use of your main income and expense records will be explained in Chapters 8 and 9.

Petty Cash Register

Date	Description	Acct #	Clear	Cash-out	Cash-in	Balance

Bank Account Checklist

❑ Obtain business checking account

❑ Prepare Check Register

❑ On a daily or weekly basis, record all checks and deposits on the Check Register

❑ On a monthly basis, reconcile your Check Register Balance with your bank statement

❑ On a monthly basis transfer information from your Check Register to the appropriate Expense Record (See Chapter 8)

❑ File your bank statements, canceled checks, and Check Registers, and retain for three years

Petty Cash Fund Checklist

❑ Buy petty cash fund cashbox or equivalent

❑ Prepare Petty Cash Register

❑ Write check to "Petty Cash" to begin petty cash fund

❑ Record all petty cash transactions in Petty Cash Register

❑ On a monthly basis, replenish petty cash fund with check for "Petty Cash"

❑ On a monthly basis, transfer information from Petty Cash Register to the appropriate Expense Record (See Chapter 8)

❑ Retain your Petty Cash Registers and cash receipts for three years

Chapter 6

Tracking Business Assets

After setting up a chart of accounts, a bank account, and a petty cash fund, the next financial recordkeeping task for a business will consist of preparing a method to keep track of the assets of the business. Recall that the assets of a business are everything that is owned by the business. They are either current assets that can be converted to cash within a year or fixed assets that are more long-term in nature. Each of these two main categories of assets will be discussed separately.

Current Assets

Following is a list of typical current assets for a business:

- Business bank checking account
- Business bank savings account
- Cash (petty cash fund and cash on hand)
- Accounts receivable (money owed to the company)
- Inventory

A company may have other types of current assets such as notes or loans receivable, but the five listed above are the basic ones for most small businesses. In complex double-entry accounting systems, the current asset account balances are constantly being changed. In a double-entry system, each time an item of inventory is sold, for example, the account balance for the inventory account must be adjusted to reflect the sale. In the type of single-entry system that is presented in this book, all asset and liability accounts are only updated when the business owner wishes to prepare a balance sheet. This may be done monthly, quarterly, or annually. At a minimum, this updating must take place at the end of the year in order to have the necessary figures available for tax purposes. The forms and instructions in this book provide a simple method for tracking and updating the required information for business assets and liabilities.

The main form for tracking your current business assets will be a Current Asset Account Record. A copy of this form follows this discussion. On this form, you will periodically track of the value of the current asset that you are following, except for your inventory. (For inventory, you will use specialized inventory records.) You should prepare a separate Current Asset Account Record for each asset. For example, if your current assets consist of a business checking account, cash on hand, and accounts receivable, you will have three separate Current Asset Accounts, one for each category of asset. These forms are very simple to use. Follow the instructions below:

① Simply fill in the Account Number for the Current Asset Account for which you are setting up the form. You will get this number from your Chart of Accounts. Also, fill in a description of the account. For example: Account Number 53: Business Banking Account.

② You must then decide how often you will be preparing a balance sheet and updating your balance sheet account balances. If you wish to keep close track of your finances, you may wish to do this on a monthly basis. For many businesses, a quarterly balance sheet may be sufficient. All businesses, no matter how small, must prepare a balance sheet at least annually, at the end of the year. Decide how often you wish to update the balances and enter the period in the space provided.

③ Next enter the date that you open the account. Under description, enter "Opening Balance." Under the "Balance" column, enter the opening value. The amount to enter for an opening balance will be as follows:
    ✦ For a bank account, this will be the opening balance of the account
    ✦ For cash on hand, this will be the opening balance of the petty cash fund and cash on hand for sales, such as the cash used in a cash register (see Chapters 5 and 9)
    ✦ For accounts receivable, this will be the total amount due from all accounts (see Chapter 9)

④ Periodically, you will enter a date and new balance. You will enter these new balances from the following sources:
    ✦ For bank accounts, this figure will come from your Check Register balance column on a particular date (see Chapter 5)
    ✦ For cash, this new figure will come from your Petty Cash Register balance (see Chapter 9) and your Monthly Cash Summary (see Chapter 9) on a certain date
    ✦ For accounts receivable, the balance will come from your Monthly Credit Sales Aging Report (see Chapter 9)

⑤ After you have entered the balances on the appropriate Current Asset Account Record, you will transfer the balances to your Balance Sheet. This will be explained in Chapter 12.

Current Asset Account

Account #:
Account Name: Period:

Date	Description of Asset	Balance

Inventory

Any business which sells an item of merchandise to a customer must have a system in place to keep track of inventory. *Inventory* is considered any merchandise or materials which are held for sale during the normal course of your business. Inventory costs include the costs of the merchandise or products themselves and the costs of the materials and paid labor which goes into creating a finished product. Inventory does not include the costs of the equipment or machinery that you need to create the finished product.

There are several reasons you will need a system of inventory control. First, if you are stocking parts or supplies to sell, you will need to keep track of what you have ordered, what is in stock, and when you will need to reorder. You will also need to keep track of the cost of your inventory for tax purposes. The amount of money which you spend on your inventory is not immediately deductible in the year spent as a business deduction. The only portion of your inventory costs which will reduce your gross profit for tax purposes is the actual cost of the goods which you have sold during the tax year.

The basic method for keeping track of inventory costs for tax purposes is to determine the cost of goods sold. First, you will need to know how much inventory is on hand at the beginning of the year. To this amount, you add the cost of any additional inventory you purchased during the year. Finally, you determine how much inventory is left at the end of the year. The difference is essentially the cost (to you) of the inventory which you sold during the year. This amount is referred to as the *Cost of Goods Sold.* Every year at tax time, you will need to figure the Cost of Goods Sold. Additionally, you may need to determine your Cost of Goods Sold monthly or quarterly for various business purposes.

Four inventory control records are provided for use in tracking inventory costs: Physical Inventory Record, Periodic Inventory Record, Perpetual Inventory Record, and Cost of Goods Sold Record.

Using our sample company, Smith Gourmet Foods, we will start her first year in business with an inventory of $0.00. When her business begins, there is no inventory. During the first year, she purchases $17,500.00 worth of products which are for selling to customers. At the end of the year, she counts all of the items which are left in her possession and determines her cost for these items. The cost of the items left unsold at the end of the year is $3,700.00.

The calculation of the Cost of Goods Sold for the first year in business is as follows:

Inventory at beginning of first year	$ 00.00
+ Plus cost of inventory added during year	$ 17,500.00
= Equals cost of inventory	$ 17,500.00
– Less inventory at end of first year	$ 3,700.00
= Equals cost of goods sold for first year	$ 13,800.00

For the second year in business, the figure for the inventory at the beginning of the year is the value of the inventory at the end of the previous year. Thus, if Smith Gourmet Foods added $25,000.00 additional inventory during the second year of operation and the value of the inventory at the end of the second year was $4,800.00, the cost-of-goods-sold calculations for the second year would be as follows:

Inventory at beginning of second year	*$ 3,700.00*
+ Plus cost of inventory added during year	*$ 25,000.00*
= Equals cost of inventory	*$ 28,700.00*
– Less inventory at end of second year	*$ 4,800.00*
= Equals cost of goods sold for second year	*$ 23,900.00*

Thus for the second year in operation the cost of goods sold would be $23,900.00. This amount would be deducted from the gross revenues that Smith's Gourmet Foods took in for the year to determine the gross profit for the second year in business.

Physical Inventory Record

This form should be used to record the results of an actual physical counting of the inventory at the end of the year and at whatever other times during the year you decide to take a physical inventory. If you decide that you will need to track your inventory monthly or quarterly, you may need to prepare this form for those time periods. To prepare this form, take the following steps:

① The quantity and description of each item of inventory should be listed, along with an item number if applicable.

② The cost (to you) of each item should be then listed under "Unit Price." A total per item cost is then calculated by multiplying the quantity of units times the unit price. This total per item cost should be listed in the far right-hand column. You will need to extract this per item unit price from your Periodic or Perpetual Inventory forms (explained next).

③ The total inventory cost should be figured by adding all the figures in the far right-hand column. The form should be dated and signed by the person doing the inventory.

Physical Inventory Report

Date: Taken by:

Quantity	Description	Item #	Unit Price	Total
			TOTAL	

Periodic Inventory Record

This is the form which you will use to keep continual track of your inventory if you have a relatively small inventory. If you have an extensive inventory, you will need to use the Perpetual Inventory Record which is supplied next. You will use the Periodic Inventory form for the purposes of keeping track of the costs of your inventory and of any orders of additional inventory. You will refer to this report when you need to order additional inventory, when you need to determine when an order should be received, and when you need to determine the cost of your inventory items at the end of the year, or other times, if desired.

① Prepare a separate Periodic Inventory Record for each item of inventory. Identify the type of item that is being tracked by description and by item number, if applicable. You may also wish to list the supplier of the item.

② The first entry on the Periodic Inventory Record should be the initial purchase of inventory. On the right-hand side of the record, list the following items:
   ◆ Date purchased
   ◆ Quantity purchased
   ◆ Price per item
   ◆ Total price paid
   ◆ *Note:* Shipping charges should not be included in the prices entered. Only the actual costs of the goods should be listed

③ When you are running low on a particular item and place an order, on the left-hand side of the record enter the following information:
   ◆ Date of the order
   ◆ Order number
   ◆ Quantity ordered
   ◆ Date the order is due to arrive

④ When the order arrives, enter the actual details about the order on the right-hand side of the page. This will allow you to keep track of your order of inventory items and also allow you to keep track of the cost of your items of inventory.

Periodic Inventory Record

Item: Item #:
Supplier:

INVENTORY ORDERED			
Date	Order #	Quantity	Due

INVENTORY RECEIVED			
Date	Quantity	Price	Total

Perpetual Inventory Record

This is the form that you will use to keep continual track of your inventory if you have a relatively extensive inventory. You will refer to this record when you need to order additional inventory, determine when an order should be received, and determine the cost of your inventory items at the end of the year. Additionally, on this form you will keep track of the number of items of each type of inventory that have been sold.

① Prepare a separate Perpetual Inventory Record for each item of inventory. Identify the type of item which is being tracked by description and by item number, if applicable. You may also wish to list the supplier for the item.

② The first entry on the Perpetual Inventory Record should be the initial purchase of inventory. On the lower left-hand side of the record, under "Inventory Received," list the following information:
   ◆ Date purchased
   ◆ Quantity purchased
   ◆ Price per item
   ◆ Total price paid
   ◆ *Note*: Shipping charges should not be included in the amounts entered

③ When you are running low on a particular item and place an order, enter the following information on the upper left-hand side of the record:
   ◆ Date of the order
   ◆ Order number
   ◆ Quantity ordered
   ◆ Date the ordered inventory is due

④ When the order arrives, enter the actual details on the lower left-hand side of the page, under "Inventory Received."

⑤ On the right-hand side of the record, keep a running total of the number of items of inventory sold. Decide how often you will be checking your stocks to update your inventory counts and stick to the schedule: weekly, monthly, or quarterly. Enter the number of items sold at each count and figure the totals. This will give you a running total of the amount of inventory you have in stock at any given time. You will, however, still need to take a physical inventory count at the end of the year (or more often) to check for lost, stolen, miscounted, or missing items, and as a check against your calculations.

Perpetual Inventory Record

Item: Item #:
Supplier:

INVENTORY ORDERED

Date	Order #	Quantity	Due

INVENTORY IN STOCK

Date	Quantity	Price	Total

INVENTORY RECEIVED

Date	Order #	Quantity	Due

Cost of Goods Sold Record

The final record for inventory control is the *Cost of Goods Sold Record*. It is on this record that you will determine the actual cost to your business of the goods which were sold during a particular time period. There are numerous methods to determine the value of your inventory at the end of a time period. The three most important are the Specific Identification method, the First-In First-Out method (called FIFO), and the Last-In First-Out method (called LIFO).

Specific Identification is the easiest to use if you have only a few items of inventory, or one-of-a-kind types of merchandise. With this method, you actually keep track of each specific item of inventory. You keep track of when you obtained the item, its cost, and when you sold the specific item.

With the FIFO method, you keep track only of general quantities of your inventory. Your inventory costs are calculated as though the oldest inventory merchandise was sold first: the first items that you purchased are the first items that you sell.

With the LIFO method, the cost values are calculated as though you sell your most-recently purchased inventory first. It is important to note that you do not necessarily have to actually sell your first item first to use the FIFO method and you do not have to actually sell your last item first to use the LIFO method of calculation.

Although there may be significant advantages in some cases to using the LIFO method, it is also a far more complicated system than the FIFO. The Specific Identification method allows you to simply track each item of inventory and deduct the actual cost of the goods which you sold during the year. The FIFO method allows you to value your inventory on hand at the end of a time period based on the cost of your most recent purchases. Using either your Periodic or Perpetual Inventory Records, valuing your inventory is a simple matter.

① At the end of your chosen time period (monthly, quarterly, or annually), take an actual physical inventory count on your Physical Inventory Record.

② Using the most recent purchases as listed on your Periodic or Perpetual Inventory Record, determine the unit price of the items left in your inventory and enter this under the Unit Price column on your Physical Inventory Record.

③ Once all of your items of inventory have been checked, counted, and a unit price determined, simply total each item and then total the value of the entire inventory. If you are conducting your final annual inventory, this final figure is your Inventory Value at year's end.

④ On the Cost of Goods Sold Record, enter this number on the line titled "Inventory Value at End of Period." If this is your first year in business, enter zero as the Inventory Value at Beginning of

Period. For later periods, the Inventory Value at Beginning of Period will be the Inventory Value at End of Period for the previous period.

⑤ Using either your Periodic Inventory or your Perpetual Inventory Record sheets, total the amounts of orders during the period which are listed under the Inventory Received column. This total will be entered on the Inventory Added During Period line. Now simply perform the calculations. You will use the figures on this sheet at tax time to prepare your taxes.

NOTE: This type of inventory calculation is not intended for manufacturing companies that manufacture finished goods from raw materials or for those with gross annual receipts over $10 million. For those type of companies, an additional calculation is necessary because of uniform capitalization rules. This tax rule requires that manufacturing inventory values include the overhead associated with the manufacturing process. Please consult an accounting professional if you fall into this category of business.

Cost of Goods Sold

Period Ending:

Inventory Value at Beginning of Period	
+ Inventory Added during Period	
= Total Inventory Value	
– Inventory Value at End of Period	
= Cost of Goods Sold	

Beginning Inventory Value for Next Period
(Take from Inventory Value at End of This Period)

Fixed Assets

The final category of assets which you will need to track are your fixed assets. Fixed assets are the more permanent assets of your business: generally the assets which are not for sale to customers. The main categories of these fixed assets are:
- Buildings
- Land
- Machinery
- Tools
- Furniture and equipment
- Vehicles

There are many more types of fixed assets such as patents, copyrights, and goodwill. However, the six listed above are the basic ones for most small businesses. If your business includes other types of fixed assets, please consult an accounting professional. For those with basic fixed assets, you will need to keep track of the actual total costs to you to acquire them. These costs include sales taxes, transportation charges, installation costs, etc. The total cost of a fixed asset to you is referred to as the asset's *cost basis*. With a major exception explained below, the cost of fixed assets are, generally, not immediately deductible as a business expense. Rather, except for the cost of land, their costs are deductible proportionately over a period of time. This proportionate deduction is referred to as *depreciation*. Since these assets generally wear out over time (except for land), each year you are allowed to deduct a portion of the initial cost as a legitimate business expense. Each type of fixed asset is given a specific time period for dividing up the cost into proportional amounts. This time period is called the *recovery period* of the asset. Depreciation is a very complex subject and one whose rules change nearly every year. The full details of depreciation are beyond the scope of this book. What follows is a general outline of depreciation rules only. It will allow you to begin to set up your fixed asset account records. However, you will need to either consult an accounting or tax professional, or consult specific tax preparation manuals for details on how your specific assets should be depreciated.

The major exception to depreciation rules is that, under the rules of IRS Code Section 179, every year a total of $125,000.00 (Note: This amount has been subject to change many times in recent years. For example, for tax year 2009, this amount was temporarily raised to $250,000.00 as part of the overall business stimulus legislation. Check with a tax professional for the current amounts)) of your fixed asset costs can be immediately used as a business deduction. This means that if your total purchases of equipment, tools, vehicles, etc. during a year amounted to less than $125,000.00, you can deduct all of the costs as current expenses. If your total fixed asset costs are over $125,000.00 (but not greater than $500,000.00), you can still deduct the first $125,000.00 in costs and then depreciate the remaining costs over time. Here are some basic rules relating to depreciation:

① The depreciation rules which were in effect at the time of the purchase of the asset will be the rules which apply to that particular asset.

② The actual cost to you of the asset is the cost basis that you use to compute your depreciation amount each year.

③ Used assets which you purchase for use in your business can be depreciated in the same manner as new assets.

④ Assets which you owned prior to going into business and which you will use in your business can be depreciated. The cost basis will be the lower of their actual market value when you begin to use them in your business or their actual cost to you. For example, you start a carpentry business and use your personal power saw in the business. It cost $150.00 new, but is now worth about $90.00. You can depreciate $90.00 (or deduct this amount as an expense if the total of your fixed asset deductions is under $125,000.00).

⑤ You may depreciate proportionately those assets which you use partially for business and partially for personal use. In the above example, if you use your saw 70 percent of the time in your business and 30 percent for personal use, you may deduct or depreciate 70 percent of $90.00, or $63.00.

The tax depreciation rules set up several categories of asset types for the purpose of deciding how long a period you must use to depreciate the asset. Cars, trucks, computer equipment, copiers, and similar equipment are referred to as five-year property. Most machinery, equipment, and office furniture is referred to as seven-year property. This means that for these types of property the actual costs are spread out and depreciated over five or seven years; that is, the costs are deducted over a period of five or seven years.

There are also several different ways to compute how much of the cost can be depreciated each year. There are three basic methods: Straight Line, MACRS, and ACRS. Straight line depreciation spreads the deductible amount equally over the recovery period. Thus, for the power saw which is worth $90.00 and is used 70 percent of the time in a business, the cost basis which can be depreciated is $63.00. This asset has a recovery period of seven years. Spreading the $63.00 over the seven-year period allows you to deduct a total of $9.00 per year as depreciation of the saw. After the first year, the saw will be valued on your books at $54.00. Thus, after seven years, the value of the saw on your books will be $0.00. It will have been fully depreciated. You will have finally been allowed to fully deduct its cost as a business expense. Of course, if you have fixed asset costs of less than $125,000.00 for the year you put the saw in service, you will be allowed to claim the entire $63.00 deduction that first year.Other methods of depreciation have more complicated rules which must be applied. For full details, please refer to a tax preparation manual or consult a tax or accounting professional.

Below are listed various types of property which are depreciable or deductible. Consult this list to determine which of your business purchases may be depreciated and which of them may be written off as an immediately deductible expense. Also, don't forget the special IRS Section 179 deduction.

DEDUCTIBLE EXPENSES

Advertising
Bad debts
Bank charges
Books and periodicals
Car and truck expenses:
   Gas, repairs, licenses,
    insurance, maintenance
Commissions to salespersons
Independent contractor costs
Donations
Dues to professional groups
Educational expenses
Entertainment of clients
Freight costs
Improvements worth less than $100
Insurance
Interest costs
Laundry and cleaning
Licenses for business
Legal and professional fees

Maintenance
Office equipment worth less than $100
Office furniture worth less than $100
Office supplies
Pension plans
Postage
Printing costs
Property taxes
Rent
Repairs
Refunds, returns, and allowances
Sales taxes collected
Sales taxes paid on purchases
Telephone
Tools worth less than $100
Uniforms
Utilities
Wages paid

DEPRECIABLE PROPERTY

Business buildings (not land)
Office furniture worth over $100
Office equipment worth over $100

Business machinery
Tools worth over $100
Vehicles used in business

Fixed Asset Account Record

Recall that fixed assets are business purchases which are depreciable, unless you elect to deduct fixed asset expenses up to $125,000.00 per year. For recordkeeping purposes, you will prepare a Fixed Asset Account Record for each fixed asset which you have if you have acquired over $125,000.00 in a calendar year. If you have acquired less than $125,000.00 worth in a year, you may put all of your fixed asset records on one Fixed Asset Account Record sheet.

To prepare your Fixed Asset Account Record sheet, follow the following instructions:

① List the date on which you acquired the property. If the property was formerly personal property, list the date on which you converted it to business property.

② Then list the property by description. Enter the actual cost of the property. If the property is used, enter the lower amount of the cost of the property or the actual market value of the property. If the property is part business and part personal, enter the value of the business portion of the property.

③ If you will have more than $125,000.00 worth of depreciable business property during the year, additionally you will need to enter information in the last three columns on the record. First, you will need to enter the recovery period for each asset. For most property other than buildings, this will be either five or seven years. Please consult a tax manual or tax professional.

④ You will need to enter the method of depreciation. Again, check a tax manual or with a tax professional.

⑤ Finally, you will need to determine the amount of the deduction for the first year (*Hint:* tax manual or tax professional).

⑥ Once you have set up a method for each fixed asset, each year you will determine the additional deduction and update the balance. You will then use that figure on your business tax return and in the preparation of your Balance Sheet (explained in Chapter 12).

Fixed Asset Account

Date	Item	Cost	Years	Method	Annual	Balance

Business Assets Checklists

❑ Prepare a Current Asset Account Record for the following assets:

> ❑ Business checking account

> ❑ Petty cash fund

> ❑ Accounts receivable

❑ Periodically update the information on your Current Asset Account Records for use in preparing a Balance Sheet. Use the following records to update your Current Asset Account Records:

> ❑ Business checking account: Check Register

> ❑ Petty cash fund: Petty Cash Register

> ❑ Accounts receivable: Credit Sales Aging Report

❑ If you will have inventory, choose to track it on either a periodic or perpetual basis. Prepare the appropriate Inventory Records

> ❑ Track your inventory orders and receipts on your Perpetual or Periodic Inventory Records

> ❑ Periodically, make a Physical Inventory Record

> ❑ Periodically, determine your Cost of Goods Sold for use on your Profit and Loss Statements

❑ Prepare a Fixed Asset Account Record for each permanent asset

> ❑ Determine the cost basis for each asset

> ❑ Determine the method of depreciation for each asset

> ❑ Periodically, determine your annual depreciation deduction for each asset and update each Fixed Asset Account balance

Chapter 7

Tracking Business Debts

Business debts are also referred to as business liabilities. However, technically, business liabilities also includes the value of the owner's equity in the business. We will deal with owner's equity more fully in Chapter 13 when we discuss balance sheets.

Business debts can be divided into two general categories. First are current debts, those which will normally be paid within one year. The second general category is long-term debts. These are generally more long-term debts or those that will not be paid off within one year.

Current debts for most small businesses consist primarily of accounts payable and taxes which are due during the year. For small businesses, the taxes which are due during a year fall into three main categories: estimated income tax payments, payment of collected sales taxes, and payroll taxes. Estimated income tax payments will be discussed in Chapter 15 when we look more closely at taxes. Payroll tax recordkeeping will be explained in Chapter 10 when we discuss payroll in depth. Since the collection and payment of sales taxes are handled differently in virtually every state, you will need to contact your state's department of revenue or similar body to determine the specific necessary recordkeeping requirements for that business debt. In Chapter 9, when we discuss the records you will need to track your income, you will be shown how to handle the recordkeeping to keep track of your sales taxes.

That leaves us only with accounts payable to track as a current debt. You will have only one simple form to use to keep track of this important category. Accounts payable are the current bills which your business owes. They may be for equipment or supplies which you have purchased on credit or they may be for items which you have ordered on account. Regardless of the source of the debt, you will need a clear system to record the debt and keep track of how much you still owe on the debt.

Long-term debts of a business are those debts which will not be paid off within one year. These can either be debts based on business loans for equipment, inventory, business-owned vehicles, or business property. In the accounting system outlined in this book, you will only keep track of the current principal and interest for these debts. For long-term debts of your business, you will fill in the Long-Term Debt Record, which is explained later in this chapter.

Combined Accounts Payable Record

On the following page, you will find an Accounts Payable Record. If you have only a few accounts which you do not pay off immediately, you can use this form. If you have many accounts payable, you will need to complete an Individual Account Payable Record for each separate account. That form and its instructions immediately follow the Accounts Payable Record.

Accounts Payable Record

On the following form, you will enter any bills or short-term debts which you do not pay immediately. If you pay the bill off upon receipt of the bill, you need not enter the amount on this sheet. Your records for expenses will take care of the necessary documentation for those particular debts. Follow these instructions to prepare and fill in this particular form:

① For those debts that you do not pay off immediately, you will need to record the following information in the left-hand column of the record:
   ✦ The date the debt was incurred
   ✦ To whom you owe the money
   ✦ Payment terms (for instance: due within 30, 60, or 90 days)
   ✦ The amount of the debt

② In the right-hand column of the Accounts Payable Record, you will record the following information:
   ✦ The date of any payments
   ✦ To whom the payments were made
   ✦ The amount of any payments made

③ By periodically totaling the left- and right-hand columns, you will be able to take a look at the total amount of your unpaid accounts payable. You may wish to do this weekly, monthly, or quarterly. You will also need the figure for your total unpaid accounts payable for the preparation of your Balance Sheet.

④ When you have totaled your accounts payable at the end of your chosen periodic interval, you should start a new record and carry the unpaid accounts over to it. Using this simple record, you will be able to check your accounts payable at a glance and also have enough information available to use to prepare a Balance Sheet for your business, as explained later in Chapter 12.

Accounts Payable Record

Period from: to:

UNPAID ACCOUNTS			
Date	Due to	Terms	Amount
		TOTAL	

PAYMENTS		
Date	Paid to	Amount
	TOTAL	

Total Unpaid Accounts
− Total Payments
= Total Accounts Payable

Individual Accounts Payable Record

If your business has many accounts payable which must be tracked, it may be a good idea to prepare an individual account payable record for each account. On the following page, you will find an Individual Account Payable Record to be used for this purpose. In order to fill in this record, follow these directions:

① You will need to enter the following information for each account to whom a bill is owed:
+ Name
+ Address
+ Contact person
+ Phone number
+ An account number, if applicable

② As you receive a bill or invoice, enter the following information off the bill or invoice:
+ Date
+ Invoice number
+ Any terms
+ Amount due

③ When an amount is paid, enter this information:
+ Check number
+ Date paid
+ Amount paid

④ Total the balance due after each transaction. Using this method of tracking accounts payable will allow you to always have a running total of your individual accounts payable available.

⑤ To prepare a balance sheet entry for accounts payable, you will simply need to total all of the various account balances for all of your accounts payable.

Individual Accounts Payable Record

Company:
Address:
Contact Person: Phone:
Account #:   Interest Rate:

Date	Invoice/Check	Terms	Amount	Balance

Long-Term Debt Record

If your business has any outstanding loans which will not be paid off within one year, you will pre-pare a Long-Term Debt Record for each loan. You will track the principal and interest paid on each long-term debt of your business. This information will enable you to have long-term debt figures for use in preparing your Balance Sheet and interest-paid figures for use in preparing your Profit and Loss Statements. On the following page, you will find a sheet to be used for this purpose. In order to fill in this sheet, follow these directions:

① You will need to enter the following information for each company to whom a loan is outstand-ing:
  ◆ Name
  ◆ Address
  ◆ Contact person
  ◆ Phone number
  ◆ Loan account number
  ◆ Loan interest rate
  ◆ Original principal amount of the loan
  ◆ Term of the loan

② You will need a loan payment book or amortization schedule in order to obtain the necessary information regarding the portions of each of your payments that are principal and interest. As you make a payment, enter the following information:
  ◆ Date of payment
  ◆ Amount of principal paid
  ◆ Amount of interest paid
  ◆ Balance due (previous balance minus payment)

③ Total the balance due after each payment. Using this method of tracking accounts payable will allow you to always have a running total of your long-term liability for each long-term debt.

④ To prepare a Balance Sheet entry for long-term debts, you will simply need to total all of the various account balances for all of your long-term debts.

⑤ You should also periodically total all of the columns on your Long-Term Debt Record. You will need the totals for interest paid for your Monthly and Annual Expense Summaries (see Chapter 8).

Long-Term Debt Record

Company:
Address:
Contact Person   Phone:
Loan Account #:   Loan Interest Rate:
Original Loan Amount: Term:

Date	Payment		Principal		Interest		Balance	
TOTALS								

Business Debts Checklists

❏ Track current debts

> ❏ Track business estimated tax liability (individual or corporate) by using quarterly Profit and Loss Statements

> ❏ Track sales tax liability on periodic Income Records

> ❏ Track payroll tax liability on Payroll Depository Record

> ❏ Track total accounts payable with Accounts Payable Record

>> ❏ Update separate accounts on Individual Account Payable Records when payments are made

> ❏ Transfer current debt information to Balance Sheet periodically

❏ Track long-term debts

> ❏ Update business loan balances on Long-Term Debt Record when payments are made

> ❏ Update mortgage balances on Long-Term Debt Record when payments are made

> ❏ Transfer long-term debt balances to Balance Sheet periodically

Chapter 8

Tracking Business Expenses

The expenses of a business are all of the transactions of the business in which money is paid out of the business, with two general exceptions. Money paid out of the business to the owner (as a draw rather than as a salary) and money paid out of the business to pay off the principal of a loan are not considered expenses of a business. Very often, the bulk of a small business's recordkeeping will consist of tracking its expenses. Because of the tax deductibility of the cost of most business expenses, it is crucial for a business to keep careful records of what has been spent to operate the business. But even beyond the need for detailed expense records for tax purposes, a small business needs a clear system which will allow for a quick examination of where business money is being spent. The tracking of business expenses will allow you to see at a glance where your money is flowing. With detailed records, it will also be an easy task to apply various financial formulas to analyze and understand your expense/income ratios in greater depth. This will allow you to see if certain costs are out-of-line, if certain expenses are increasing or decreasing, and if your business expenses make clear business sense.

In order to track your business expenses, you will use two main forms, either a Daily or a Weekly Expense Record (depending on the volume of your business expenses), and a Monthly Expense Summary. You may also need to use a number of additional specialized forms if your business needs dictate their use. The specialized forms that are included will cover the additional recordkeeping which is necessary to document travel expenses, meals and entertainment expenses, and vehicle expenses. There is also an Annual Expense Summary for totaling your expense payments.

Tracking Expenses

All of your expenses will initially be recorded on either the Daily or Weekly Expense Record sheet. You will have to choose if you desire to track your expenses on a daily form or a weekly form. If you anticipate having a great number of entries, choose a daily sheet for recording the expenses. If your expense transactions will generally number under 30 per week, you can use the weekly record. Regardless of which time period you choose to have on each sheet, you should record the expenditures at least weekly so that you do not fall too far behind in keeping it up-to-date. You may switch between recording periods if your level of expenses changes.

On your expense record sheet, you will record all of your business expenses in chronological order. The expense transactions will generally come from two main sources: your business bank account check register and your petty cash register. You will transfer all of the expenses from these two sources to the main expense record sheets. This will provide you with a central listing of all of the expenditures for your business.

From this record sheet (whether it is a daily or weekly record), you will transfer your expenses to a Monthly Expense Summary sheet. On the Monthly Expense Summary sheet, you will enter a line for each expense type which you have listed on your business Chart of Accounts (see Chapter 4). You will then go through your Daily or Weekly Expense Record sheets for each month and total the expenses for each account. You will enter this total in the column for the specific type of expense.

Finally, on a monthly basis, you will transfer the totals for your various expense categories to the Annual Expense Summary sheet. On this sheet, you collect and record the total monthly expenses. With these figures, you will be able to easily total your expense amounts to ascertain your quarterly and annual expenses.

By recording your business expenses in this manner, you should have little difficulty being able to keep track of the money flowing out of your business on a daily, weekly, monthly, quarterly, and annual basis. You will have all of the information that you will need to easily provide the necessary expenditure figures for preparing a Profit and Loss Statement (which will be explained in Chapter 11).

On the next few pages you will be given a detailed explanation of how to fill in these various simplified forms. Remember that you must tailor the forms to fit your particular business.

Daily and Weekly Expense Records

On the following pages are both the Daily Expense Record and Weekly Expense Record forms. These forms are identical except for the time period that they are intended to cover. To use these forms, follow these steps:

① Decide which time period you wish to use for completing the forms. If you anticipate over 30 expense transactions a week, you should probably choose the Daily Expense Record. Otherwise, the Weekly Expense Record should be sufficient.

② Fill in the date or dates that the form will cover at the top where indicated.

③ Beginning with your Bank Account Check Register, transfer the following information from the register to the Expense Record:
- ✦ The date of the transaction
- ✦ The check number
- ✦ To whom the amount was paid
- ✦ The expense account number (off your Chart of Accounts)
- ✦ The amount of the transaction

④ Next, using your Petty Cash Register, transfer the following information from your Petty Cash Register to the Expense Record:
- ✦ The date of the transaction
- ✦ In the column for "Check Number," put "PC" to indicate that the expense was a petty cash expense
- ✦ To whom the amount was paid
- ✦ The expense account number (off your Chart of Accounts)
- ✦ The amount of the transaction
- ✦ *Note*: Do not list the checks that you make out to "Petty Cash" as an expense

⑤ For credit card transactions, follow these rules:
- ✦ Do not list the payment to a credit card company as an expense
- ✦ List the monthly amount on the credit card bill for interest as an interest expense
- ✦ Individually, list each of the business purchases on the credit card as a separate expense item, assigning an account number to each separate business charge. Make a notation for the date, to whom the expense was paid, and the amount. In the column for "Check Number," provide the type of credit card (for example: "V" for Visa)
- ✦ Do not list any personal charge items as business expenses
- ✦ If a charged item is used partially for business and partially for personal reasons, list only that portion that is used for business reasons as a business expense

⑥ At the end of the period (daily or weekly), total the Amount column. You will use this daily or weekly total expense amount to cross-check your later calculations.

⑦ It is a good idea to keep all of your various business expense receipts for at least three years after the tax period to which they relate. You may wish to buy envelopes for each weekly period, label each appropriately, and file your weekly business expense receipts in them. This will make it easy to find each specific receipt, if necessary.

Annual Recordkeeping Tasks Checklist

- ❑ Cash Basis businesses: Adjust your accounts for end-of-the-year as explained in Chapter 13

- ❑ Finalize your Annual Income Summary

- ❑ Finalize your Annual Expense Summary

- ❑ Finalize your Annual Travel Expense Summary

- ❑ Finalize your Annual Auto Expense Summary

- ❑ Finalize your Annual Meals and Entertainment Expense Summary

- ❑ Finalize your Annual Payroll Summary

- ❑ Do a full Inventory using your Physical Inventory Record

- ❑ Determine your Cost of Goods Sold

- ❑ Prepare an Annual Profit and Loss Statement

- ❑ Check your progress against your Estimated Profit and Loss Statement

- ❑ Update your Current Asset Account Records

- ❑ Update your Fixed Asset Account Records, if desired

- ❑ Update your Long-Term Debt Records

- ❑ Prepare an Annual Balance Sheet

- ❑ Analyze your financial records using Ratio Comparison Chart

- ❑ Prepare an Estimated Profit and Loss Statement for the next year

- ❑ Photocopy the necessary forms for the next year's records

Weekly Expense Record

Week of:

Date	Check #	To Whom Paid	Account #	Amount

Monthly Expense Summary

Using this record sheet, you will compile and transfer the total expense amount for each expense category. In this way, you will be able to keep a monthly total of all of the expenses, broken down by category of expense. To fill in this form, do the following:

① Indicate the month that the Summary will cover where indicated at the top.

② In the first column on the left-hand side, list all of your expense account numbers from your business Chart of Accounts.

③ In the next column, using your Daily or Weekly Expense Records, transfer the amounts for each expense. If you have more than four expense amounts for any account, use a second Monthly Expense Record to record additional amounts.

④ In the Total column, list the total expenses in each category for the month.

⑤ At the bottom of the page, total the amount for all of the categories for the month. Don't forget to include any amounts from any additional records in your totals.

⑥ To double-check your transfers and your calculations, total all of your Daily or Weekly Expense Record total amounts. This figure should equal your Monthly Expense Summary total for that month. If there is a discrepancy, check each of your figures until you discover the error.

Monthly Expense Summary

Month of:

Account Name/#	Amount	Amount	Amount	Amount	Total
					TOTAL	

Annual Expense Summary

① Fill in the year. Fill in your account numbers from your Chart of Accounts across the top row. If you have more than nine expense accounts, use a second and third page, if necessary.

② On a monthly basis, carry the totals from all of the rows on your Monthly Expense Summaries to the appropriate column of the Annual Expense Summary.

③ At the end of each quarter, total all of the monthly entries to arrive at your quarterly totals for each category.

④ To double-check your monthly calculations, total your categories across each month and put this total in the final column. Compare this total with the total on your Monthly Expense Summaries. If there is a discrepancy, check each of your figures until you discover the error. Don't forget to include your extra records if you have more than nine expense accounts to list.

⑤ To double-check your quarterly calculations, total your monthly totals in the final quarterly column. This figure should equal the total of the quarterly category totals across the quarterly row. If there is a discrepancy, check each of your figures until you discover the error.

⑥ Finally, total each of your quarterly amounts to arrive at the annual totals. To cross-check your calculations, total the quarterly totals in the final column. This figure should equal the total for all of the annual totals in each category across the Annual Total row. If there is a discrepancy, check each of your figures until you discover the error.

Annual Expense Summary

Year of:

Account # ⇨									Total
January									
February									
March									
1st Quarter									
April									
May									
June									
2nd Quarter									
July									
August									
September									
3rd Quarter									
October									
November									
December									
4th Quarter									
Annual TOTAL									

Travel, Auto, and Meals and Entertainment Expenses

Travel, auto, and meals and entertainment expenses are treated slightly differently than other business expenses because you are required by the Internal Revenue Service to support your expenses with adequate additional records or evidence. These records can be in the form of trip diaries, account books, or similar items. Weekly and Monthly Travel Expense Records and Annual Travel Expense Summary sheets are provided to assist in keeping accurate records for IRS and your own accounting purposes. Weekly and Monthly Auto Expense Records and Annual Auto Expense Summary sheets are included to track your business auto expenses. In addition, Weekly and Monthly Meals and Entertainment Expense Records and Annual Meals and Entertainment Expense Summary sheets are included to track your meals and entertainment expenses.

The following list is a general guide to those travel, auto, meals, and entertainment expenses which can be deducted as legitimate business expenses:

- **Transportation**: the cost of plane, train, or bus travel to the business destination. Also the cost of a taxi, bus, or limousine between airports, stations, hotels, and business locations. This includes any costs for baggage transfers.
- **Car**: The cost of operating your car when away from home on business. You can deduct your actual expenses or you may use the standard mileage rate. If you use the standard rate, you can also deduct tolls and parking expenses. For 2010, the standard mileage rate is 50 cents per mile, but is generally changed for each tax year.
- **Lodging**: If your business trip is overnight, you can deduct the cost of your lodging.
- **Meals**: If your business trip is overnight, you can deduct the cost of meals, beverages, and tips. You may also choose instead to use a standard meal allowance. For 2010, the standard meal allowance is, generally, $65 per day for meals, depending where your business trip is located. For complete information on this, please refer to IRS Publication 463: *Travel, Entertainment, Gift, and Car Expenses* and IRS Publication 1542: *Per Diem Rates*. Whether you choose to deduct the actual cost or the standard allowance, your deduction is limited to 50 percent of your expenses.
- **Entertainment**: You can deduct the cost of business-related entertainment if you entertain a client, customer, or employee and it is directly related to your business. As with meals, entertainment expense deductions are limited to 50 percent of your actual expenses.

For travel, car, and meals and entertainment expenses, you should also keep additional records that indicate the dates the expenses were incurred, the location of the expenses, and the business reason for the expenses. These can be noted on any receipts for the expenses.

Weekly or Monthly Travel Expense Records

① Decide whether you will need to track your travel expenses on a weekly or monthly basis. For most businesses, a monthly record will be adequate.

② Fill in the time period and the employee name.

③ For each separate expense, fill in the date and a description of the item. Place the amount for the item in the appropriate column (Travel, Lodging, Meals, or Other). Carry the amount over to the Total column.

④ At the end of the month (or week if you are keeping records on a weekly basis), total each column in the final Total row. To check for accuracy, the totals of the Travel, Lodging, Meals, and Other columns should equal the total for the Total column.

Weekly Travel Expense Record

Week of: Employee Name:

Date	Item	Travel	Lodging	Meals	Others	Total
	Weekly Total					

Monthly Travel Expense Record

Month of: Employee Name:

Date	Item	Travel	Lodging	Meals	Others	Total
Weekly Total						

Annual Travel Expense Summary

① Fill in the year and employee name.

② On a monthly basis, carry the totals from all of the columns on your Weekly or Monthly Travel Expense Record forms to the appropriate column of the Annual Travel Expense Summary form.

③ At the end of each quarter, total all of the monthly entries to arrive at your quarterly totals for each category.

④ To double-check your monthly calculations, total your categories across each month and put this total in the final column. Compare this total with the total on your Weekly or Monthly Travel Expense Record sheets. If there is a discrepancy, check each of your figures until you discover the error.

⑤ To double-check your quarterly calculations, total your monthly totals in the final quarterly column. This figure should equal the total of the quarterly category totals across the quarterly row. If there is a discrepancy, check each of your figures until you discover the error.

⑥ Finally, total each of your quarterly amounts to arrive at the annual totals. To cross- check your calculations, total the quarterly totals in the final column. This figure should equal the total for all of the annual totals in each category across the Annual Totals row. If there is a discrepancy, check each of your figures until you discover the error.

⑦ When you use the information on this form, remember that duplicate expenses may be recorded on this form and on the Annual Expense Summary. The purpose of this form is to keep track of your annual travel expenses as required by the IRS.

Annual Auto Expense Summary

Week of: Employee Name:

Car Make/Model: License Number:

Date	Description	Mileage	Gas/Oil	Other	Total
January					
February					
March					
1st Quarter					
April					
May					
June					
2nd Quarter					
July					
August					
September					
3rd Quarter					
October					
November					
December					
4th Quarter					
Annual TOTAL					

Weekly or Monthly Auto Expense Records

① Decide whether you will need to track your auto expenses on a weekly or monthly basis. For most businesses, a monthly record will be adequate.

② Fill in the time period, the employee name, car make and model, and license number.

③ For each separate expense, fill in the date and a description of the item. Place the amount for the item in the appropriate column (Gas/Oil or Other). Carry the amount over to the Total column. List the mileage driven for the period.

④ At the end of the month (or week, if you are keeping records on a weekly basis), total each column in the final Weekly or Monthly Total row. To check for accuracy, the totals of the Gas/Oil and Other columns should equal the total for the Total column.

Weekly Auto Expense Record

Week of: Employee Name:

Car Make/Model: License Number:

Date	Description	Mileage	Gas/Oil	Other	Total
	Weekly TOTAL				

Monthly Auto Expense Record

Month of: Employee Name:

Car Make/Model: License Number:

Date	Description	Mileage	Gas/Oil	Other	Total
	Weekly TOTAL				

Annual Auto Expense Summary

① Fill in the year, employee name, car make and model, and license number.

② On a monthly basis, carry the totals from all of the columns on your Weekly or Monthly Auto Expense Record forms to the appropriate column of the Annual Auto Expense Summary form.

③ At the end of each quarter, total all of the monthly entries to arrive at your quarterly totals for each category.

④ To double-check your monthly calculations, total your categories across each month and put this total in the final column. Compare this total with the total on your Weekly or Monthly Auto Expense Record sheets. If there is a discrepancy, check each of your figures until you discover the error.

⑤ To double-check your quarterly calculations, total your monthly totals in the final quarterly column. This figure should equal the total of the quarterly category totals across the quarterly row. If there is a discrepancy, check each of your figures until you discover the error.

⑥ Finally, total each of your quarterly amounts to arrive at the annual total. To cross- check your calculations, total the quarterly totals in the final column. This figure should equal the total for all of the annual totals in each category across the Annual Total row. If there is a discrepancy, check each of your figures until you discover the error.

⑦ When you use the information on this form, remember that duplicate expenses may be recorded on this form and on the Annual Expense Summary. The purpose of this form is to keep track of your annual auto expenses as required by the IRS.

Annual Auto Expense Summary

Week of:

Employee Name:

Car Make/Model:

License Number:

Date	Description	Mileage	Gas/Oil	Other	Total
January					
February					
March					
1st Quarter					
April					
May					
June					
2nd Quarter					
July					
August					
September					
3rd Quarter					
October					
November					
December					
4th Quarter					
Annual TOTAL					

Weekly or Monthly Meals and Entertainment Expense Records

① Decide whether you will need to track your meals and entertainment expenses on a weekly or monthly basis. For most businesses, a monthly record will be adequate.

② Fill in the time period and the employee name.

③ For each separate expense, fill in the date, description of the item, and business purpose. Place the amount for the item in the appropriate column (Meals or Entertainment). Carry the amount over to the Total column.

④ At the end of the month (or week if you are keeping records on a weekly basis), total each column in the final Weekly or Monthly Totals row. To check for accuracy, the totals of the Meals and Entertainment columns should equal the total for the Total column.

Weekly Meals & Entertainment Expense Record

Week of: Employee Name:

Date	Item	Business Purpose	Meals	Entertainment	Total
		Weekly TOTAL			

I confirm that the information on this form is true and correct, and that all of the expenses are business-related. All receipts are attached to this form.

_____   _____
Signature   Date

Monthly Meals & Entertainment Expense Record

Month of: _____   Employee Name: _____

Date	Item	Business Purpose	Meals	Entertainment	Total
		Weekly TOTAL			

I confirm that the information on this form is true and correct, and that all of the expenses are business-related. All receipts are attached to this form.

_____   _____
Signature   Date

Annual Meals and Entertainment Expense Summary

① Fill in the year and employee name.

② On a monthly basis, carry the totals from all of the columns on your Weekly or Monthly Meals and Entertainment Expense Record forms to the appropriate column of the Annual Meals and Entertainment Expense Summary form.

③ At the end of each quarter, total all of the monthly entries to arrive at your quarterly totals for each category.

④ To double-check your monthly calculations, total your categories across each month and put this total in the final column. Compare this total with the total on your Weekly or Monthly Meals and Entertainment Expense Record sheets. If there is a discrepancy, check each of your figures until you discover the error.

⑤ To double-check your quarterly calculations, total your monthly totals in the final quarterly column. This figure should equal the total of the quarterly category totals across the quarterly row. If there is a discrepancy, check each of your figures until you discover the error.

⑥ Finally, total each of your quarterly amounts to arrive at the annual totals. To cross- check your calculations, total the quarterly totals in the final column. This figure should equal the total for all of the annual totals in each category across the Annual Totals row. If there is a discrepancy, check each of your figures until you discover the error.

⑦ When you use the information on this form, remember that duplicate expenses may be recorded on this form and on the Annual Expense Summary. The purpose of this form is to keep track of your annual meals and entertainment expenses as required by the IRS.

Annual Meals & Entertainment Expense Summary

Year of: Employee Name:

Date	Item	Meals	Entertainment	Total
January				
February				
March				
1st Quarter				
April				
May				
June				
2nd Quarter				
July				
August				
September				
3rd Quarter				
October				
November				
December				
4th Quarter				
Annual TOTAL				

Purchase Orders

Two final forms which may be used for business expenses are the *Purchase Order* and the *Purchase Order Record*. A Purchase Order is used for placing orders for business merchandise when a credit account has been established with a company in advance. You should use the Purchase Order on the next page in conjunction with the Purchase Order Record which follows. Your Purchase Order Record provides you with a simple record of what you have ordered using your Purchase Orders.

① Place your business card in the upper left-hand corner of the blank Purchase Order form from this book and make a master copy on a copy machine. Make a number of copies of the master copy of your Purchase Order. Number your Purchase Orders consecutively.

② Using your first numbered Purchase Order, enter the date. Under "Ship via," enter how you wish the order to be shipped to you (i.e., UPS ground, US Mail, Freight Carrier, etc.).

③ If you have a delivery deadline date, enter under "Deliver by."

④ Enter the appropriate information under "Bill to" and "Ship to."

⑤ For each item ordered, enter the following:
- ◆ Item number
- ◆ Quantity
- ◆ Description
- ◆ Price and amount

⑥ Subtotal and add tax and shipping if you know the correct amounts. Check the appropriate box under "Terms."

⑦ Upon completing each Purchase Order, enter the following information on your Purchase Order Record:
- ◆ purchase order number
- ◆ Date
- ◆ Vendor name
- ◆ Brief description of what was ordered
- ◆ Date when due
- ◆ Amount of the purchase order

Purchase Order

Date:

Purchase Order #:

Ship via:

Deliver by:

Bill to:	Ship to:

Item #	Qty.	Description	Price Each	Total

Terms

❑ Cash
❑ COD
❑ On Account
❑ MC/VISA/CREDIT CARD

Subtotal	
Tax	
Shipping	
TOTAL	

Purchase Order Record

PO Number	Date	Issued to	For	Due	Amount

Business Expense Checklist

❑ On a daily or weekly basis, transfer the details of your business expenses from your Check Register and Petty Cash Register to your Expense Record sheets

> ❑ On a monthly basis, transfer the totals for your expenses to your Monthly Expense Summary

> ❑ On a monthly basis, transfer the totals for your expenses to your Annual Expense Summary

❑ Periodically, record your travel expenses on your Travel Expense Record sheets

> ❑ On a monthly basis, transfer the totals for your travel expenses to your Annual Travel Expense Summary

❑ Periodically, record your auto expenses on your Auto Expense Record sheets

> ❑ On a monthly basis, transfer the totals for your auto expenses to your Annual Auto Expense Summary

❑ Periodically, record your meal and entertainment expenses on your Meal and Entertainment Expense Record sheets

> ❑ On a monthly basis, transfer the totals for your meal and entertainment expenses to your Annual Meal and Entertainment Expense Summary

❑ As needed, prepare Purchase Orders

> ❑ Each time you prepare a Purchase Order, enter the information from the Purchase Order on your Purchase Order Record

Chapter 9

Tracking Business Income

The careful tracking of your business's income is one of the most important accounting activities you will perform. It is essential for your business that you know intimately where your income comes from. Failure to accurately track income and cash is one of the most frequent causes of business failure. You must have in place a clear and easily-understood system to track your business income. There are three separate features of tracking business income that must be incorporated into your accounting system. You will need a system in place to handle cash, track all of your sales and service income, and handle credit sales.

The first system you will need is a clear method for handling cash on a daily or weekly basis. This is true no matter how large or small your business may be and regardless of how much or how little cash is actually handled. You must have a clear record of how much cash is on hand and of how much cash is taken in during a particular time period. You will also need to have a method to tally this cash flow on a monthly basis. For these purposes, three forms are provided: a Daily Cash Report, a Weekly Cash Report, and a Monthly Cash Report Summary.

The second feature of your business income tracking system should be a method to track your actual income from sales or services. This differs from your cash-tracking. With these records you will track taxable and nontaxable income whether the income is in the form of cash, check, credit card payment, or on account. Please note that when *nontaxable income* is referred to, it means only income that is not subject to any state or local sales tax (generally, this will be income from the performance of a service). These records will also track your intake of sales taxes, if applicable. For this segment of your income tracking, you will have either a Daily or Weekly Income Record, depending on your level of income activity. You will also track your income on Monthly and Annual Income Summaries, which will provide you with a monthly, quarterly, and annual report of your taxable income, non-taxable income, and sales taxes collection.

The third feature of your business income tracking consists of a method to track and bill credit sales. With this portion of income-tracking, you will list and track all of your sales to customers which are made on account or on credit. The accounts that owe you money are referred to as your *accounts receivable*. They are the accounts from whom you hope to receive payment. The tracking of these credit sales will take place on either a Daily, Weekly, or Monthly Credit Sales Record. You will also use a Credit Sales Aging Report to see how your customers are doing over time. The actual billing of these credit sales will incorporate an Invoice, Statement, and Past Due Statement. Finally, a Credit Memo will be used to track those instances when a customer is given credit for any returned items.

Tracking Your Cash

Most businesses will have to handle cash in some form. Here we are not talking about the use of petty cash. Petty cash is the cash that a business has on hand for the payment of minor expenses which may crop up and for which the use of a business check is not convenient. The cash handling discussed in this section is the daily handling of cash used to take money in from customers or clients and the use of a cash drawer or some equivalent. You must have some method to accurately account for the cash used in your business in this regard. Three forms are provided: a Daily Cash Report, a Weekly Cash Report, and a Monthly Cash Report Summary. The use of these forms is explained below.

Daily or Weekly Cash Reports

This form is used each day or week to track the cash received in the business from customer payments to the business, not petty cash. The cash may be in a cash box or some type of cash register. Regardless of how your cash is held, you need a method to account for the cash. Please follow these instructions:

① First, you will need to decide if you wish to track your cash transactions on a daily or weekly basis. Depending on the level of your business, choose to use either a Daily or Weekly Cash Report.

② You must decide how much cash you will need to begin each period with sufficient cash to meet your needs and make change for cash sales. Usually $100.00 should be sufficient for most needs. Choose a figure and begin each period with that amount in your cash drawer. Excess cash that has been collected should be deposited in your business bank account. Each period, fill in the date and the cash on hand on your Cash Report.

③ As you take in cash and checks throughout the period, record each item of cash taken in, checks taken in, and any instances of cash paid out. "Cash Out" does not mean change that has been made, but rather cash paid out for business purposes (for example, a refund).

④ Your business may have so much daily cash flow that it will be burdensome to record each item of cash flow on your sheet. In that case, you will need a cash register of some type. Simply total the cash register at the end of the day and record the total cash in, checks in, and cash out in the appropriate places on the Daily Cash Report.

⑤ At the end of each period, total your Cash In and Checks In. Add these two amounts to your Cash on Hand at the beginning of the period. This equals your Total Receipts for the period. Subtract any Cash Out from this amount. This figure should equal your actual cash on hand at the end of the period. Make a bank deposit for all of the checks and for all of the cash in excess of the amount that you will need to begin the next period.

⑥ In the space for deposits, note the following: a deposit number, if applicable; the date of the deposit; the deposit amount; and the name and signature of the person who made the deposit. Don't forget to also record your deposit in your business Bank Account Check Register.

Daily Cash Report

Week of: _____   Cash on Hand Beginning: _____

Week	CASH IN Name	Amount	CHECKS IN Name	Amount	CASH OUT Name	Amount
1						
2						
3						
4						
5						
6						
7						
8						
9						
10						
11						
12						
TOTAL						

Deposit #:	
Deposit Date:	
Deposit Amount:	
Deposited by:	
Signed:	

Total Cash in _____

+ Total Checks in _____

+ Cash on Hand Beginning _____

= Total Receipts _____

– Total Cash Out _____

= Balance on Hand _____

– Bank Deposit _____

= Cash on Hand Ending _____

Weekly Cash Report

Week of: _____   Cash on Hand Beginning: _____

Week	CASH IN Name	Amount	CHECKS IN Name	Amount	CASH OUT Name	Amount
1						
2						
3						
4						
5						
6						
7						
8						
9						
10						
11						
12						
TOTAL						

Deposit #:	
Deposit Date:	
Deposit Amount:	
Deposited by:	
Signed:	

Total Cash in _____

+ Total Checks in _____

+ Cash on Hand Beginning _____

= Total Receipts _____

− Total Cash Out _____

= Balance on Hand _____

− Bank Deposit _____

= Cash on Hand Ending _____

Monthly Cash Report Summary

This form will be used to keep a monthly record of your Daily or Weekly Cash Reports. It serves as a monthly listing of your cash flow and of your business bank account deposits. You will, of course, also record your bank deposits in your business Bank Account Check Register. To use this form, follow these instructions:

① On a daily or weekly basis, collect your Daily or Weekly Cash Reports. From each Record, record the following information:
- ◆ Cash on hand at the beginning of the period
- ◆ Cash taken in
- ◆ Checks taken in
- ◆ Cash paid out
- ◆ The amount of the daily or weekly bank deposit
- ◆ Cash on hand at the end of the period and after the bank deposit

② You can total the Deposit column as a cross-check against your Bank Account Check Register record of deposits.

Monthly Cash Report Summary

Month:

Date	On Hand	Cash in	Checks in	Cash out	Deposit	On Hand
1						
2						
3						
4						
5						
6						
7						
8						
9						
10						
11						
12						
13						
14						
15						
16						
17						
18						
19						
20						
21						
22						
23						
24						
25						
26						
27						
28						
29						

Tracking Income

The second feature of your business income tracking system should be a method to keep track of your actual income. This portion of the system will provide you with a list of all taxable and non-taxable income and of any sales taxes collected, if applicable. For sales tax information, please contact your state's sales tax revenue collection agency. If your state has a sales tax on the product or service which you provide, you will need accurate records to determine your total taxable and non-taxable income and the amount of sales tax which is due. For this purpose and for the purpose of tracking all of your income for your own business analysis, you should prepare a Daily or Weekly Income Record. The information from these reports will then be used to prepare Monthly and Annual Income Summaries.

Daily or Weekly Income Records

To use this form, do the following:

① Depending on the level of your business, decide which time period you would like to track on each form: daily or weekly. Fill in the appropriate date or time period.

② You will need to contact your state taxing agency for information on how to determine if a sale or the provision of a service is taxable or nontaxable. You also will need to determine the appropriate rates for sales tax collection.

③ For each item, record the following information:
   ✦ Invoice number
   ✦ Taxable income amount
   ✦ Sales tax amount
   ✦ Nontaxable income amount
   ✦ Total income (Taxable, sales tax, and nontaxable amounts combined)

④ On a daily or weekly basis, total the amounts in each column to determine the totals for the particular time period. These figures will be carried over to the Monthly and Annual Income Summary sheets that will be explained next.

Daily Income Record

Date of:

Invoice #	Taxable income	Sales Tax	Nontaxable Income	Total Income
Daily TOTAL				

Weekly Income Record

Week of:

Invoice #	Taxable Income	Sales Tax	Nontaxable Income	Total Income
Weekly TOTAL				

Monthly Income Summary

To use this form, do the following:

① Fill in the appropriate month.

② Using your Daily or Weekly Income Records, record the following information for each day or week:
  ✦ Total taxable income amount
  ✦ Total sales tax amount
  ✦ Total nontaxable income amount
  ✦ Total income (taxable, sales tax, and nontaxable amounts combined)

③ On a monthly basis, total the amounts in each column to determine the totals for the particular month. These figures will be carried over to the Annual Income Summary that will be explained next.

Monthly Income Summary

Month of:

Invoice #	Taxable Income	Sales Tax	Nontaxable Income	Total Income
Monthly TOTAL				

Annual Income Summary

① Fill in the year.

② On a monthly basis, carry the totals from all of the columns on your Monthly Income Summary form to the appropriate column of the Annual Income Summary form.

③ At the end of each quarter, total all of the monthly entries to arrive at your quarterly totals for each category.

④ To double-check your monthly calculations, total your categories across each month and put this total in the final column. Compare this total with the total on your Monthly Income Summary sheets. If there is a discrepancy, check each of your figures until you discover the error.

⑤ To double-check your quarterly calculations, total your monthly totals in the final quarterly column. This figure should equal the total of the quarterly category totals across the quarterly row. If there is a discrepancy, check each of your figures until you discover the error.

⑥ Finally, total each of your quarterly amounts to arrive at the annual totals. To cross check your calculations, total the quarterly totals in the final column. This figure should equal the total for all of the annual totals in each category across the Annual Total row. If there is a discrepancy, check each of your figures until you discover the error.

Annual Income Summary

Year of:

Date	Taxable Income	Sales Tax	Nontaxable Income	Total Income
January				
February				
March				
1st Quarter				
April				
May				
June				
2nd Quarter				
July				
August				
September				
3rd Quarter				
October				
November				
December				
4th Quarter				
Annual TOTAL				

Tracking Credit Sales

The final component of your business income tracking system will be a logical method to track your credit sales. You will use a Daily, Weekly, or Monthly Credit Sales Record to track the actual sales on credit and a Credit Sales Aging Report to track the payment on these sales. In addition, several forms are provided for the billing of these credit sales: an Invoice, Statement, Past Due Statement, and Credit Memo.

Daily, Weekly, or Monthly Credit Sales Records

To keep track of sales made to customers on credit or on account, follow these directions:

① Depending on your particular level of business activity, decide whether you will need to use a Daily, Weekly, or Monthly Credit Sales Record.

② Fill in the appropriate date or time period.

③ For each sale that is made on credit, fill in the following information from the customer Invoice (see Invoice instructions later in this chapter):
   ✦ Invoice number
   ✦ Date of sale
   ✦ Customer name
   ✦ Total sale amount

④ The final column is for recording the date that the credit sale has been paid in full.

⑤ The information from your Daily, Weekly, or Monthly Credit Sales Record will also be used to prepare your Credit Sales Aging Report on a monthly basis.

Daily Credit Sales Record

Date:

Invoice #	Sale Date	Customer	Sale Total	Date Paid

Weekly Credit Sales Record

Week of:

Invoice #	Sale Date	Customer	Sale Total	Date Paid

Monthly Credit Sales Record

Month:

Invoice #	Sale Date	Customer	Sale Total	Date Paid

Credit Sales Aging Report

This report is used to track the current status of your credit sales or accounts receivables. Through the use of this form you will be able to track whether or not the people or companies that owe you money are falling behind on their payments. With this information, you will be able to determine how to handle these accounts: sending past due notices, halting sales to them, turning them over to a collection agency, etc. To use this form, do the following:

① Decide on which day of the month you would like to perform your credit sales aging calculations. Enter this date on the first line of the form.

② For each credit sales account, enter the name of the account from your Daily, Weekly, or Monthly Credit Sales Records.

③ In the Total column, enter the total current amount that is owed to you. If this figure is based on credit sales during the current month, enter this figure again in the Current column. Do this for each credit account.

④ Each month you will prepare a new Credit Sales Aging Report on a new sheet. On the same date in the next month, determine how much of the originally-owed balance has been paid off. Enter the amount of the unpaid balance from the previous month in the 30–60 days column. Enter any new credit sales for the month under the Current column. The figure in the Total column should be the total of all of the columns to the right of the Total column.

⑤ Each month, determine how much was paid on the account, deduct that amount from the oldest amount due, and shift the amounts due over one column to the right. Add any new credit sales to the Current column and put the total of the amounts in the Total column.

⑥ After entering the information for each month, total each of the columns across the Total line at the bottom of the report. The Total column is 100 percent of the amount due. Calculate what percentage of 100 percent each of the other columns is to determine how much of your accounts receivable are 30, 60, 90, or more than 90 days overdue.

Credit Sales Aging Report

Account Name	Total	Current	30–60 Days	60–90 Days	90 Days +
TOTALS					
PERCENT	100%				

Invoices and Statements

For credit sales, you will need to provide each customer with a current Invoice. You will also need to send them a Statement if the balance is not paid within the first 30 days. You will also need to send a Past Due Statement if the balance becomes overdue. Finally, a form is provided to record instances when a customer is given credit for a returned item. You will need to provide two copies of each of these forms: one for your records and one for the customer.

Invoice

The invoice is your key credit sales document. To prepare and track invoices, follow these directions:

① Make a number of copies of the invoice form. You can insert your business card in the upper-left corner before copying. Number each form consecutively. Make a copy of the form when the form is sent out to the customer using either carbon paper or a copier.

② For each order, fill in the following information:
   - ✦ Date
   - ✦ The name and address of who will be billed for the order
   - ✦ The name and address where the order will be shipped
   - ✦ The item number of the product or service sold
   - ✦ The quantity ordered
   - ✦ The description of the item
   - ✦ The per unit price of the item
   - ✦ The total amount billed (quantity times per unit price)

③ Subtotal all of the items where shown. Add any sales taxes and shipping costs and total the Balance.

④ Record the pertinent information from the Invoice on the appropriate Daily, Weekly, or Monthly Credit Sales Record.

⑤ Record the pertinent information from the Invoice on the appropriate Daily or Weekly Income Record or Monthly Income Summary.

⑥ Send one copy of the Invoice to the customer with the order and file the other copy in a file for your invoices.

Invoice

Date:

Invoice No.:

Bill to:

Ship to:

Item #	Qty.	Description	Price Each	Total
				0.00
				0.00
				0.00
				0.00
				0.00
				0.00
				0.00
				0.00
				0.00
				0.00
				0.00
				0.00
				0.00
				0.00
				0.00
		Subtotal		0.00
		Tax		
		Shipping		

Statement and Past Due Statement

Statements are used to send your credit customers a notice of the amount that is currently due. Statements are generally sent at 30-day intervals, beginning either 30 days after the invoice is sent, or at the beginning of the next month or the next cycle for sending statements. Follow these instructions for preparing your statements:

① You should decide on a statement billing cycle. Generally, this is a specific date each month (for example: the first, tenth, or fifteenth of each month).

② Make a copy of the Statement form using your business card in the upper-left corner. Fill in the date and the account name and address.

③ In the body of the form, enter information from any Invoice that is still unpaid as of the date you are completing the Statement. You should enter the following items for each unpaid Invoice:
+ The date of the Invoice
+ A description (including Invoice number) of the Invoice
+ Any payments received since the last statement or since the sale
+ The amount still owed on that Invoice

④ When all of the invoice information for all of the customer's invoices has been entered, total the Amounts column and enter in Balance.

⑤ The information on the Statement then can be used to enter information on your Credit Sales Aging Report.

⑥ The Past Due Statement is simply a version of the basic Statement that includes a notice that the account is past due. This Past Due Statement should be sent when the account becomes overdue. Fill it out in the same manner used for Statements.

Statement

Date:

Account:

Date	Description	Payment	Amount Due

Please pay this BALANCE

Past Due Statement

Date:

Account:

This account is now past due. Please pay upon receipt to avoid collection costs

Date	Description	Payment	Amount Due

Please pay this BALANCE

Credit Memo

The final form for tracking your business income is the Credit Memo. This form is used to provide you and your customer with a written record of any credit given for goods that have been returned by the customer. You will need to set a policy regarding when such credit will be given, (for example: whether only for a certain time period after the sale, or for defects, or other limitations). To use the Credit Memo, follow these instructions:

① Make copies of the Credit Memo using your business card in the upper-left corner. You will need to make two copies of the Credit Memo when filled in: one for your records and one for your customer to keep.

② Fill in the date, the number of the original Invoice, and the customer's name and address.

③ Fill in the following information in the body of the Credit Memo:
  ✦ Item number of item returned
  ✦ Quantity of items returned
  ✦ Description of item returned
  ✦ Unit price of item returned
  ✦ Total amount of credit (quantity times unit price)

④ Subtotal the credit for all items. Add any appropriate sales tax credit and total the amount in the Credit box. This is the amount that will be credited or refunded to the customer.

⑤ In the lower-left box, indicate the reason for the return, any necessary approval, and the date of the approval.

⑥ Handle the Credit Memo like a negative Invoice. Record the amount of credit as a negative on the appropriate Daily or Weekly Income Record.

⑦ Record the pertinent information from the Credit Memo as a negative amount on the appropriate Daily, Weekly, or Monthly Credit Sales Record, if the Credit Memo applies to a previous sale on credit that was recorded on a Credit Sales Record.

Credit Memo

Date:

Invoice #:

Credit to:

GOODS RETURNED

Item #	Qty.	Description	Price Each	Total

Reason for return:

Approved by:

Date:

Subtotal

Tax

CREDIT

Business Income Checklist

❑ Track your cash handling

> ❑ On a daily or weekly basis, prepare a Cash Record

>> ❑ As required, make any appropriate deposits of cash and checks to your Business Bank Account

>> ❑ Record any deposits in your Check Register

> ❑ On a monthly basis, prepare a Monthly Cash Summary

❑ Track your income

> ❑ On a daily or weekly basis, record all nontaxable and taxable income taken in, and sales tax proceeds on an appropriate Income Record

>> ❑ On a monthly basis, transfer information from your Income Records to your Monthly and Annual Income Summaries

❑ Track your credit sales

> ❑ For every sale on credit, prepare an Invoice and record the appropriate information on a Daily, Weekly, or Monthly Credit Sales Record and an appropriate Income Record

> ❑ On a monthly basis, prepare a Credit Sales Aging Report using the information from your Credit Sales Records and Statements

> ❑ On a monthly basis, prepare Statements and Past Due Statements

> ❑ As needed, prepare Credit Memos and record the information on the appropriate Income Record and Credit Sales Record, if applicable

Chapter 10

Tracking Payroll

One of the most difficult and complex accounting functions that small businesses face is their payroll. Because of the various state and federal taxes which must be applied and because of the myriad government forms which must be prepared, the handling of a business payroll often causes accounting nightmares. Even if there is only one employee, there is a potential for problems.

First, let's examine the basics. If your business is a sole proprietorship and you are the only one who works in the business, there is no need for a formal payroll system. You may pay for yourself on a periodic schedule, but these payments are not considered deductions for the business. They are simply draws and no taxes are withheld. You will need to file and pay estimated taxes as an individual on the amount of money that you expect your business to net each year. These payments are made quarterly and are handled on IRS Form 1040-ES: *Estimated Tax for Individuals*. You also will be required to pay a self-employment tax to the federal government. This is equivalent to a payroll deduction for Social Security and Medicare taxes. This is handled with IRS Schedule SE: *Self-Employment Tax* and is filed with your annual personal income taxes. This form is also found in Chapter 15.

If you operate as a partnership and there are no employees, the same rules apply. The partnership net income will be passed through to you as a partner and you will be liable for individual income taxes on your share. Any draws which you take against the partnership will not be considered business deductions for the business. If your business is a corporation, all pay must be handled as payroll, even if you are the only employee. The corporation is a separate entity and the corporation itself will be the employer. You and any other people which you hire will be the employees. Follow the instructions for business payroll explained later in this chapter.

If you operate as a sole-proprietorship or partnership and you will have employees, you must also follow the entire business payroll details which are explained in this chapter. Business payroll entails a great deal of paperwork and has numerous government tax filing deadlines. You will be required to make payroll tax deposits, file various quarterly payroll tax returns, and make additional end-of-the-year reports.

Initially, if you have any employees, you must take certain steps to set up your payroll and official status as an employer. The following information contains only the instructions for meeting federal requirements. Please check with your particular state and local governments for information regarding any additional payroll tax, state unemployment insurance, or worker's compensation requirements. The requirements below will apply to any business which decides to become an employer, whether it is a sole proprietorship, limited liability company, partnership, or an S- or C-corporation.

Setting Up Your Payroll

① The first step in becoming an employer is to file IRS Form SS-4: *Application for Employer Identification Number* (FEIN). This will officially register your business with the federal government as an employer. This form and instructions are included in Chapter 15.

② Next, each employee must fill in an IRS Form W-4: *Employee's Withholding Allowance Certificate*. This will provide you with the necessary information regarding withholding allowances to enable you to prepare your payroll.

③ You must then determine the gross salary or wage that each employee will earn. For each employee, complete an Employee Payroll Record and prepare a Quarterly Payroll Time Sheet as explained later in this chapter.

④ You will then need to consult the tables in IRS Circular E: *Employer's Tax Guide*. From the tables in this publication, you will be able to determine the proper deductions for each employee for each pay period. If your employees are paid on an hourly basis and the number of hours worked is different each pay period, you will have to perform these calculations for each pay period.

⑤ Before you pay your employee, you should open a separate business bank account for handling your business payroll tax deductions and payments. This will allow you to immediately deposit all taxes due into this separate account and help prevent the lack of sufficient money available when the taxes are due.

⑥ Next you will pay your employee and record the deduction information on the employee's Employee Payroll Record.

⑦ When you have completed paying all of your employees for the pay period, you will write a separate check for the total amount of all of your employee's deductions and for the total amount of any employer's share of taxes. You will then deposit this check into your Business Payroll Tax Bank Account that you set up in item number five on the previous page.

⑧ At the end of every month, you will need to transfer the information regarding employee deductions to your Payroll Depository Record and Annual Payroll Summary. Copies of these forms are included later in this chapter. You will then also calculate your employer share of Social Security and Medicare taxes. Each month (or quarter if your tax liability is less than $2,500.00 per quarter), you will need to deposit the correct amount of taxes due with the Federal government. This is done either by making a monthly payment for the taxes due to your bank with IRS Form 8109: *Tax Deposit Coupon,* or by making the payment on a quarterly basis when you file IRS Form 941: *Employer's Quarterly Federal Tax Return.* A copy of this form is included in Chapter 15.

⑨ On a quarterly or annual basis, you also will need to make a tax payment for Federal Unemployment Tax, using IRS Form 940: *Employer's Annual Federal Unemployment Tax Return* (FUTA). This tax is solely the responsibility of the employer and is not deducted from the employee's pay. Also on a quarterly basis, you will need to file IRS Form 941: *Employer's Quarterly Federal Tax Return.* If you have made monthly deposits of your taxes due, there will be no quarterly taxes to pay, but you still will need to file these forms quarterly.

⑩ Finally, to complete your payroll, at the end of the year you must do the following:
  ✦ Prepare IRS Form W-2: *Wage and Tax Statement* for each employee
  ✦ File IRS Form W-3: *Transmittal of Wage and Tax Statements*

Remember that your state and local tax authorities generally will have additional requirements and taxes that will need to be paid. In many jurisdictions, these requirements are tailored after the Federal requirements and the procedures and due dates are similar.

Quarterly Payroll Time Sheet

On the following page is a Quarterly Payroll Time Sheet. If your employees are paid an hourly wage, you will prepare a sheet like this for each employee for each quarter during the year. On this sheet you will keep track of the following information:

- Number of hours worked (daily, weekly, and quarterly)
- Number of regular and overtime hours worked

The information from this Quarterly Payroll Time Sheet will be transferred to your individual Employee Payroll Record in order to calculate the employee's paycheck amounts. This is explained following the Quarterly Payroll Time Sheet.

Quarterly Payroll Time Sheet

Week of	Sun	Mon	Tue	Wed	Thu	Fri	Sat	Reg	OT	Total
Quarterly TOTAL										

Employee Payroll Record

You will use this form to track each employee's payroll information.

① For each employee, fill in the following information at the top of the form:
  ✦ Name and address of employee
  ✦ Employee's Social Security number
  ✦ Number of exemptions claimed by employee on Form W-4
  ✦ Regular and overtime wage rates
  ✦ Pay period (ie., weekly, biweekly, monthly, etc.)

② For each pay period, fill in the number of regular and overtime hours worked from the employee's Quarterly Payroll Time Sheet. Multiply this amount by the employee's wage rate to determine the gross pay. For example: 40 hours at the regular wage of $8.00/hour = $320.00; plus five hours at the overtime wage rate of $12.00/hour = $60.00. Gross pay for the period is $320.00 + $60.00 = $380.00.

③ Determine the federal withholding tax deduction for the pay amount by consulting the withholding tax tables in IRS Circular E: *Employer's Tax Guide.* Enter this figure on the form. For example: In 2006 for a single person with no dependents, claiming only one exemption, and paid weekly, the withholding tax for $380.00 would be $36.00.

④ Determine the employee's share of Social Security and Medicare deductions, as found in IRS Circular E: *Employer's Tax Guide.* As of 2010, the employee's Social Security share rate is 12.4 percent and the employee's Medicare share rate is 2.9 percent. Multiply these rates times the employee's gross wages and enter the figures in the appropriate places. For example: for $380.00, the Social Security deduction would be $380.00 x .124 = $47.12 and the Medicare deduction would be $380.00 x .029 = $11.02.

⑤ Determine any state or local taxes and enter in the appropriate column.

⑥ Subtract all of the deductions from the employee's gross wages to determine the employee's net pay. Enter this figure in the final column and prepare the employee's paycheck using the deduction information from this sheet. Also, prepare a check to your Payroll Tax Bank Account for a total of the federal withholding amount and two times the Social Security and Medicare amounts. This includes your employer share of these taxes. The employer's share of Social Security and Medicare taxes is equal to the employee's share.

Employee Payroll Record

Employee: Social Security #:
Address: Number of Exemptions:
                                          Rate of Pay: Overtime Rate:
                                          Pay Period:

Date	Check #	Pay Period	Reg. Hours	OT Hours	Gross Pay	Fed. W/H	S/S Ded.	Medic. Ded.	State Taxes	Net Pay
Pay Period TOTAL										

Payroll Depository Record

You will be required to deposit taxes with the IRS on a monthly or quarterly basis (unless your total employment taxes totaled over $50,000.00 for the previous year, in which case you should obviously consult an accountant). If your employment taxes total less than $2,500.00 per quarter, you may pay your payroll tax liability when you quarterly file your IRS Form 941: *Employer's Quarterly Tax Return.* If your payroll tax liability is over $2,500.00 per quarter, you must deposit your payroll taxes on a monthly basis with a bank using IRS Form 8109: *Federal Tax Deposit Coupon.* The IRS will send you deposit coupons around the same time it assigns you an employee identification number (EIN). Use IRS Form 8109-B (as shown in Chapter 14) *only* if you are a new employer and have received your EIN, but not your preprinted coupons, or you have run out of the preprinted coupons and have not yet received a resupply. To track your payroll tax liability, use the Payroll Depository Record following these instructions:

① On a monthly basis, total each column on all of your Employee Payroll Records. This will give you a figure for each employee's federal withholding tax, Social Security tax, and Medicare tax for the month.

② Total all of the federal withholding taxes for all employees for the month and enter this figure in the appropriate column on the Payroll Depository Record.

③ Total Social Security and Medicare taxes for all of your employees for the entire month and enter this figure in the appropriate columns on the Payroll Depository Record. Note that SS/EE refers to Social Security/Employee's Share and that MC/EE refers to Medicare/Employee's Share.

④ Enter identical amounts in the SS/ER and MC/ER columns as you have entered in the SS/EE and MC/EE columns. Note that SS/ER refers to Social Security/Employer's Share and that MC/ER refers to Medicare/Employer's Share. The employer's share of Social Security and Medicare is the same as the employee's share, but is not deducted from the employee's pay.

⑤ Total all of the deductions for the month. This is the amount of your total monthly federal payroll tax liability. If necessary, write a check to your local bank for this amount and deposit it using IRS Form 8109: *Federal Tax Deposit Coupon.*

⑥ If you must file only quarterly, total all three of your monthly amounts on a quarterly basis and pay this amount when you file your IRS Form 941: *Employer's Quarterly Federal Tax Return.* On a yearly basis, total all of the quarterly columns to arrive at your total annual federal payroll tax liability.

Payroll Depository Record

Month	Fed. W/H		SS/EE		SS/ER		MC/EE		MC/ER		Total	
January												
February												
March												
1st Quarter												

1st Quarter Total Number of Employees: Total Wages Paid:

Month	Fed. W/H		SS/EE		SS/ER		MC/EE		MC/ER		Total	
April												
May												
June												
2nd Quarter												

2nd Quarter Total Number of Employees: Total Wages Paid:

Month	Fed. W/H		SS/EE		SS/ER		MC/EE		MC/ER		Total	
July												
August												
September												
3rd Quarter												

3rd Quarter Total Number of Employees: Total Wages Paid:

Month	Fed. W/H		SS/EE		SS/ER		MC/EE		MC/ER		Total	
October												
November												
December												
4th Quarter												

4th Quarter Total Number of Employees: Total Wages Paid:

Yearly TOTAL												

Yearly Total Number of Employees: Total Wages Paid:

Annual Payroll Summary

The final payroll form is used to total all of the payroll amounts for all employees on a monthly, quarterly, and annual basis. Much of the information on this form is similar to the information which you compiled for the Payroll Depository Record form. However, the purpose of this form is to provide you with a record of all of your payroll costs, including the payroll deduction costs. This form will be useful for both tax and planning purposes as you examine your business profitability on a quarterly and annual basis. Follow these directions to prepare this form:

① For each month, transfer the amounts for federal withholding taxes from the Payroll Depository Record to this form.

② For each month, total the columns on your Payroll Depository form for SS/EE and SS/ER and also for MC/EE and MC/ER. You will then simply need to transfer the totals for Social Security and Medicare taxes to this form. Recall that SS refers to Social Security, MC refers to Medicare, EE refers to Employee, and ER refers to Employer.

③ For each month, total all of your employees' gross and net pay amounts from their individual Employee Payroll Records and transfer these totals to this form.

④ On a quarterly basis, total the columns to determine your quarterly payroll costs. Annually, total the quarterly amounts to determine your annual costs.

Annual Payroll Summary

	Gross Pay		Federal W/H		S/S Taxes		Medicare Taxes		State Taxes		Net Pay	
January												
February												
March												
1st Quarter Total												
April												
May												
June												
2nd Quarter Total												
July												
August												
September												
3rd Quarter Total												
October												
November												
December												
4th Quarter Total												
Yearly TOTAL												

Payroll Checklist

❏ File IRS Form SS-4: *Application for Employer Identification Number* and obtain Federal Employer Identification Number (FEIN)

❏ Obtain IRS Form W-4: *Employee's Withholding Allowance Certificate* for each employee

❏ Set up Quarterly Payroll Time Sheets and Employee Payroll Records for employees

❏ Open separate business payroll tax bank account

❏ Consult IRS Circular E: *Employer's Tax Guide* and use tables to determine withholding tax amounts

❏ Obtain information on any applicable state or local taxes

❏ List Federal withholding, Social Security, Medicare, and any state or local deductions on Employee Payroll Record

❏ Pay employees and deposit appropriate taxes in payroll tax bank account

❏ Fill in Payroll Depository Record and Annual Payroll Summary

❏ Pay payroll taxes

   ❏ Monthly, using IRS Form 8109: *Federal Tax Deposit Coupon*, if your payroll tax liability is more than $2500 per quarter

   ❏ Quarterly, using IRS Form 941: *Employer's Quarterly Federal Tax Return*, if your payroll tax liability is less than $2500 per quarter

   ❏ Annually, file IRS Form 940: *Employer's Annual Federal Unemployment (FUTA) Tax Return*

❏ Annually, prepare and file IRS Form W-2: *Wage and Tax Statement* and IRS Form W-3: *Transmittal of Wage and Tax Statement* for each employee

Chapter 11

Preparing a Profit and Loss Statement

A profit and loss statement is the key financial statement for your business which presents how your business is performing over a period of time. The profit and loss statement illuminates both the amounts of money which your business has spent on expenses and the amounts of money that your business has taken in over a specific period of time. You may choose to prepare a profit and loss statement monthly, quarterly, or annually, depending on your particular needs. You will, at a minimum, need to have an annual profit and loss statement in order to streamline your tax return preparation.

A profit and loss statement, however, provides much more than assistance in easing your tax preparation burdens. It allows you to clearly view the performance of your business over a particular time period. As you begin to collect a series of profit and loss statements, you will be able to conduct various analyses of your business. For example, you will be able to compare monthly performances over a single year to determine which month was the best or worst for your business. Quarterly results will also be able to be contrasted. The comparison of several annual expense and revenue figures will allow you to judge the growth or shrinkage of your business over time. Numerous other comparisons are possible, depending on your particular business. How have sales been influenced by advertising expenses? Are production costs higher this quarter than last? Do seasons have an impact on sales? Are certain expenses becoming a burden on the business? The profit and loss statement is one of the key financial statements for the analysis of your business. Along with the balance sheet, which is discussed in Chapter 12, the profit and loss statement should become an integral part of both your short- and long-range business planning.

This chapter will explain how to compile the information which you will need to prepare your profit and loss statements. All of the necessary information to prepare your profit and loss statement will be obtained from the financial records which you have prepared using this book. No other sources will be necessary to complete your profit and loss statements. Various methods to analyze the information on your profit and loss statements will be outlined in Chapter 13.

There are several types of profit and loss statements provided for your use. The first two are Monthly and Quarterly Short Profit and Loss Statements. These are very simple forms which provide few details beyond your total income and expenses and your net pre-tax profit for the month. These Short Profit and Loss Statements are used primarily to determine any estimated tax liability. Monthly, Quarterly, and Annual Profit and Loss Statements are also included for those who wish to periodically extract more details from their records.

Finally, an Estimated Profit and Loss Statement is provided to allow you to estimate your future profits and losses over any time period. The Estimated Profit and Loss Statement can serve as a valuable business planning service by allowing you to project estimated changes to your business over various time periods and examine what the results may be. Projections of various business plans can be examined in detail and decisions can then be made on the basis of clear pictures of future scenarios. Your estimates for your business profits and losses can take into account industry changes, economic factors, and personal business decisions. Your estimates are primarily for internal business planning purposes, although it may be useful to use an Estimated Profit and Loss Statement to convey your future business plans to others. As a trial exercise, you should prepare an Estimated Profit and Loss Statement using your best estimates before you even begin business. You may wish to prepare such pre-business statements for monthly, quarterly, and annual time periods.

Short Profit and Loss Statements

The first two forms are Monthly and Quarterly Short Profit and Loss Statements. These forms are useful if the only information that you wish to obtain regarding your business on a monthly or quarterly basis is the bottom line: the net pre-tax profit. This figure may be necessary to determine your individual or corporate estimated federal income tax liability. The use of this form also gives you a quick method to gauge the basic performance of your business. However, if you wish to have a more detailed and comprehensive presentation of your business income and expenses, please use the various Profit and Loss Statements provided next. You will always need to prepare a full Annual Profit and Loss Statement. To prepare a Short Profit and Loss Statement, follow these instructions:

① Choose either the Monthly or Quarterly Short Profit and Loss Statement. The first figure you will need will be your Gross Sales Income. This figure will come from your monthly or quarterly Total Sales figures on your Annual Income Summary sheet. If your business is a pure service business, put your income on the Service Income Total line. If your business income comes from part sales and part service, place the appropriate figures on the correct lines.

② Next, if your business sells items from inventory, you will need to calculate your monthly or quarterly Cost of Goods Sold. You may need to do a quick inventory count in order to have the necessary figures to make this computation. Fill in the Cost of Goods Sold figure on the Profit and Loss Statement. If your business is a pure service business, skip this line. Determine your Net Sales Income by subtracting your Cost of Goods Sold from your Gross Sales Income.

③ Calculate your Total Income for the period by adding your Net Sales Income, your Total Service Income, and any Miscellaneous Income (for example, interest earned on a checking account).

④ To obtain your Expenses figure, consult your Annual Expense Summary sheet. Transfer either the monthly or quarterly totals for all of your expenses to the appropriate Short Profit and Loss Statement. Add in any Miscellaneous Expenses.

⑤ Simply subtract your Total Expense figure from your Total Income figure to determine your Pre-Tax Profit for the time period. You may use this figure for a quick check of your business profitability or to determine your estimated income tax liability for the appropriate period.

Monthly Short Profit and Loss Statement

For the month of:

INCOME				
Income	Gross Sales Income			
	Less Cost of Goods Sold			
	Net Sales Income Total			
	Service Income Total			
	Estimated Miscellaneous Income Total			
	TOTAL INCOME			
EXPENSES				
Expenses	General Expenses			
	Miscellaneous Expenses			
	TOTAL EXPENSES			
Pre-Tax Profit (income less expenses)				

Quarterly Short Profit and Loss Statement

For the quarter of:

INCOME			
Income	Gross Sales Income		
	Less Cost of Goods Sold		
	Net Sales Income Total		
	Service Income Total		
	Estimated Miscellaneous Income Total		
	TOTAL INCOME		
EXPENSES			
Expenses	General Expenses		
	Miscellaneous Expenses		
	TOTAL EXPENSES		
Pre-Tax Profit (income less expenses)			

Profit and Loss Statements

You may use this more detailed Profit and Loss Statement to obtain a clearer picture of your business performance. At a minimum, each year at year's end, you will need to prepare the Annual Profit and Loss Statement to assist you in tax preparation. If you desire, you may prepare a Monthly or Quarterly version of this form to help with your business planning. To prepare this form:

① Choose either the Monthly, Quarterly, or Annual Profit and Loss Statement. The first figure you will need will be your Gross Sales Income. This figure will come from your monthly, quarterly, or annual Total Sales figures on your Annual Income Summary sheet. If your business is a pure service business, put your income on the Service Income Total line. If your business income comes from part sales and part service, place the appropriate figures on the correct lines.

② Next, if your business sells items from inventory, you will need to calculate your monthly, quarterly, or annual Cost of Goods Sold. Monthly or quarterly, you may need to do a quick inventory count in order to have the necessary figures to make this computation. Annually, you will need to perform a thorough inventory. Fill in the Cost of Goods Sold figure on the Profit and Loss Statement. If your business is a pure service business, skip this line. Determine your Net Sales Income by subtracting your Cost of Goods Sold from your Gross Sales Income.

③ Calculate your Total Income for the period by adding your Net Sales Income, your Total Service Income, and any Miscellaneous Income (for example, interest earned on a checking account).

④ To obtain your Expenses figure, consult your Annual Expense Summary sheet. Fill in the appropriate Expense Account categories on the appropriate Profit and Loss Statement. If you have a large number of categories, you may need to prepare a second sheet. Transfer either the monthly, quarterly, or annual totals for each of your separate expense accounts to the Profit and Loss Statement. Add in any Miscellaneous Expenses.

⑤ Total all of your expenses and subtract your Total Expense figure from your Total Income figure to determine your Pre-Tax Profit for the time period. To analyze your Profit and Loss Statement, see Chapter 13.

Monthly Profit and Loss Statement

For the month of:

INCOME			
Income	Estimated Gross Sales Income		
	Less Estimated Cost of Goods Sold		
	Estimated Net Sales Income Total		
	Estimated Service Income Total		
	Estimated Miscellaneous Income Total		
	Estimated Total Income		
EXPENSES			
Expenses	Account Number		
	Account Number		
	Account Number		
	Account Number		
	Account Number		
	Account Number		
	Account Number		
	Account Number		
	Account Number		
	Account Number		
	Account Number		
	Account Number		
	Account Number		
	Account Number		
	General Expenses Total		
	Miscellaneous Expenses		
	TOTAL EXPENSES		
Pre-Tax Profit (income less expenses)			

Quarterly Profit and Loss Statement

For the quarter of:

INCOME			
Income	Gross Sales Income		
	Less Cost of Goods Sold		
	Net Sales Income Total		
	Service Income Total		
	Miscellaneous Income Total		
	Total Income		
EXPENSES			
Expenses	Account Number		
	Account Number		
	Account Number		
	Account Number		
	Account Number		
	Account Number		
	Account Number		
	Account Number		
	Account Number		
	Account Number		
	Account Number		
	Account Number		
	Account Number		
	Account Number		
	General Expenses Total		
	Miscellaneous Expenses		
	TOTAL EXPENSES		
Pre-Tax Profit (income less expenses)			

Annual Profit and Loss Statement

For the year of:

INCOME			
Income	Gross Sales Income		
	Less Cost of Goods Sold		
	Net Sales Income Total		
	Service Income Total		
	Miscellaneous Income Total		
	Total Income		
EXPENSES			
Expenses	Account Number		
	Account Number		
	Account Number		
	Account Number		
	Account Number		
	Account Number		
	Account Number		
	Account Number		
	Account Number		
	Account Number		
	Account Number		
	Account Number		
	Account Number		
	Account Number		
	General Expenses Total		
	Miscellaneous Expenses		
	TOTAL EXPENSES		
Pre-Tax Profit (income less expenses)			

Estimated Profit and Loss Statement

The Estimated Profit and Loss Statement differs from the other type of profit and loss statements in that the figures used are projections that you will estimate based on expected business income and expenses for a time period in the future. The value of this type of financial planning tool is to allow you to see how various scenarios will affect your business. You may prepare this form as either a monthly, quarterly, or annual projection. To prepare this form, do the following:

① The first figure that you will need will be your Gross Sales Income. Using either past Profit and Loss Statements or your Total Income figures on your Annual Income Summary sheet and future estimates of income, fill in this amount. If your business is a pure service business, put your estimated income on the Service Income Total line. If your business income comes from part sales and part service, place the appropriate figures on the correct lines.

② Next, if your business sells items from inventory, you will need to calculate your estimated Cost of Goods Sold. In order to have the necessary figures to make this computation, you will need to prepare a projection of your inventory costs and how many items you expect to sell. Fill in the Cost of Goods Sold figure on the Profit and Loss Statement. If your business is a pure service business, skip this line. Determine your Estimated Net Sales Income by subtracting your Cost of Goods Sold from your Gross Sales Income.

③ Calculate your Estimated Total Income for the period by adding your Net Sales Income, your Total Service Income, and any estimated Miscellaneous Income (for example: interest earned on a checking account).

④ Fill in the appropriate Expense Account categories on the Estimated Profit and Loss Statement. If you have a large number of categories, you may need to prepare a second sheet. To obtain your Estimated General Expenses figure, consult your Annual Expense Summary sheet or prior Profit and Loss Statements. Based on your future projections, fill in the totals for each of your separate expense accounts. Add in any estimated Miscellaneous Expenses.

⑤ Total all of your expenses and subtract your Total Estimated Expense figure from your Total Estimated Income figure to determine your Estimated Pre-Tax Profit for the time period.

Estimated Profit and Loss Statement

For the period of:

ESTIMATED INCOME			
Income	Estimated Gross Sales Income		
	Less Estimated Cost of Goods Sold		
	Estimated Net Sales Income Total		0.00
	Estimated Service Income Total		
	Estimated Miscellaneous Income Total		
	Estimated Total Income		0.00
ESTIMATED EXPENSES			
Expenses	Advertising expenses		
	Auto expenses		
	Cleaning and maintenance expenses		
	Charitable contributions		
	Dues and publications		
	Office equipment expenses		
	Freight and shipping expenses		
	Business insurance expenses		
	Business interest expenses		
	Legal and accounting expenses		
	Business meals and lodging		
	Miscellaneous expenses		
	Postage expenses		
	Office rent/mortgage expenses		
	Repair expenses		
	Office supplies		
	Sales taxes		
	Federal unemployment taxes		

Profit and Loss Statement Checklist

❏ If you only need basic pre-tax profit information in order to determine your individual or corporate estimated tax liability, prepare a Short Profit and Loss Statement

> ❏ Fill in your Gross Sales Income from your Annual Income Summary

> ❏ Fill in Cost of Goods Sold and calculate Net Sales Income

> ❏ Fill in any Service and Miscellaneous Income and calculate Total Income for the period

> ❏ Fill in any Miscellaneous Income and calculate Total Expenses for the period

> ❏ Calculate pre-tax profit for the time period

❏ If you need more detailed information for business planning purposes, prepare a full Monthly or Quarterly Profit and Loss Statement. Every business should prepare a full Annual Profit and Loss Statement, at a minimum. Prepare an Estimated Profit and Loss Statement, if desired

> ❏ Fill in your Gross Sales Income from your Annual Income Summary

> ❏ Fill in Cost of Goods Sold and calculate Net Sales Income

> ❏ Fill in any Service and Miscellaneous Income and calculate Total Income for the period

> ❏ Fill in General Expenses information for each separate expense account from your Annual Expense Summary

> ❏ Fill in any Miscellaneous Income and calculate Total Expenses for the period

> ❏ Calculate pre-tax profit for the time period

Special Instructions for Cash Method Accounting

The forms and instructions in this book are designed to be used primarily for *accrual method accounting*, as opposed to *cash method*. The accrual method of accounting records income when it is earned rather than when it is received and records expenses when they are incurred rather than when they are actually paid. In contrast, the cash method of accounting records income only when it is received and expenses only when they are actually paid. As explained in Chapter 2, businesses that have an inventory may keep their books using the cash method (if their annual gross revenue is under $1 million) or the accrual method. If your business has an extensive inventory, it may still be wise to use the accrual method of accounting. Once a method has been chosen, you will need written IRS approval to switch to another method. All the forms in this book will still be able to be used for those businesses that elect to use the cash method of accounting. Follow these minor alterations in how you handle your income and expenses:

① The major difference in accrual vs. cash accounting procedures regarding business expenses is that when using the cash method, unpaid expenses are not deductible as business expenses. Thus, all of your accounting procedures will be identical for cash and accrual except the treatment of your Accounts Payable. Recall that you record your unpaid bills as a current liability on an Accounts Payable Record. As you total your expenses at the end of the year, the unpaid bills and expenses which are recorded as accounts payable are simply not counted as current expenses for cash-method businesses. Only those business expenses which have actually been paid by the end of the year are deductible as business expenses for the year. The accounts payable figures are not used.

② The difference between cash and accrual method accounting in the area of income concerns the handling of your credit sales. Recall that you record all of your sales as income on your periodic Income Records. This includes both cash and credit sales. You also record your credit sales on your Credit Sales Records. For cash method businesses, you will simply not record any of your credit sales on your Income Records until they are actually paid. You will continue to record your credit sales as explained in Chapter 8. However, at tax time, you will not count any of your unpaid credit sales as business income. Only those sales for which you have actually taken in income will be counted. You may wish to retitle your Income Record sheets as "Cash Income Records." Your Credit Sales Records will also remain the same, but you will not transfer any of the credit sales to your (Cash) Income Records until they have been paid.

③ Refunds are handled a little differently for cash-method businesses. If the sale was for cash or was a credit sale which has been paid, record any refund as a negative sale. List the returned amount on your Income Record as a negative amount. This is the same as for accrual-method businesses. However, if the sale for which a refund is being made was a credit sale which has not yet been paid, simply list the refund as a negative credit sale. Do not make any entry on your Income Record. The reason for this is since you have not recorded the income from the original sale, you may not record the refund as a deduction against the income.

④ Bad debts are also handled slightly differently for cash-method companies. Customers who were billed for a service but who have not paid and whose accounts are deemed uncollectible are not "bad debts" for cash method businesses. The reason is that since the income from the account was never included as business income (remember: cash method only counts income when actually received), you can't count a bad debt deduction against that income. You simply never record the income as received. If you have received a check for a payment and included that payment as income, and later that check is returned as unpaid, you may then deduct that amount as a bad debt. The reasoning is the same: you included the check as income, thus you are entitled to a deduction to remove that income from your books because of the bounced check.

⑤ When you prepare your Profit and Loss Statements, cash-method businesses will not record any accounts payable (from their Accounts Payable Records) as expenses. Cash-method companies will also not use the accounts receivable figures (from their Credit Sales Records) to determine their current income. Expenses for a particular period will be limited to those expenses which have actually been paid (as shown on your Check Register and Petty Cash Register). Income for a particular period will be limited to that income which has actually been taken in (as shown on your Income Record and not your Credit Sales Record). Using these figures will give you an accurate Profit and Loss Statement for the period in question.

With these few simple alterations, you may use the forms and instructions in this book for cash-method accounting.

Chapter 12

Preparing a Balance Sheet

A profit and loss statement provides a view of business operations over a particular period of time. It allows a look at the income and expenses and profit or losses of the business during the time period. In contrast, a Balance Sheet is designed to be a look at the financial position of a company on a specific date. It shows what the business owns and owes on a fixed date. Its purpose is to depict the financial strength of a company as shown by its assets and liabilities. Recall that the assets minus liabilities equals equity (or net worth). Essentially, the Balance Sheet shows what the company would be worth if all of the assets were sold and all of the liabilities were paid off. A value is placed on each asset and each liability. These figures are then balanced by adjusting the value of the owner's equity figure in the equation.

In order to prepare a Balance Sheet for your business, you will need to update your Asset and Liability Accounts. Once you have updated these account balances, it will be a simple matter of transferring the balances to your Balance Sheet and performing the necessary calculations. On the next page, you will find the instructions for preparing Balance Sheets. Chapter 13 provides information on analyzing your Balance Sheets.

Balance Sheets

Your Balance Sheet will total your current and fixed assets and your current and long-term liabilities. You may choose to prepare a Balance Sheet monthly, quarterly, or annually. Forms for each time period are included. You will, at a minimum, need to prepare a Balance Sheet at year's end. For corporations and partnerships, this is a requirement. For sole proprietorships, this is highly recommended. Obtain all of the figures you need on the same date after updating all of your accounts.

① Your Current Assets consist of the following items. Where to obtain the correct figure for the asset amount is shown after each item:
- ✦ Cash in Bank (from your Check Register Balance)
- ✦ Cash on Hand (from your Petty Cash Register and Monthly Cash Report Summary)
- ✦ Accounts Receivable (from your Credit Sales Aging Reports)
- ✦ Inventory (from a Physical Inventory Record annually or from a review of your Perpetual or Periodic Inventory Record monthly or quarterly)
- ✦ Prepaid Expense (These may be rent, insurance, prepaid supplies, or similar items which have been paid for prior to their actual use. You will have to check through your Monthly Expense Summary to determine which items may be considered prepaid expenses)

② Total all of your Current Assets on your Balance Sheet.

③ Your Fixed Assets consist of the following items. Where to obtain the correct figure for the asset amount is shown after each item:
- ✦ Equipment (from your Fixed Asset Account sheets. You will need to update these sheets to include any equipment purchased since your last update. Update from your Monthly Expense Summary sheets)
- ✦ Autos and Trucks (from your Fixed Asset Account sheets. You will need to update these sheets to include any vehicles purchased since your last update. Update from your Monthly Expense Summary sheets)
- ✦ Buildings (from your Fixed Asset Account sheets. You will need to update these sheets to include any buildings purchased since your last update. Update from your Monthly Expense Summary sheets)

④ Total your Fixed Assets (except land) on your Balance Sheet. Now, returning to your Fixed Asset sheets, total all of the depreciation which you have previously deducted for all of your fixed assets (except land). Include in this figure any business deductions which you have taken for Section 179 write-offs of business equipment. Enter this total depreciation figure under Depreciation and subtract this figure from the total Fixed Assets (except land) figure.

⑤ Now, enter the value for any land which your business owns. Recall that land may not be depreciated. Add the Fixed Asset amount less Depreciation and the value of the land. This is your total Fixed Asset value.

⑥ Add any Miscellaneous Assets not yet included. These may consist of stocks, bonds, or other business investments. Total your Current, Fixed, and Miscellaneous Assets to arrive at your Total Assets figure.

⑦ Your Current Liabilities consist of the following items. Where to obtain the correct figure for the liability amount is shown after each item:
- ✦ Accounts Payable (from your Accounts Payable Record sheets)

+ Taxes Payable (from two sources: your sales taxes payable figure will come from your Monthly Income Summary sheets and your payroll taxes payable will come from the Check Register of your special payroll tax bank account. Include any amounts which have been collected but not yet paid to the state or federal government)
+ Miscellaneous Current Liabilities (include here the principal due on any short-term notes payable. Also include any interest on credit purchases, notes, or loans which has accrued but not been paid. Also list the current amounts due on any long-term liabilities. Finally, list any payroll which has accrued but has not yet been paid)

⑧ Your Fixed Liabilities consist of the principal of any long-term note, loan, or mortgage due. Any current amounts due should be listed as a Current Liability.

⑨ Total your Current and Long-Term Liabilities to arrive at a Total Liabilities Figure.

⑩ Subtract your Total Liabilities from your Total Assets to arrive at your Owner's Equity. For a sole proprietor, this figure represents the Net Worth of your business. For a partnership, this figure represents the value of the partner's original investments plus any earnings and less any partner draws. For a corporation, this figure represents the total of contributions by the owners or stockholders plus earnings after paying any dividends. Also for corporations, the Owner's Equity equals the *stock value* of the company plus any money which the corporation's owners have decided to set aside as *capital surplus*. Thus, to determine the *value of each share* of a corporation's outstanding stock, the calculation is:

Total Owner's Equity – any Capital Surplus
÷ Total number of outstanding corporate shares
= Value of each share of corporate stock

Monthly Balance Sheet

As of:

ASSETS			
Current Assets	Cash in Bank		
	Cash on Hand		
	Accounts Receivable		
	Inventory		
	Prepaid Expenses		
	Total Current Assets		
Fixed Assets	Equipment (actual cost)		
	Autos and Trucks (actual cost)		
	Buildings (actual cost)		
	Total Fixed Assets (except land)		
	(less depreciation)		
	Net Total		
	Add Land (actual cost)		
	Total Fixed Assets		
	Total Miscellaneous Assets		
	Total Assets		
LIABILITIES			
Current Liabilities	Accounts Payable		
	Miscellaneous Payable		
	Total Current Liabilities		
Fixed Liabilities	Loans Payable (long-term)		
	Total Fixed Liabilities		
	Total Liabilities		
Owner's Equity	Net Worth or Capital Surplus + Stock Value		

Quarterly Balance Sheet

As of:

ASSETS			
Current Assets	Cash in Bank		
	Cash on Hand		
	Accounts Receivable		
	Inventory		
	Prepaid Expenses		
	Total Current Assets		
Fixed Assets	Equipment (actual cost)		
	Autos and Trucks (actual cost)		
	Buildings (actual cost)		
	Total Fixed Assets (except land)		
	(less depreciation)		
	Net Total		
	Add Land (actual cost)		
	Total Fixed Assets		
	Total Miscellaneous Assets		
	Total Assets		
LIABILITIES			
Current Liabilities	Accounts Payable		
	Miscellaneous Payable		
	Total Current Liabilities		
Fixed Liabilities	Loans Payable (long-term)		
	Total Fixed Liabilities		
	Total Liabilities		
Owner's Equity	Net Worth or Capital Surplus + Stock Value		

Annual Balance Sheet

As of:

ASSETS			
Current Assets	Cash in Bank		
	Cash on Hand		
	Accounts Receivable		
	Inventory		
	Prepaid Expenses		
	Total Current Assets		
Fixed Assets	Equipment (actual cost)		
	Autos and Trucks (actual cost)		
	Buildings (actual cost)		
	Total Fixed Assets (except land)		
	(less depreciation)		
	Net Total		
	Add Land (actual cost)		
	Total Fixed Assets		
	Total Miscellaneous Assets		
	Total Assets		
LIABILITIES			
Current Liabilities	Accounts Payable		
	Miscellaneous Payable		
	Total Current Liabilities		
Fixed Liabilities	Loans Payable (long-term)		
	Total Fixed Liabilities		
	Total Liabilities		
Owner's Equity	Net Worth or Capital Surplus + Stock Value		

Balance Sheet Checklist

- ❏ Decide on frequency for Balance Sheet preparation

- ❏ Update your Current Asset accounts and transfer to Balance Sheet

    - ❏ Update your Cash in Bank (from Check Register)

    - ❏ Update your Cash on Hand (Petty Cash Register and Monthly Cash Report Summary)

    - ❏ Update your Accounts Receivable (from Credit Sales Aging Report)

    - ❏ Update your Inventory (from Physical, Perpetual, or Periodic Inventory Record)

    - ❏ Include any prepaid expenses

- ❏ Update Fixed Asset accounts and transfer to Balance Sheet

    - ❏ Enter any depreciation taken on Fixed Assets

    - ❏ Enter the value of any land owned by business

- ❏ Update Current Liabilities and transfer to Balance Sheet

    - ❏ Update Accounts Payable (from Accounts Payable Record Sheets)

    - ❏ Update Taxes Payable (from Annual Payroll Summary, Monthly Income Summary, or Check Register)

    - ❏ Update Miscellaneous Current Liabilities

    - ❏ Update Fixed Liabilities and transfer to Balance Sheet

    - ❏ Total all figures and calculate Owner's Equity

Chapter 13

Analyzing the Financial Statements

Once you have prepared your Profit and Loss Statements and your Balance Sheets, you still need to know how to analyze them. You need to know how to effectively use the information they contain to more clearly understand your business. In this chapter, you will learn the use of simple ratio and proportion analysis in order to derive more meaning from your financial records. Looking at your assets, liabilities, income, and expenses in different ways will allow you to exercise more control over your business finances.

Ratio analysis sounds intimidating. It isn't. Ratios are simply fractions used as a manner of comparison. We use them everyday to make different facts easier to understand. When you use 10 gallons of gas to drive 150 miles in your car, it is easier to explain if you say that your car gets 15 miles per gallon. 15 MPG is a ratio. It is derived from the simple fraction of 150/10 or 150 divided by 10. The answer of 15 is the ratio of miles driven to gas consumed or, simply put, miles per gallon. If you were to check your miles per gallon with every tankful of gasoline, you would have an effective method to check your car's performance. You would be performing a *ratio analysis* of your car's fuel consumption.

Ratios measure relationships between particular numbers. This manner of analyzing your business will allow you to look at your operations in various manners. You will simply be using the figures on your two central financial records (your Profit and Loss Statement and your Balance Sheet). By periodically plugging figures from those two records into certain simple ratio equations, you will be able to track certain aspects of your business.

Let's look at a simple financial ratio: a comparison of the amount of debt of a business versus the amount of the net worth of a business. We will use the figures from our original business example: Smith's Gourmet Foods. Recall that in our first look at Smith's business, it had a net worth of $1,670.00 and Smith owed a total of $400.00 in total debt. The ratio equation that we will use is simply:

Debt Ratio = Debt/Net Worth

Plugging our financial figures into this equation, we get:

400/1670 = .2395 or about 24%

This means that currently Smith's debt amounts to about 24 percent of her business net worth. This is a very stable situation. Smith could take these figures to a bank and would, most likely, be able to borrow considerably more money to purchase additional equipment for expansion. If Smith tracks this particular ratio for several months or even years, she will be able to gain an understanding of how her debt and net worth are in proportion. If, for example, Smith chooses to take out another loan to buy additional equipment for $1,200.00, her total debt will increase by that amount and her net worth will stay the same. The new debt ratio would be:

1600/1670 = .958 or about 96%

Smith's business debt is now fully 96 percent of its net worth. As long as she is able to bring in enough income to make timely payments on the loan for the new equipment, her business will still be financially sound. However, it would be unlikely that she would be given further loans for equipment unless she were able to decrease this percentage by either paying off a portion of the loan or increasing the business net worth in some way.

Another way to use balance sheet figures to analyze a business is to look at the *current ratio*. This simply means how many times the current debts could be paid off with the current assets. Our equation for this is:

Current Ratio = Current Assets/Current Debts

Again, for Smith's Gourmet Foods, we have the following figures:

Current Ratio = $2,070.00/$400.00 = 5.175

Smith would be able to pay off her current debt about five times with her current assets. Her business is in a very sound cash position. A current ratio of two or more, that is, the ability to pay off current debts twice with current assets, is considered adequate for most businesses. If a business has a relatively unstable cash flow, however, it might be necessary to maintain a current ratio of more than two.

Thus, based on our first two methods of analyzing the finances of our sample company, we have seen that it appears to be in sound financial shape. Its debt/net worth ratio is about 24 percent and its current ratio or ability to pay of current debts is a healthy 5.175.

We will look at 12 separate ways to use the figures from your Profit and Loss Statements and Balance Sheets to analyze your business. The first three methods will look at the profitability of your business: Net Profit Margin, Gross Profit Margin, and Return on Sales. The next six will examine the liquidity of your business or the ability of your business to meet its obligations: Current Ratio, Quick Ratio, Cash Turnover, and three separate Debt Ratios. The final three methods will look at the debt and investment aspects of your business: Collection Ratio, Investment Turnover, and Return on Investment. The meaning and use of each analysis method will be explained.

Each of these analysis methods consists of using figures from your Profit and Loss Statements or Balance Sheets in simple equations. Once you have performed the various analyses, you must then use the information which you have obtained to determine why the business trends which you have uncovered in your business have occurred. This will require an honest analysis of your business.

For each type of analysis, we will use the following figures from our sample company as examples:

Smith's Gourmet Foods Profit and Loss Statement

		2008		2009
Income:				
Gross Sales:	$	24,000.00	$	30,000.00
Cost of Goods Sold:	$	8,000.00	$	16,000.00
Gross Profit:	$	16,000.00	$	14,000.00
Expenses:				
Advertising:	$	1,200.00	$	2,400.00
Bad Debt	$	100.00	$	400.00
Depreciation	$	100.00	$	200.00
Insurance	$	200.00	$	400.00
Interest	$	150.00	$	300.00
Repairs	$	50.00	$	150.00
Sales Tax	$	1,200.00	$	1,500.00
Supplies	$	350.00	$	700.00
Telephone	$	400.00	$	750.00
Wages	$	4,000.00	$	6,000.00
Total Expenses:	$	7,750.00	$	12,800.00
Net Profit before tax:	$	8,250.00	$	1,200.00

Smith's Gourmet Foods Balance Sheet

		2008		2009
Assets:				
Current Assets:				
Cash	$	100.00	$	200.00
Accounts Receivable	$	150.00	$	450.00
Inventory	$	350.00	$	700.00
Total Current Assets:	$	600.00	$	1,350.00
Long-Term Assets:				
Equipment	$	1,200.00	$	2,400.00
Total Long-Term Assets:	$	1,200.00	$	2,400.00
Total Assets:	$	1,800.00	$	3,750.00
Liabilities:				
Current Liabilities:				
Notes Payable:	$	100.00	$	200.00
Accounts Payable:	$	350.00	$	1,000.00
Total Current Liabilities:	$	450.00	$	1,200.00
Long-Term Liabilities:				
Notes Payable:	$	1,000.00	$	2,000.00
Total Liabilities:	$	1,450.00	$	3,200.00
Net Worth:	$	350.00	$	550.00
Net Worth + Liabilities:	$	1,800.00	$	3,750.00

Net Profit Margin

The net profit margin that a business makes is determined by dividing its actual sales by its net profit figure without taking interest or income taxes into account. This figure will depend on earnings and expenses. By factoring out interest and taxes, you can use this figure to compare your business to other similar businesses without taking into account high debts or high income taxes. To perform this analysis, you will need to look at three figures from your Profit and Loss Statement:

- Gross Sales
- Interest Expenses
- Net Profit (before taxes)

The ratio that you will use is:

Net Profit – Interest/Gross Sales = Net Profit Margin

The higher the Net Profit Margin, the more profitable the business is.

To use the figures from our example, we would get:

$8,250.00 – $150.00/$24,000.00 = 33.75% for 2008

$1,200.00 – $300.00/$30,000.00 = 3% for 2009

For 2005, Smith made a 33.75 percent net profit on sales and in 2006, Smith's net profit margin dropped to three percent. This signals a danger sign for Smith. In 2006, although the amount of gross sales has gone up, the net profit has gone down. Smith must now carefully examine her business income and expenses to determine why this has happened.

Gross Profit Margin

The gross profit margin is an indication of the markup on goods that are sold to customers. It is only useful for businesses which sell goods from inventory. For this calculation, you will need the following figures from your Profit and Loss Statement:

- Gross Profit
- Gross Sales

The equation for gross profit margin is:

Gross Profit/Gross Sales = Gross Profit Margin

The higher the Gross Profit Margin, the better for business.

Looking at our sample company, we see the following:

$16,000.00/$24,000.00 = 66.66% Gross Profit Margin for 2008

$14,000.00/$30,000.00 = 46.66% Gross Profit Margin for 2009

We can see that although the actual profit margin in 2006 is still relatively high at nearly 47 percent, it has fallen 20 percent in one year. This also signals Smith that something may be wrong. With this clue, we can examine the Profit and Loss Statements more closely. Looking at the Smith Profit and Loss Statement, we can see that the Cost of Goods Sold has doubled in one year (from $8,000.00 to $16,000.00), and yet Gross Sales have only increased 25 percent (from $24,000.00 to $30,000.00).

Smith must now attempt to determine what may have caused the cost of her goods sold to increase without a proportionate increase in sales income. Was food in inventory lost, stolen, or spoiled? Did her wholesale prices increase? Should she now increase her retail prices? This is where honest analysis of a business will come in. The use of financial ratios can give you insight into financial problems, but it will take your own knowledge of the business to determine how to solve the financial problems that may be uncovered.

Return on Sales Ratio

This ratio allows a business to determine how much net profit was derived from its gross sales. This ratio is very similar to the Net Profit Margin but it factors in all expenses, including interest. It provides an indication of whether your expenses are under control and also whether your business is generating enough income from sales to pay for its costs. The figures that you will need from your Profit and Loss Statement are:

- Gross Sales
- Net Profit (before taxes)

The equation for Return on Sales Ratio is:

Net Profit/Gross Sales = Return on Sales Ratio

The higher the Return on Sales Ratio, the better for business

Plugging in our sample company's figures, we get:

$8,250.00/$24,000.00 = 34.375% for 2008

$1,200.00/$30,000.00 = 4% for 2009

We can see immediately that Smith has suffered a huge decrease in the rate of return on her sales, in fact an 800 percent drop. This signals a very serious problem for her business. Why? Although her gross sales are up in 2006 (from $24,000.00 to $30,000.00), her cost of goods sold are up even more (doubled from $8,000.00 to $16,000.00). In addition, her expenses have also nearly doubled (from $7,750.00 to $12,800.00). Thus, her expenses and goods costs are going up at a higher rate than her actual sales, leading to a precipitous drop in her net profit. She must either get her business expenses under control, increase her prices to account for higher cost of goods sold expenses, or find cheaper products to sell.

Current Ratio

The current ratio is the ability of a company to meet its short-term obligations. It measures how many times a company's current debt could be paid off by using its current assets. A general rule of thumb is that current assets should be about two times current debts. Too high a ratio may mean that too many assets are held in unproductive manners. Too low a ratio may mean that the business is too short on cash and may be unable to make timely payments to suppliers. The figures from your Balance Sheet which you will need are:

- Total Current Assets
- Total Current Liabilities

Current Assets/Current Liabilities = Current Ratio

Current Ratio should be around 2 on average

Looking at our sample company, we see the following:

$600.00/$450.00 = 1.333% for 2008

$1,350.00/$1,200.00 = 1.125% for 2009

We can see that the Current Ratio for Smith's Gourmet Foods is falling slightly. A close examination shows that accounts payable for 2006 have nearly tripled. Although Current Assets have more than doubled, Current Liabilities have nearly tripled. If this trend continues, Smith will be in trouble.

We can also look at a similar ratio, termed a Quick Ratio. This is essentially a Current Ratio with inventory factored out of the equation. It should be held to under one to indicate a strong business.

Current Assets – Inventory/Current Debt = Quick Ratio

For Smith's Gourmet Foods, we see little change in the two-year period:

$600.00 – $350.00/$450.00 = .555 for 2005

$1,350.00 – $700.00/$1,200.00 = .542 for 2006

Debt to Net Worth Ratio

This figure indicates the relationship between a business net worth and the debt which a business carries. It is an indication to banks and other creditors whether a business can handle additional debt. It is also a indication of business risk, in that a high debt to net worth ratio may indicate that the business is overly burdened by interest payments and hampered in its ability to borrow any additional funds which may be necessary. Too low a ratio, however, may indicate that a business is too conservative and could effectively borrow more funds to generate more profits. To calculate this ratio, use the following figures from your Balance Sheet:

- Total Liabilities
- Net Worth

The equation to use is as follows:

Total Debt/Net Worth = Total Debt Ratio

Over 1 indicates too much debt for net worth

Using the figures for our sample company, we find that:

$1,450.00/$350.00 = 4.14 Debt/Worth Ratio for 2008

$3,200.00/$550.00 = 5.82 Debt/Worth Ratio for 2009

Again, this calculation seems to indicate that Smith's Gourmet Foods may be in trouble financially. The 2008 Debt/Worth ratio is already too high and it increases in 2009. Smith's business owes nearly six times as much as its Net Worth. Clearly, this company would not be a safe credit risk for new debt.

We could also look at the debt in terms of current and long-term liabilities by using similar equations:

Current Debt/Net Worth = Current Debt Ratio

Long-Term Debt/Net Worth = Long-Term Debt Ratio

Cash Turnover Ratio

The final liquidity ratio provides an indication of how often cash flow turns over to finance your sales. Your working cash is the amount of money which you need daily to operate your business: pay salaries, utilities, supplies, inventory, etc. If your cash supply is too tight this can restrict your ability to meet your current obligations. The figures you will need to make this calculation are:

- Current Assets
- Current Debt
- Gross Sales

The equation to determine your cash turnover is:

Gross Sales/Current Assets – Current Debt = Cash Turnover Ratio

Generally, your cash turnover should be between 4 and 7

Let's look at Smith's Gourmet Foods figures:

$24,000.00/$600.00 – $450.00 = 160

$30,000.00/$1,350.00 – $1,200.00 = 200

We can easily see that Smith's Cash Turnover begins in 2008 at too high a rate and then increases in 2009. This indicates that the business operates on too little cash and may have a worsening ability to meet its obligations. It may soon be unable to pay its creditors, meet its salary obligations, or even buy additional inventory. There simply is not enough working capital in the form of cash available. Examining the Balance Sheet, we can see that Smith has let her available cash dwindle by not collecting her accounts receivable quickly enough and by not keeping up with her own bills (her accounts payable). This has led to her current cash-poor position.

Collection Ratio

The collection ratio provides a clear indication of the average period of time that it takes to collect your accounts receivable or credit sales. The ratio shows the average number of days it takes for your business to get paid for credit sales. This figure should be near the point at which you declare an account overdue (for example: 30 days). Too long a period and you are overextending your credit and basically becoming a banker for your slow-paying customers. The figures you will need for this calculation are:

- Accounts Receivable
- Gross Sales

The equation for calculating your collection period success rate is:

Accounts Receivable x 365/Gross Sales = Average Collection Period

The period should be no more than 1.5 times your credit overdue period

Let's see how Smith is doing in this regard:

$150.00 x 365/$24,000.00 = 2.28 days for 2008

$450.00 x 365/$30,000.00 = 5.475 days for 2009

Although her overall collection period is very low, note that it more than doubled in one year. This is an indication that her customers are beginning to pay at a slower rate. If this continues, it may prove to be trouble for her, particularly in light of the other indications that her business is operating on a very tight cash flow. She may wish to exert more effort at getting prompt payment for her goods in order to keep her cash levels high enough to meet her obligations.

Investment Turnover Ratio

This figure indicates the ability of a business to use its assets to generate sales income. The ability to generate greater and greater sales from a stable asset base is a good indication of business health. If the ratio is going down, this may indicate that the growth of the business is not being met with a growth in sales proportionate to the investment in assets. The figures you will need for this calculation are:

- Gross Sales
- Long-Term Assets

The calculation is:

Gross Sales/Long-Term Assets = Investment Turnover Ratio

In general, the higher the ratio the stronger the business.

For Smith's Gourmet Foods, the figures look like this:

$24,000.00/$1,200.00 = 20% for 2008

$30,000.00/$2,400.00 = 12.5% for 2009

Again, we can see that Smith's financial position is weakening. Her ability to generate sales from her assets has fallen considerably in 2009. Despite having twice as many assets, she was only able to increase sales by 25 percent. If you couple this analysis with her increasing Cost of Goods Sold and expenses, you can readily see why her Net Profit has fallen from $8,250 in 2008 to only $1,200 in 2006. She was not able to translate her higher wage costs, increased equipment costs, and higher advertising into a proportionately higher sales income. If she hopes to continue as a viable business, she must get her expenses back in line with gross sales, generate more sales from her new equipment, rein in her Cost of Goods Sold, and perhaps, increase her prices to bring in more income to her business.

Return on Investment Ratio

Our final financial ratio analysis tool is the return on investment ratio. This analysis provides a clear a indication of business profitability. It shows how much profit a business is able to generate in proportion to its net worth. This figure shows what level of actual return you are getting on the money that you have invested in your company. You should strive for a healthy return on your business investment or your business has little chance to grow. The figures you will need from both your Balance Sheet and Profit and Loss Statement are:

- Net Profit
- Net Worth

The calculation is:

Net Profit/Net Worth = Return on Investment

Your business should strive for at least a 12% return to be healthy

Let's check on Smith's Gourmet Foods one final time:

$8,250.00/$350.00 = 2,357% Return for 2008

$1,200.00/$550.00 =218% Return for 2009

Although Smith has an extremely high return on her investment for both years, her return rate has fallen by 90 percent in one year. Also, it is clear that her high return rate stems from her extremely low actual Net Worth. Although she was able to generate a very high return for her low investment for both years, her rapidly falling profits and rising expenses are a clear indication of a business in trouble. She needs to use the information obtained from all of the ratios to carefully analyze what has gone wrong with her initially-profitable business.

Ratio Comparison Chart

On the following page is a Ratio Comparison Chart for use in your business. It will allow you to compare key ratios over three time periods which you select (months, quarters, or years). By using this method of comparison you will be able to detect trends in your business, whether the trends involve profitability, liquidity, collections success, or general business prosperity.

To prepare your Ratio Comparison Chart, simply do the following:

①   Decide which of the ratios will be most beneficial for your business to track.

②   Determine over what time periods you will track the selected ratios.

③   Using the Comparison Chart, your Balance Sheets, and your Profit and Loss Statements, compute each selected ratio.

④   Repeat this for each time period.

⑤   Compare and contrast the business financial trends that become apparent in your Ratio Comparison Chart.

⑥   Using the information from the highlighted trends, carefully examine your Profit and Loss Statements and Balance Sheets to determine the business reasons behind the trends.

Ratio Comparison Chart

Ratio	Period	Period	Period
Net Profit Margin			
Gross Profit Margin			
Return on Sales			
Current Ratio			
Quick Ratio			
Total Debt/Net Worth			
Current Debt/Net Worth			
Long Term Debt/Net Worth			
Cash Turnover Ratio			
Collection Ratio			
Investment Turnover			
Return on Investment			

Chapter 14

Mechanics and Schedules of Recordkeeping

Once you have read through this entire book, you should take the time to carefully analyze your business in light of its recordkeeping needs. No two businesses will have identical financial recordkeeping requirements. You must determine which financial facts and figures will be most important in the successful operation of your individual business. Keep in mind that as your business grows, your needs may change. In addition, as you become more familiar with your recordkeeping, you may decide that you need additional methods of tracking certain aspects of your operations. You may decide that some of the information that you are collecting is unnecessary in your particular type of business. Don't be afraid to alter your recordkeeping system as your business changes. Your system is only valuable to you if it fits your own needs.

Once you have attempted to analyze your recordkeeping needs, you will need to actually set up your financial recordkeeping system. The forms in this book are designed to be photocopied and used in this system. The forms are not, however, designed to be torn out of this book (especially if you are reading a library copy of this book!)

Setting Up Your Recordkeeping System

① Carefully go through this book and note which recordkeeping forms you will need. A checklist of forms is provided at the end of this chapter. Your list may seem extensive. Many of the forms, however, may only be used once a year.

② Make a photocopy of each of the necessary forms. Also make a photocopy of each checklist that applies, and the Recordkeeping Schedule and specific Tax Schedule (see Chapter 14). If the form to be used is a monthly form, make 12 copies. If the form to be used is a quarterly form, make four copies. Make enough copies for one year's worth of records.

③ Purchase a three-ring binder and at least 15 tabbed dividers. Label the tabbed dividers in order as follows, deleting those items which do not apply to your particular business:
- ◆ Checklists and Schedules
- ◆ Business Chart of Accounts
- ◆ Check Register
- ◆ Petty Cash Register
- ◆ Assets
- ◆ Inventory
- ◆ Accounts Payable
- ◆ Liabilities
- ◆ Business Expenses
- ◆ Cash Records
- ◆ Credit Sales
- ◆ Payroll
- ◆ Profit and Loss Statements
- ◆ Balance Sheets
- ◆ Ratio Comparison Charts

④ Three-hole punch all of the forms, schedules, and checklists. Place each form behind the appropriate divider in the binder. Label and fill in the preliminary information on the forms. Certain forms such as Invoices, Statements, and Past Due Statements will not be punched but will be kept in folders.

⑤ Now you are ready to begin filling in the forms. Beginning with your Business Chart of Accounts, follow the instructions in this book to initially prepare each form. Then follow the Schedule of Recordkeeping and Tax Schedule to keep up with your financial recordkeeping tasks.

Financial Recordkeeping Schedules

Use these schedules of tasks to keep track of your schedule of recordkeeping functions. Don't forget also to keep up with the Tax Schedule included in Chapter 14 for your particular type of business.

Daily Recordkeeping Tasks Checklist

- ❏ Record payments and deposits in Check Register

- ❏ Record payments and additions in Petty Cash Register

- ❏ Record any Inventory received

- ❏ Prepare Daily Cash Record, if desired

- ❏ Prepare Daily Income Record, if desired

- ❏ Record any Invoices in Daily Credit Sales Record, if desired

- ❏ Record Purchase Orders in Purchase Order Record

- ❏ Record expenses in Daily Expense Record, if desired

- ❏ Prepare and record any Credit Memos, if required

- ❏ Fill in any Payroll time sheets

Weekly Recordkeeping Tasks Checklist

- ❏ Prepare Weekly Cash Record, if desired

- ❏ Prepare Weekly Income Record, if desired

- ❏ Record any Invoices in Weekly Credit Sales Record, if desired

- ❏ Record any accounts payable on your Accounts Payable Record and/or Individual Accounts Payable Record

❏ Record expenses in Weekly Expense Record, if desired

❏ Record travel expenses in Weekly Travel Expense Record, if desired

❏ Record auto expenses in Weekly Auto Expense Record, if desired

❏ Record meal and entertainment expenses in Weekly Meals and Entertainment Expense Record, if desired

❏ Prepare payroll, if necessary

❏ Make proper payroll deposits, if necessary

Monthly Recordkeeping Tasks Checklist

❏ Reconcile your Check Register against your Bank Statement

❏ Transfer the information from your Check Register and Petty Cash Register to your Expense Records

❏ Record any Invoices in Monthly Credit Sales Record, if desired

❏ Prepare Credit Sales Aging Report

❏ Prepare and mail Statements and Past Due Statements

❏ Prepare Monthly Cash Summary

❏ Prepare Monthly Income Summary and transfer the information to your Annual Income Summary

❏ Record monthly travel expenses in Monthly Travel Expense Record and transfer the information to your Annual Travel Expense Summary

❏ Record monthly auto expenses in Monthly Auto Expense Record and transfer the information to your Annual Auto Expense Summary

❏ Record monthly meal and entertainment expenses in Monthly Meals and Entertainment Expense Record and transfer the information to your Annual Meals and Entertainment Expense Summary

❏ Prepare a Monthly Expense Summary and transfer the information to your Annual Expense Summary

❏ Do a quick inventory check

❏ Determine your Cost of Goods Sold, if desired

❏ Prepare a Monthly Profit and Loss Statement, if desired

❏ Check your progress against your Estimated Profit and Loss Statement

❏ Update your Current Asset Account Records, if desired

❏ Update your Fixed Asset Account Records, if desired

❏ Update your Long-Term Debt Records, if desired

❏ Prepare a Monthly Balance Sheet, if desired

❏ Prepare payroll, if necessary, and transfer the information to your Annual Payroll Summary

❏ Make proper payroll deposits, if necessary

Quarterly Recordkeeping Tasks Checklist

☐ Do a quick inventory check

☐ Determine your quarterly Cost of Goods Sold, if desired

☐ Calculate quarterly totals on your Annual Income Summary

☐ Calculate quarterly totals on your Annual Expense Summary

☐ Calculate quarterly totals on your Annual Auto Expense Summary

☐ Calculate quarterly totals on your Annual Travel Expense Summary

☐ Calculate quarterly totals on your Annual Meals and Entertainment Expense Summary

☐ Calculate quarterly totals on your Quarterly Payroll Time Sheet(s)

☐ Calculate quarterly totals on your Annual Payroll Summary

☐ Prepare a Quarterly Profit and Loss Statement, if desired

☐ Check your progress against your Estimated Profit and Loss Statement

☐ Update your Current Asset Account Records, if desired

☐ Update your Fixed Asset Account Records, if desired

☐ Prepare a Quarterly Balance Sheet, if desired

☐ Update your Long-Term Debt Records, if desired

☐ Analyze your financial records using Ratio Comparison Chart, if desired

Annual Recordkeeping Tasks Checklist

❏ Cash Basis businesses: Adjust your accounts for end-of-the-year as explained in Chapter 12

❏ Finalize your Annual Income Summary

❏ Finalize your Annual Expense Summary

❏ Finalize your Annual Travel Expense Summary

❏ Finalize your Annual Auto Expense Summary

❏ Finalize your Annual Meals and Entertainment Expense Summary

❏ Finalize your Annual Payroll Summary

❏ Do a full Inventory using your Physical Inventory Record

❏ Determine your Cost of Goods Sold

❏ Prepare an Annual Profit and Loss Statement

❏ Check your progress against your Estimated Profit and Loss Statement

❏ Update your Current Asset Account Records

❏ Update your Fixed Asset Account Records, if desired

❏ Update your Long-Term Debt Records

❏ Prepare an Annual Balance Sheet

❏ Analyze your financial records using Ratio Comparison Chart

❏ Prepare an Estimated Profit and Loss Statement for the next year

❏ Photocopy the necessary forms for the next year's records

❏ Set up all of the financial recordkeeping for next year and file your old records and retain for three years

Financial Forms Checklist

❏ Chart of Accounts

❏ Check Register

❏ Monthly Bank Statement Reconciliation

❏ Petty Cash Register

❏ Current Asset Account Record

❏ Physical Inventory Record

❏ Perpetual Inventory Record

❏ Cost of Goods Sold Record

❏ Fixed Asset Account Record

❏ Accounts Payable Record

❏ Individual Accounts Payable Record

❏ Long-Term Debt Record

❏ Daily or Weekly Expense Record

❏ Monthly Expense Summary

❑ Annual Expense Summary

❑ Weekly or Monthly Travel Expense Record

❑ Annual Travel Expense Summary

❑ Weekly or Monthly Auto Expense Record

❑ Annual Auto Expense Summary

❑ Weekly or Monthly Meals and Entertainment Expense Record

❑ Annual Meals and Entertainment Expense Summary

❑ Purchase Order

❑ Purchase Order Record

❑ Daily or Weekly Cash Record

❑ Monthly Cash Summary

❑ Daily or Weekly Income Record

❑ Monthly Income Summary

❑ Annual Income Summary

❑ Daily, Weekly, or Monthly Credit Sales Record

❑ Credit Sales Aging Report

❑ Invoice

❑ Statement

Chapter 15

Business Tax Forms

A basic comprehension of the information required on federal tax forms will help you understand why certain financial records are necessary. Understanding tax reporting will also assist you as you decide how to organize your business financial records. A checklist of tax forms is provided that details which IRS forms are necessary for each type of business. In addition, various schedules of tax filing are also provided to assist you in keeping your tax reporting timely. Finally, a sample of each form is included on the Forms-on-CD. Taxation details for all five basic business entities follow:

Taxation of Sole Proprietorships

The taxation of sole proprietorships is a relatively easy concept to understand. The sole proprietorship is not considered a separate entity for federal tax purposes. Thus, all of the profits and losses of the business are simply reported as personal profits or losses of the sole owner. They are reported on IRS Schedule C: Profits or Losses of a Business which is included in the calculations for completing the owner's joint or single IRS Form 1040.

Please note that many of the tax forms in this chapter will only apply to a sole proprietorship that actually hires employees. Simply because a sole proprietorship business is owned by one owner does not in any way restrict the sole owner from hiring employees or independent contractors to assist in the operation of the business. In fact, there have been sole proprietorships that have operated with many, many employees and at different locations and even in many states.

Sole Proprietorship Tax Forms Checklist

❑ IRS Form 1040: U.S. Individual Income Tax Return

❑ IRS Schedule C: Profit or Loss From Business. Must be filed with IRS Form 1040 by all sole proprietorships, unless Schedule IRS Schedule C-EZ is filed

❑ IRS Schedule C-EZ: Net Profit From Business. May be filed if expenses are under $5,000 and other qualifications are met (See Schedule C-EZ)

❑ IRS Form 1040-SS: Self-Employment Tax. Required for any sole proprietor who shows $400 income from his or her business on IRS Schedule C or C-EZ

❑ IRS Form 1040-ES: Estimated Tax for Individuals. Must be used by all sole proprietors who expect to make a profit requiring estimated taxes

❑ IRS Form SS-4: Application for Employer Identification Number. Must be filed by all sole proprietors who will hire one or more employees

❑ IRS Form W-2: Wage and Tax Statement. Must be filed by all sole proprietors who have one or more employees

❑ IRS Form W-3: Transmittal of Wage and Tax Statement .Must be filed by all sole proprietors who have one or more employees

❑ IRS Form W-4: Employee's Withholding Allowance Certificate. Must be provided to employees of sole proprietors. Not filed with the IRS

❑ IRS Form 940: Employer's Annual Federal Unemployment Tax Return (FUTA). Must be filed by all sole proprietors who have employees

❑ IRS Form 941: Employer's Quarterly Federal Tax Return. Must be filed by all sole proprietors who have one or more employees

❑ IRS Form 8109: Federal Tax Deposit Coupon. Used by all employers with quarterly employee tax liability over $2,500.00 (Obtain from IRS)

❑ IRS Form 8829: Expenses for Business Use of Your Home. Filed with annual IRS Form 1040, if necessary

❑ Any required state and local income and sales tax forms

Sole Proprietorship Monthly Tax Schedule

❑ If you have employees, and your payroll tax liability is over $2,500.00 quarterly, you must make monthly tax payments using IRS Form 8109

❑ If required, file and pay any necessary state or local sales tax

Sole Proprietorship Quarterly Tax Schedule

❑ Pay any required estimated taxes using vouchers from IRS Form 1040-ES

❑ If you have employees, file IRS Form 941 and make any required payments of FICA and withholding taxes

❑ If you have employees and your unpaid FUTA tax liability is over $500.00, make FUTA deposit using IRS Form 8109

❑ If required, file and pay any necessary state or local sales tax

Sole Proprietorship Annual Tax Schedule

❑ If you have employees, prepare IRS Forms W-2 and provide to employees by January 31

❑ File IRS Form W-3 and copies of all IRS Forms W-2 with IRS by January 31

❑ If you have paid any independent contractors over $600 annually, prepare IRS Forms 1099 and provide to recipients by January 31; and file IRS Form 1096 and copies of all IRS Forms 1099 with IRS by January 31

❑ Make required unemployment tax payment and file IRS Form 940

❑ File IRS Form 1040-SS with your annual IRS Form 1040

❑ File IRS Schedule C and IRS Form 1040

❑ If you are required, file and pay any necessary state or local sales, income, or unemployment taxes

❑ File IRS Form 8829 with your annual IRS Form 1040, if necessary

Taxation of Partnerships

There may be certain tax advantages to the operation of a business as a partnership. The profits generated by a partnership may be distributed directly to the partners without incurring any "double" tax liability, as is the case with the distribution of corporate profits in the form of dividends to the shareholders. Income from a partnership is taxed at personal income tax rates. Note, however, that depending on the individual tax situation of each partner, this aspect could prove to be a disadvantage. The losses of a partnership are also distributed directly to each partner at the end of each fiscal year and may be written off as deductions by each individual partner. Tax credits are also handled in a similar fashion.

For detailed understanding about the individual tax consequences of operating your business as a partnership, a competent tax professional should be consulted. A basic comprehension of the information required on federal tax forms will help you understand why certain financial records are necessary. Understanding tax reporting will also assist you as you decide how to organize your business financial records.

A chart of tax forms is provided which details which IRS forms may be necessary. In addition, a schedule of tax filing is also provided to assist you in keeping your tax reporting timely. Finally, a sample of each form is presented on the Forms-on-CD that accompanied this book.

Partnership Tax Forms Checklist

☐ IRS Form 1040: U.S. Individual Income Tax Return. Must be filed by all partners. Do not use IRS Form 1040-A or IRS Form 1040-EZ

☐ IRS Form 1065: U.S. Partnership Return of Income. Must be completed by all partnerships

☐ IRS Form 1065 - Schedule K-1: Partner's Share of Income, Credit, Deductions, etc. Must be filed by all partners

☐ IRS Form 1040-SS: Self Employment Tax. Required for any partner who shows $400+ income from their business on Schedule K-1

☐ IRS Form W-2: Wage and Tax Statement. Must be filed by all partnerships who have one or more employees

☐ IRS Form 1040-ES: Estimated Tax for Individuals. Must be used by all partners who expect to make a profit requiring estimated taxes

☐ IRS Form SS-4: Application for Employer Identification Number. Must be filed by all partnerships who will hire one or more employees

☐ IRS Form W-3: Transmittal of Wage and Tax Statement. Must be filed by all partnerships who have one or more employees

☐ IRS Form W-4: Employee's Withholding Allowance Certificate. Must be provided to employees of partnerships. It is not filed with the IRS

☐ IRS Form 940: Employer's Annual Federal Unemployment Tax Return (FUTA). Must be filed by all partnerships with employees

☐ IRS Form 941: Employer's Quarterly Federal Tax Return. Must be filed by all partnerships who have one or more employees

☐ IRS Form 8109: Federal Tax Deposit Coupon. Must be filed by all partnerships with employees and a quarterly income tax liability over $2,500, or a quarterly federal unemployment liability of over $500.00

☐ Any required state and local income and sales tax forms. Please check with the appropriate tax authority for more information

Partnership Monthly Tax Schedule

❑ If you have employees, and your payroll tax liability is over $2,500 quarterly, you must make monthly tax payments using Form 8109

❑ If required, file and pay any necessary state or local sales tax

Partnership Quarterly Tax Schedule

❑ Pay any required estimated taxes using vouchers from IRS Form 1040-ES

❑ If you have employees: file IRS Form 941 and make any required payments of FICA and Withholding Taxes

❑ If you have employees and your unpaid FUTA tax liability is over $500 quarterly, make FUTA deposit using IRS Form 8109

❑ If required, file and pay any necessary state or local sales tax

Partnership Annual Tax Schedule

❑ If you have employees, prepare W-2 forms and provide to employees by January 31st and file Form W-3 and copies of all W-2 forms with IRS by January 31st

❑ If you have paid any independent contractors over $600 annually, prepare 1099 Forms and provide to recipient by January 31st and file Form 1096 and copies of all 1099 forms with IRS by January 31st

❑ Make required unemployment tax payment and file IRS Form 940

❑ File IRS Form 1040-SS with your annual 1040 Form

❑ If required, file and pay any necessary state or local sales, income, or unemployment tax

❑ File IRS Form 1065 and Schedule K-1. Also provide a copy of Schedule K-1 to each partner by January 31st

Taxation of Corporations

Corporations are a separate entity under the law and as such are subject to taxation at both the state and federal levels. In general corporations are subject to federal income tax on the annual profits in many ways similar to the tax on individual income. However, there are significant differences. The most important aspect is the "double" taxation on corporate income if it is distributed to the shareholders in the form of dividends. At the corporate level, corporate net income is subject to tax at the corporate level.

Corporate funds that are distributed to officers or directors in the form of salaries, expense reimbursements, or employee benefits may be used by a corporation as a legitimate business deduction against the income of the corporation. Corporate surplus funds that are paid out to shareholders in the form of dividends on their ownership of stock in the corporation, however, are not allowed to be used as a corporate deduction. Thus, any funds used in this manner have been subject to corporate income tax prior to distribution to the shareholders. The dividends are then also subject to taxation as income to the individual shareholder and so are subject to a "double" taxation.

S-corporations are taxed similarly to partnerships, with the corporation acting only as a conduit and all of the deductions and income passing to the individual shareholders where they are subject to income tax. Corporations may be used by businesses in many ways to actually lessen the federal and state income tax burdens. A competent tax professional should be consulted. A brief study of the federal tax forms your business will use will provide you with an overview of the method by which corporations are taxed. A basic comprehension of the information required on federal tax forms will help you understand why certain financial records are necessary. Understanding tax reporting will also assist you as you decide how to organize your business financial records.

A checklist of tax forms is provided detailing which IRS forms may be necessary. In addition, a schedule of tax filing is also provided to assist you in keeping your tax reporting timely. Finally, a sample of each IRS tax form mentioned is included on the enclosed Forms-on-CD.

Corporation Tax Forms Checklist

☐ IRS Form 1120: U.S. Corporation Income Tax Return. This forms must be filed by all corporations

☐ IRS Form 1120-W: Estimated Tax for Corporations. Must be completed by all corporations expecting a profit requiring estimated tax payments

☐ IRS Form W-4: Employee's Withholding Allowance Certificate. Must be provided to employees of corporations. It is not filed with the IRS

☐ IRS Form W-2: Wage and Tax Statement. Must be filed by all corporations

☐ IRS Form 1040, 1040-A, 1040-EZ: U. S. Individual Income Tax Return. One of these forms must be filed by all shareholders

☐ IRS Form SS-4: Application for Employer identification Number. Must be filed by all corporations

☐ IRS Form W-3: Transmittal of Wage and Tax Statements. Must be filed by all corporations

☐ IRS Form 940: Employer's Annual Federal Unemployment (FUTA) Tax Return Must be filed by all corporations. If the amount of FUTA tax due for any calendar quarter is over $500, the tax due must be deposited at a financial institution (using IRS Form 8190) within the month following the end of the quarter

☐ IRS Form 941: Employer's Quarterly Federal Tax Return. Must be filed by all corporations, within the month following the end of each quarter. When filed, the corporation must pay any income, social security, and Medicare taxes which are due and have not been deposited monthly using IRS Form 8109. You may pay these taxes quarterly with Form 941 if you total tax liability for the quarter is less than $2,500. If you deposited all taxes when due (using IRS Form 8109), you have 10 additional days from the normal due date to file Form 941

☐ IRS 8109: Federal Tax Deposit Coupon. Must be filed by all corporations with a quarterly income, social security and Medicare tax liability of over $2,500 or with a quarterly federal unemployment liability of over $500

☐ Any required state and local income and sales tax forms. Please check with the appropriate tax authority for more information

Corporation Monthly Tax Schedule

❑ If corporate payroll tax liability is over $2,500 quarterly, the corporation must make monthly tax payments using IRS Form 8109: Federal Tax Deposit Cou-pon

❑ If required: file and pay any necessary state or local sales tax

Corporation Quarterly Tax Schedule

❑ Pay any required corporate estimated taxes using IRS Form 8109

❑ File IRS Form 941: Employer's Quarterly Federal Tax Return and make any required payments of FICA and withholding taxes

❑ If corporate unpaid quarterly FUTA tax liability is over $500, make FUTA deposit using IRS Form 8109

❑ If required, file and pay any necessary state or local sales tax

Corporation Annual Tax Schedule

❑ Prepare IRS Form W-2: Wage and Tax Statement and provide to each employee by January 31st. Also file IRS Form W-3: Transmittal of Wage and Tax Statements for each employee and copies of all W-2 forms with the Social Security Administration by January 31st

❑ If corporation has paid any independent contractors over $600 annually, prepare IRS Form 1099-MISC: Miscellaneous Income and provide to recipients by January 31. Also file IRS Form 1096: Annual Summary and Transmittal of U.S. Information Returns and copies of all 1099 forms with IRS by January 31

❑ Make required unemployment tax payment and file IRS Form 940: Employer's Annual Federal Unemployment (FUTA) Tax Return

❑ File IRS Form 1120: U.S. Corporation Income Tax Return

❑ If required: file and pay any necessary state or local sales, income, or unemployment tax

Taxation of S-Corporations

Corporations are a separate entity under the law and as such are subject to taxation at both the state and federal levels. There are two types of corporations: C-corporations and S-corporations. The difference between the two is in the area of taxation. In general, C-corporations are subject to federal income tax on the annual profits in many ways similar to the tax on individual income. However, there are significant differences. The most important aspect is the "double" taxation on corporate income if it is distributed to the shareholders in the form of dividends. At the corporate level, corporate net income is subject to tax at the corporate level. Corporate funds that are distributed to officers or directors in the form of salaries, expense reimbursements, or employee benefits may be used by a corporation as a legitimate business deduction against the income of the corporation. Corporate surplus funds that are paid out to shareholders in the form of dividends on their ownership of stock in the corporation, however, are not allowed to be used as a corporate deduction. Thus, any funds used in this manner have been subject to corporate income tax prior to distribution to the shareholders. The dividends are then also subject to taxation as income to the individual shareholder and so are subject to a "double" taxation.

S-corporations are taxed similarly to partnerships, with the corporation acting only as a conduit and all of the deductions and income passing to the individual shareholders where they are subject to income tax. The S-corporation does not pay a corporate tax and files a different type of tax return than does a standard corporation. Taxation of the profits of the S-corporation falls to the individuals who own shares in the corporation. This also allows for each individual shareholder to personally deduct their share of any corporate losses. A competent tax professional should be consulted. A brief study of the federal tax forms your business will use will provide you with an overview of the method by which corporations are taxed. A basic comprehension of the information required on federal tax forms will help you understand why certain financial records are necessary. Understanding tax reporting will also assist you as you decide how to organize your business financial records.

A chart of tax forms is provided detailing which IRS forms may be necessary. In addition, a schedule of tax filing is also provided to assist you in keeping your tax reporting timely. Finally, a sample of each IRS tax form mentioned is included on the enclosed Forms-on-CD.

S-Corporation Tax Forms Checklist

☐ IRS Form 1040: Must be filed by all S-corporation shareholders. Do not use IRS form 1040-A or IRS form 1040-EZ

☐ IRS Form 2553: Election by a Small Business Corporation. Must be filed by all S-corporations

☐ IRS Form 1120-S: U.S. Income Tax Return for an S-Corporation. Must be filed by all S-corporations

☐ IRS Form 1120-S, Schedule K-1: Shareholder's Share of Income, Credit, Deductions, etc. Must be completed by all S-corporations

☐ IRS Form 1040-ES: Estimated Tax for Individuals. Must be used by all S-corporation shareholders who expect a profit requiring estimated taxes

☐ IRS Form SS-4: Application for Employer Identification Number. Must be filed by all S-corporations who will hire employees

☐ IRS Form W-2: Wage and Tax Statement. Must be filed by all S-corporations who have one or more employees

☐ IRS Form W-3: Transmittal of Wage and Tax Statement. Must be filed by all S-corporations who have one or more employees

☐ IRS Form W-4: Employee's Withholding Allowance Certificate. Must be provided to employees of S-corporations. It is not filed with the IRS

☐ IRS Form 940: Employer's Annual Federal Unemployment (FUTA) Tax Return. Must be filed by all S-corporation employers

☐ IRS Form 941: Employer's Quarterly Federal Tax Return. Must be filed by all S-corporations who have one or more employees

☐ IRS Form 8109: Federal Tax Deposit Coupon. Must be filed by all S-corporations with a quarterly income tax liability over $2,500.00 or a quarterly FUTA tax liability of over $500

☐ Any required State and Local Income and Sales Tax forms. Please check with the appropriate tax authority for more information

S-Corporation Monthly Tax Schedule

❑ If corporation has employees, and corporate payroll tax liability is over $2,500 quarterly, the corporation must make monthly tax payments using Form 8109: Federal Tax Deposit Coupon

❑ If required: file and pay any necessary state or local states tax

S-Corporation Quarterly Tax Schedule

❑ Pay any required estimated taxes using vouchers from IRS Form 1040-ES: Estimated Tax for Individuals

❑ If corporation has employees: file IRS Form 941 and make any required payments of FICA and Withholding Taxes

❑ If corporation has employees and corporate unpaid FUTA tax liability is over $500, make FUTA deposit using IRS Form 8109

❑ If required: file and pay any necessary state or local sales tax

S-Corporation Annual Tax Schedule

❑ Prepare IRS Form W-2: Wage and Tax Statement and provide to each employee by January 31st. Also file IRS Form W-3: Transmittal of Wage and Tax Statements for each employee and copies of all W-2 forms with the Social Security Administration by January 31st

❑ If corporation has paid any independent contractors over $600 annually, prepare IRS Form 1099-MISC: Miscellaneous Income and provide to recipients by January 31. Also file IRS Form 1096: Annual Summary and Transmittal of U.S. Information Returns and copies of all 1099 forms with IRS by January 31

❑ Make required unemployment tax payment and file IRS Form 940

❑ File IRS Form 1120-S and Schedule K-1 of IRS Form 1120-S. Also provide a copy of Schedule K-1 to each shareholder by January 31st

❑ If required: file and pay any necessary state or local sales, income, or unemployment taxes

Taxation of a Limited Liability Company

There may be certain tax advantages to the operation of a business as a limited liability company. There are three methods by which a limited liability company can be taxed at the federal level. The choice of method is, for the most part, up to the member(s) of the company. The checklists provided in this chapter are separated into these three general divisions.

LLC Taxation As a Partnership

All limited liability companies that have more than one member will be taxed at the federal level as a partnership, unless the members elect otherwise. The partnership taxation is automatic and does not require any election or filing of any form for the election. If, however, a limited liability company elects to be taxed as a regular corporation, the members must vote to make this election and they must file Internal Revenue Service Form 8832: Entity Classification Election. If corporate taxation is elected, see below under "Taxation As a Corporation." If the limited liability company is to be taxed as a partnership, the profits generated by the limited liability company may be distributed directly to the members without incurring any "double" tax liability, as is the case with the distribution of corporate profits in the form of dividends to the shareholders. Income from a limited liability company is taxed at the personal income tax rate of each individual member. Note, however, that depending on the individual tax situation of each member, this aspect could prove to be a disadvantage. The losses of a limited liability company are also distributed directly to each member at the end of each fiscal year and may be written off as deductions by each individual member. Tax credits are also handled in a similar fashion. A list of necessary tax forms for limited liability companies being taxed as partnerships is included at the end of this chapter.

LLC Taxation As a Corporation

All limited liability companies, whether they have only one member or many, may elect to be taxed at the federal level as a corporation. This corporate taxation is not automatic and requires the filing of IRS Form 8832: Entity Classification Election. The company should complete this form, checking the box stating "Initial classification by a newly-formed entity (or change in current classification of an existing entity to take effect on January 1, 1997)." Under "Form of Entity" on this form, the limited liability company should check the box in front of the statement: "A domestic eligible entity electing to be classified as an association taxable as a corporation." This will cause the limited liability company to be taxed as a corporation. If the limited liability company is to be taxed as a corporation, the profits generated by the limited liability company will not pass through directly to the member, as with taxation of sole proprietorships or partnerships. Indeed, taxation of corporations opens the company up to "double" tax liability, in that any corporate profits are first taxed at the corporate level, and then the distribution of corporate profits in the form of dividends to the shareholders (or members) is taxed at the individual level at the personal income tax rates of the members. Note, however, that depending on the individual tax situation of the member, this aspect could prove to be an advantage. For a limited liability company that elects to be taxed as a corporation, the business losses are also not distributed directly to the member as individual deductions, but rather serve as deductions only for the company against company income. Tax credits are also handled in a similar fashion. A list of necessary tax forms for limited liability companies being taxed as corporations is included at the end of this chapter.

LLC Taxation As Sole Proprietorship

All limited liability companies that have only one member will be taxed at the federal level as a sole proprietorship, unless the sole member elects otherwise. The sole proprietorship taxation requires the filing of IRS Form 8832: Entity Classification Election. The single-member company should complete this form, checking the box stating "Initial classification by a newly-formed entity (or change in current classification of an existing entity to take effect on January 1, 1997)." Under "Form of Entity" on this form, the single-member limited liability company should check the box in front of the statement: "A domestic eligible entity with a single owner electing to be disregarded as a separate entity." This will cause the single-member limited liability company to be taxed as a sole proprietorship. If, however, a single-member limited liability company elects to be taxed as a regular corporation, the member must also file IRS Form 8832: Entity Classification Election. If corporate taxation is elected, see above under "Taxation As a Corporation." If the limited liability company is to be taxed as a sole proprietorship, the profits generated by the limited liability company pass through directly to the sole member without incurring any "double" tax liability, as is the case with the distribution of corporate profits in the form of dividends to the shareholders. Income from a limited liability company is taxed at the personal income tax rate of the sole member. Note, however, that depending on the individual tax situation of the member, this aspect could prove to be a disadvantage. The losses of a limited liability company are also distributed directly to the member as individual deductions. Tax credits are also handled in a similar fashion. A list of necessary tax forms for limited liability companies being taxed as sole proprietorships is included at the end of this chapter.

For a detailed understanding of the individual tax consequences of operating your business as a limited liability company, a competent tax professional should be consulted. The federal tax forms that are mentioned in this chapter are contained on the Forms-on-CD. A brief study of the tax forms will provide you with an overview of the method by which limited liability companies are taxed. A basic comprehension of the information required on federal tax forms will help you understand why certain financial records are necessary. Understanding tax reporting will also assist you as you decide how to organize your business financial records.

Various checklists of tax forms are provided that detail which IRS forms may be necessary for each method of taxation of limited liability companies. In addition, various schedules of tax filing are also provided to assist you in keeping your tax reporting timely.

Limited Liability Company Tax Forms Checklist
Taxed As a Sole Proprietorship

☐ IRS Form 8832: Entity Classification Election. This form must be completed and filed by all limited liability companies electing to be treated as a corporation

☐ IRS Form 1040: U.S. Individual Income Tax Return. Do not use IRS Form 1040A or IRS Form 1040EZ: Income Tax Return for Single and Joint Filers With No Dependents

☐ IRS Schedule C (Form 1040): Profit or Loss From Business (Sole Proprietorship) must be filed with IRS Form 1040 by all limited liability companies electing to be treated as sole proprietorships, unless Schedule IRS Schedule C-EZ: Net Profit From Business (Sole Proprietorship) is filed

☐ IRS Schedule C-EZ (Form 1040): Net Profit From Business (Sole Proprietorship) may be filed if expenses are under $5000 and other qualifications are met

☐ IRS Form 1040-SS: U.S. Self-Employment Tax Return. Required for any sole proprietor who shows $400+income from his or her limited liability company business on IRS Schedule C or IRS Schedule C-EZ

☐ IRS Form 1040-ES: Estimated Tax for Individuals must be used by all companies that expect to make a profit requiring estimated taxes

☐ IRS Form SS-4: Application for Employer Identification Number must be filed by all companies who will hire one or more employees

☐ IRS Form W-2: Wage and Tax Statement must be filed by all companies that have one or more employees

☐ IRS Form W-3: Transmittal of Wage and Tax Statements must be filed by all companies that have one or more employees

☐ IRS Form W-4: Employee's Withholding Allowance Certificate must be provided to employees of companies. Not filed with the IRS

☐ IRS Form 940: Employer's Annual Federal Unemployment (FUTA) Tax Return must be filed by all companies that have employees

☐ IRS Form 941: Employer's Quarterly Federal Tax Return must be filed by all companies that have one or more employees

☐ IRS Form 8109: Federal Tax Deposit Coupon. Used by all companies with quarterly employee tax liability over $2500. (Obtain from IRS)

☐ IRS Form 8829: Expenses for Business Use of Your Home. Filed with annual IRS Form 1040, if necessary

☐ Any required state and local income and sales tax forms

Limited Liability Company Tax Forms Checklist
Taxed As a Partnership

☐ IRS Form 1040: U.S. Individual Income Tax Return must be filed by all members. Do not use IRS Form 1040A or IRS Form 1040-EZ: Income Tax Return for Single and Joint Filers With No Dependents

☐ IRS Form 1065: U.S. Return of Partnership Income must be completed by all limited liability companies which are taxed as partnerships

☐ IRS Schedule K-1 (Form 1065): Partner's Share of Income, Credits, Deductions, etc. must be filed by all members

☐ IRS Form 1040-SS: U.S. Self-Employment Tax Return. Required for any member who shows $400+income from his or her business on Schedule K-1

☐ IRS Form 1040-ES: Estimated Tax for Individuals must be used by all members who expect to make a profit requiring estimated taxes

☐ IRS Form SS-4: Application for Employer Identification Number must be filed by all companies that will hire one or more employees

☐ IRS Form W-2: Wage and Tax Statement must be filed by all companies that have one or more employees

☐ IRS Form W-3: Transmittal of Wage and Tax Statements must be filed by all companies that have one or more employees

☐ IRS Form W-4: Employee's Withholding Allowance Certificate must be provided to employees of companies. Not filed with the IRS

☐ IRS Form 940: Employer's Annual Federal Unemployment (FUTA) Tax Return must be filed by all companies that have employees

❑ IRS Form 941: Employer's Quarterly Federal Tax Return must be filed by all partnerships that have one or more employees.

❑ IRS Form 8109: Federal Tax Deposit Coupon. Used by all companies with quarterly employee tax liability over $2500. (Obtain from IRS)

❑ Any required state and local income and sales tax forms. Please check with the appropriate tax authority for more information

Limited Liability Company Tax Forms Checklist
Taxed As a Corporation

❑ IRS Form 8832: Entity Classification Election. This form must be completed and filed by all limited liability companies electing to be treated as a corporation

❑ IRS Form 1040: U.S .Individual Income Tax Return must be filed by all members. Do not use IRS Form 1040A or IRS Form 1040EZ: Income Tax Return for Single and Joint Filers With No Dependents

❑ IRS Form 1120: U.S. Corporation Income Tax Return. This form must be filed by all limited liability companies electing to be treated as a corporation

❑ IRS Form 1120-W (Worksheet): Estimated Tax for Corporations must be completed by all limited liability companies expecting a profit requiring estimated tax payments

❑ IRS Form SS-4: Application for Employer Identification Number must be filed by all limited liability companies

❑ IRS Form W-2: Wage and Tax Statement must be filed by all limited liability companies

❑ IRS Form W-3: Transmittal of Wage and Tax Statements must be filed by all limited liability companies

❑ IRS Form W-4: Employee's Withholding Allowance Certificate must be provided to employees of limited liability companies. It is not filed with the IRS

❑ IRS Form 940: Employer's Annual Federal Unemployment (FUTA) Tax Return must be filed by all limited liability companies

❑ IRS Form 941: Employer's Quarterly Federal Tax Return must be filed by all limited liability companies

❑ IRS Form 8109: Federal Tax Deposit Coupon. Used by companies with quarterly employee tax liability over $2500. (Obtain from IRS)

❑ Any required state and local income and sales tax forms. Please check with the appropriate tax authority for more information

Limited Liability Company Monthly Tax Schedule

❑ If you have employees, and your payroll tax liability is over $2500 quarterly, you must make monthly tax payments using IRS Form 8109: Federal Tax Deposit Coupon

❑ If required, file and pay any necessary state or local sales tax Quarterly Tax Schedule

Limited Liability Company Quarterly Tax Schedule

❑ Pay any required estimated taxes using vouchers from IRS Form1040-ES: Estimated Tax for Individuals

❑ If you have employees, file IRS Form 941: Employer's Quarterly Federal Tax Return and make any required payments of FICA and withholding taxes

❑ If you have employees and your quarterly unpaid FUTA tax liability is over $500, make FUTA deposit using IRS Form 8109: Federal Tax Deposit Coupon

❑ If required, file and pay any necessary state or local sales tax Annual Tax Schedule

Limited Liability Company Annual Tax Schedule

❑ If you have employees, prepare IRS Form W-2: Wage and Tax Statement for each employee and provide to employees by January 31; and file IRS Form W-3: Transmittal of Wage and Tax Statements and copies of all W-2 Forms with IRS by January 31

❑ If you have paid any independent contractors over $600 annually, prepare IRS Form 1099-MISC: Miscellaneous Income and provide to recipient by January 31; and file IRS Form 1096: Annual Summary and Transmittal of U.S. Information Returns and copies of all 1099 Forms with IRS by January 31

❑ Make required unemployment tax payment and file IRS Form 940: Employer's Annual Federal Unemployment (FUTA) Tax Return

☐ File IRS Form 1040-SS: U.S. Self-Employment Tax Return with your annual IRS Form 1040: U.S. Individual Income Tax Return

☐ File IRS Form 1065: U.S. Return of Partnership Income and Schedule K-1 (Form 1065): Partner's Share of Income, Credits, Deductions, etc. (treatment as a partnership)

☐ File IRS Form 1120: U.S. Corporation Income Tax Return (treatment as a corporation)

☐ File IRS Schedule C (Form 1040): Profit or Loss From Business (Sole Proprietorship) and IRS Form 1040: U.S. Individual Income Tax Return (treatment as a sole proprietorship)

☐ If you are required, file and pay any necessary state or local sales, income, or unemployment taxes

---

ATTENTION:
The U.S. IRS Tax Forms included in this book on pages 211–261 are provided for informational purposes only and should not be reproduced or photocopied for filing purposes by taxpayers. Additionally, tax forms are subject to change at any time to comply with everchanging tax laws. For filing purposes, taxpayers should use the most current forms available. Any of the IRS tax forms included in this book may be obtained, free of charge, by calling 1-800-TAXFORM (1-800-829-3676). Be sure to order using the IRS publication number. You can also access forms and instructions on the web at www.irs.gov and go to the Forms and Publications page. Some downloaded forms are not acceptable for filing. Check the FAQ's on the IRS publications website for current IRS restrictions.

Quick and Easy Access to IRS Tax Help and Tax Products

Internet

To get IRS information, forms and publications in Spanish, select **Español** in upper right corner of **www.irs.gov.**

Online Services & Tax Help

Access the IRS website 24 hours a day, 7 days a week at *www.irs.gov* to obtain information on:

- *Online Services* — Conduct business with the IRS electronically
- *Taxpayer Advocate Service* — Helps taxpayers resolve problems with the IRS.
- *Free File and e-file* — Free Federal Online Filing
- *Where's My Refund*— Your refund status anytime from anywhere
- *Free Tax Return Preparation*— Free tax assistance and preparation
- *Recent Tax Changes* — Highlights on newly-enacted tax law
- *Innocent Spouses* — Tax Information for Innocent Spouses
- *Disaster Tax Relief* — Tax relief provisions for disaster situations
- *Identity Theft and Your Tax Records* — Safeguard your identity and tax records
- *Online Payment Agreement (OPA) Application* — Online agreements
- *Applying for Offers in Compromise* — Information on Offers in Compromise

View & Download Products

Visit the IRS website at *www.irs.gov* and select *Forms and Publications,* or simply type *www.irs.gov/formspubs* in your Internet search window to:

- view or download current and previous year tax products
- order current year tax products online

The *Forms and Publications* page provides links to access and acquire both electronic and print media. Additionally, the *Search* function provides basic and advanced search capabilities for published products available on IRS.gov.

Online Ordering of Products

To order Tax Products delivered by mail, go to *www.irs.gov/formspubs*

- For current year products, select "Forms and publications by U.S. mail"
- For a tax booklet of forms and instructions, select "Tax packages"
- For Employer Products (e.g. W-4, Pub. 15) and Information Returns (e.g. W-2, W-3, 1099 series), select "Employer forms and instructions"
- For tax products on a DVD, select "Tax products on DVD (Pub. 1796)" See DVD below

Telephone

Tax Forms & Publications

1-800-829-3676

Call to order current and prior year forms, instructions, and publications.

You should receive your order within 10 working days.

National Taxpayer Advocate Helpline
1-877-777-4778

Tax Help & Questions

Individuals: 1-800-829-1040

Business & Specialty Tax: 1-800-829-4933

Hearing Impaired TTY/TDD: 1-800-829-4059

TeleTax - 24 hour tax information: 1-800-829-4477

See instructions 1040, 1040A, or 1040EZ for topic numbers and details.

Refund Hotline: 1-800-829-1954

Community Locations

You can pick up some of the most requested forms, instructions, and publications at many IRS offices, post offices, and libraries.

Also some grocery stores, copy centers, city and county government offices, and credit unions have reproducible tax form products available to photocopy or print from a DVD.

Mail

You can receive tax products within 10 working days after receipt of your order.

Do not send your tax return to the address shown here. Instead, see the tax form instructions.

Send written request to:

Internal Revenue Service
1201 N. Mitsubishi Motorway
Bloomington, IL 61705-6613

DVD

Purchase the IRS Publication 1796 (IRS Tax Products).
Internet:

- National Technical Information Service (NTIS) at *www.irs.gov/cdorders*

  or

- Government Printing Office (GPO) at *http://bookstore.gpo.gov* (search for Pub. 1796)

Telephone:
- NTIS at 1-877-233-6767

  or

- GPO at 1-866-512-1800

Availability: First release—early January
Final release—early March

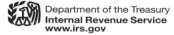

Department of the Treasury
Internal Revenue Service
www.irs.gov

Publication 2053-A (Rev. 9-2009)
Cat. No. 23267Z

Form **SS-4**	**Application for Employer Identification Number**	OMB No. 1545-0003

Form **SS-4**
(Rev. January 2009)
Department of the Treasury
Internal Revenue Service

Application for Employer Identification Number
(For use by employers, corporations, partnerships, trusts, estates, churches, government agencies, Indian tribal entities, certain individuals, and others.)
► See separate instructions for each line. ► Keep a copy for your records.

OMB No. 1545-0003

EIN

Type or print clearly.

1 Legal name of entity (or individual) for whom the EIN is being requested

2 Trade name of business (if different from name on line 1) | **3** Executor, administrator, trustee, "care of" name

4a Mailing address (room, apt., suite no. and street, or P.O. box) | **5a** Street address (if different) (Do not enter a P.O. box.)

4b City, state, and ZIP code (if foreign, see instructions) | **5b** City, state, and ZIP code (if foreign, see instructions)

6 County and state where principal business is located

7a Name of principal officer, general partner, grantor, owner, or trustor | **7b** SSN, ITIN, or EIN

8a Is this application for a limited liability company (LLC) (or a foreign equivalent)? . . . . ☐ Yes ☐ No | **8b** If 8a is "Yes," enter the number of LLC members . . . . ►

8c If 8a is "Yes," was the LLC organized in the United States? . . . . ☐ Yes ☐ No

9a **Type of entity** (check only one box). **Caution.** If 8a is "Yes," see the instructions for the correct box to check.

☐ Sole proprietor (SSN) _____
☐ Partnership
☐ Corporation (enter form number to be filed) ► _____
☐ Personal service corporation
☐ Church or church-controlled organization
☐ Other nonprofit organization (specify) ► _____
☐ Other (specify) ►

☐ Estate (SSN of decedent) _____
☐ Plan administrator (TIN) _____
☐ Trust (TIN of grantor) _____
☐ National Guard ☐ State/local government
☐ Farmers' cooperative ☐ Federal government/military
☐ REMIC ☐ Indian tribal governments/enterprises
Group Exemption Number (GEN) if any ►

9b If a corporation, name the state or foreign country (if applicable) where incorporated | State | Foreign country

10 **Reason for applying** (check only one box)

☐ Started new business (specify type) ► _____
☐ Hired employees (Check the box and see line 13.)
☐ Compliance with IRS withholding regulations
☐ Other (specify) ►

☐ Banking purpose (specify purpose) ► _____
☐ Changed type of organization (specify new type) ► _____
☐ Purchased going business
☐ Created a trust (specify type) ► _____
☐ Created a pension plan (specify type) ► _____

11 Date business started or acquired (month, day, year). See instructions. | **12** Closing month of accounting year

13 Highest number of employees expected in the next 12 months (enter -0- if none).

Agricultural	Household	Other

14 Do you expect your employment tax liability to be $1,000 or less in a full calendar year? ☐ Yes ☐ No (If you expect to pay $4,000 or less in total wages in a full calendar year, you can mark "Yes.")

15 First date wages or annuities were paid (month, day, year). **Note.** If applicant is a withholding agent, enter date income will first be paid to nonresident alien (month, day, year) . . . . ►

16 Check **one** box that best describes the principal activity of your business.
☐ Construction ☐ Rental & leasing ☐ Transportation & warehousing ☐ Accommodation & food service ☐ Health care & social assistance ☐ Wholesale-agent/broker
☐ Real estate ☐ Manufacturing ☐ Finance & insurance ☐ Other (specify) ☐ Wholesale-other ☐ Retail

17 Indicate principal line of merchandise sold, specific construction work done, products produced, or services provided.

18 Has the applicant entity shown on line 1 ever applied for and received an EIN? ☐ Yes ☐ No
If "Yes," write previous EIN here ►

Third Party Designee	Complete this section **only** if you want to authorize the named individual to receive the entity's EIN and answer questions about the completion of this form.	
	Designee's name	Designee's telephone number (include area code) ( )
	Address and ZIP code	Designee's fax number (include area code) ( )

Under penalties of perjury, I declare that I have examined this application, and to the best of my knowledge and belief, it is true, correct, and complete.
Name and title (type or print clearly) ►

Applicant's telephone number (include area code) ( )

Signature ► Date ►

Applicant's fax number (include area code) ( )

For Privacy Act and Paperwork Reduction Act Notice, see separate instructions. Cat. No. 16055N Form **SS-4** (Rev. 1-2009)

Form **1040** Department of the Treasury—Internal Revenue Service
U.S. Individual Income Tax Return 20**09** (99) IRS Use Only—Do not write or staple in this space.

For the year Jan. 1–Dec. 31, 2009, or other tax year beginning , 2009, ending , 20	OMB No. 1545-0074

Label

(See instructions on page 14.)

Use the IRS label.

Otherwise, please print or type.

L A B E L

H E R E

Your first name and initial — Last name — **Your social security number**

If a joint return, spouse's first name and initial — Last name — **Spouse's social security number**

Home address (number and street). If you have a P.O. box, see page 14. — Apt. no. — ▲ You **must** enter your SSN(s) above. ▲

City, town or post office, state, and ZIP code. If you have a foreign address, see page 14. — Checking a box below will not change your tax or refund.

Presidential Election Campaign ► Check here if you, or your spouse if filing jointly, want $3 to go to this fund (see page 14) ► ☐ **You** ☐ **Spouse**

Filing Status

Check only one box.

- 1 ☐ Single
- 2 ☐ Married filing jointly (even if only one had income)
- 3 ☐ Married filing separately. Enter spouse's SSN above and full name here. ►
- 4 ☐ Head of household (with qualifying person). (See page 15.) If the qualifying person is a child but not your dependent, enter this child's name here. ►
- 5 ☐ Qualifying widow(er) with dependent child (see page 16)

Exemptions

- 6a ☐ **Yourself.** If someone can claim you as a dependent, **do not** check box 6a . . . . .
- b ☐ **Spouse** . . . .

Boxes checked on 6a and 6b ___

No. of children on 6c who:
- **lived with you** ___
- **did not live with you due to divorce or separation (see page 18)** ___

c **Dependents:**

(1) First name Last name	(2) Dependent's social security number	(3) Dependent's relationship to you	(4) ✓ if qualifying child for child tax credit (see page 17)
			☐
			☐
			☐
			☐

If more than four dependents, see page 17 and check here ► ☐

Dependents on 6c not entered above ___

Add numbers on lines above ► ___

- d Total number of exemptions claimed . . . .

Income

Attach Form(s) W-2 here. Also attach Forms W-2G and 1099-R if tax was withheld.

If you did not get a W-2, see page 22.

Enclose, but do not attach, any payment. Also, please use Form 1040-V.

7	Wages, salaries, tips, etc. Attach Form(s) W-2	7	
8a	**Taxable** interest. Attach Schedule B if required	8a	
b	**Tax-exempt** interest. **Do not** include on line 8a . . .	8b		
9a	Ordinary dividends. Attach Schedule B if required	9a	
b	Qualified dividends (see page 22)	9b		
10	Taxable refunds, credits, or offsets of state and local income taxes (see page 23) . .	10	
11	Alimony received	11	
12	Business income or (loss). Attach Schedule C or C-EZ	12	
13	Capital gain or (loss). Attach Schedule D if required. If not required, check here ► ☐	13	
14	Other gains or (losses). Attach Form 4797	14	
15a	IRA distributions . 15a	b Taxable amount (see page 24)	15b	
16a	Pensions and annuities 16a	b Taxable amount (see page 25)	16b	
17	Rental real estate, royalties, partnerships, S corporations, trusts, etc. Attach Schedule E	17	
18	Farm income or (loss). Attach Schedule F	18	
19	Unemployment compensation in excess of $2,400 per recipient (see page 27) . . .	19	
20a	Social security benefits 20a	b Taxable amount (see page 27)	20b	
21	Other income. List type and amount (see page 29) _____	21	
22	Add the amounts in the far right column for lines 7 through 21. This is your **total income** ►	22	

Adjusted Gross Income

23	Educator expenses (see page 29)	23		
24	Certain business expenses of reservists, performing artists, and fee-basis government officials. Attach Form 2106 or 2106-EZ	24		
25	Health savings account deduction. Attach Form 8889 .	25		
26	Moving expenses. Attach Form 3903	26		
27	One-half of self-employment tax. Attach Schedule SE .	27		
28	Self-employed SEP, SIMPLE, and qualified plans . .	28		
29	Self-employed health insurance deduction (see page 30)	29		
30	Penalty on early withdrawal of savings	30		
31a	Alimony paid b Recipient's SSN ►	31a		
32	IRA deduction (see page 31)	32		
33	Student loan interest deduction (see page 34) . . .	33		
34	Tuition and fees deduction. Attach Form 8917 . . .	34		
35	Domestic production activities deduction. Attach Form 8903	35		
36	Add lines 23 through 31a and 32 through 35	36	
37	Subtract line 36 from line 22. This is your **adjusted gross income** . . . . . ►	37	

For Disclosure, Privacy Act, and Paperwork Reduction Act Notice, see page 97. Cat. No. 11320B Form **1040** (2009)

Form 1040 (2009)   Page **2**

Tax and Credits	38	Amount from line 37 (adjusted gross income)	38	
	39a	Check if: ☐ **You** were born before January 2, 1945, ☐ Blind. ☐ **Spouse** was born before January 2, 1945, ☐ Blind. } Total boxes checked ▶ 39a		
Standard Deduction for—	b	If your spouse itemizes on a separate return or you were a dual-status alien, see page 35 and check here ▶ 39b ☐		
● People who check any box on line 39a, 39b, or 40b **or** who can be claimed as a dependent, see page 35.	40a	**Itemized deductions** (from Schedule A) **or** your **standard deduction** (see left margin) . .	40a	
	b	If you are increasing your standard deduction by certain real estate taxes, new motor vehicle taxes, or a net disaster loss, attach Schedule L and check here (see page 35) . ▶ 40b ☐		
	41	Subtract line 40a from line 38	41	
	42	**Exemptions.** If line 38 is $125,100 or less and you did not provide housing to a Midwestern displaced individual, multiply $3,650 by the number on line 6d. Otherwise, see page 37 .	42	
● All others:	43	**Taxable income.** Subtract line 42 from line 41. If line 42 is more than line 41, enter -0- . .	43	
Single or Married filing separately, $5,700	44	**Tax** (see page 37). Check if any tax is from: **a** ☐ Form(s) 8814 **b** ☐ Form 4972 .	44	
	45	**Alternative minimum tax** (see page 40). Attach Form 6251	45	
Married filing jointly or Qualifying widow(er), $11,400	46	Add lines 44 and 45 . . . . ▶	46	
	47	Foreign tax credit. Attach Form 1116 if required	47		
	48	Credit for child and dependent care expenses. Attach Form 2441	48		
Head of household, $8,350	49	Education credits from Form 8863, line 29	49		
	50	Retirement savings contributions credit. Attach Form 8880	50		
	51	Child tax credit (see page 42)	51		
	52	Credits from Form: **a** ☐ 8396 **b** ☐ 8839 **c** ☐ 5695	52		
	53	Other credits from Form: **a** ☐ 3800 **b** ☐ 8801 **c** ☐	53		
	54	Add lines 47 through 53. These are your **total credits**	54	
	55	Subtract line 54 from line 46. If line 54 is more than line 46, enter -0- . . . . ▶	55	
Other Taxes	56	Self-employment tax. Attach Schedule SE	56	
	57	Unreported social security and Medicare tax from Form: **a** ☐ 4137 **b** ☐ 8919 . .	57	
	58	Additional tax on IRAs, other qualified retirement plans, etc. Attach Form 5329 if required . .	58	
	59	Additional taxes: **a** ☐ AEIC payments **b** ☐ Household employment taxes. Attach Schedule H	59	
	60	Add lines 55 through 59. This is your **total tax** . . . . ▶	60	
Payments	61	Federal income tax withheld from Forms W-2 and 1099 . .	61		
	62	2009 estimated tax payments and amount applied from 2008 return	62		
	63	Making work pay and government retiree credits. Attach Schedule M	63		
If you have a qualifying child, attach Schedule EIC.	64a	**Earned income credit (EIC)**	64a		
	b	Nontaxable combat pay election	64b			
	65	Additional child tax credit. Attach Form 8812	65		
	66	Refundable education credit from Form 8863, line 16 . . .	66		
	67	First-time homebuyer credit. Attach Form 5405	67		
	68	Amount paid with request for extension to file (see page 72) .	68		
	69	Excess social security and tier 1 RRTA tax withheld (see page 72)	69		
	70	Credits from Form: **a** ☐ 2439 **b** ☐ 4136 **c** ☐ 8801 **d** ☐ 8885	70		
	71	Add lines 61, 62, 63, 64a, and 65 through 70. These are your **total payments** . . . ▶	71	
Refund	72	If line 71 is more than line 60, subtract line 60 from line 71. This is the amount you **overpaid**	72	
Direct deposit? See page 73 and fill in 73b, 73c, and 73d, or Form 8888.	73a	Amount of line 72 you want **refunded to you.** If Form 8888 is attached, check here . ▶ ☐	73a	
	▶ b	Routing number ▶ c Type: ☐ Checking ☐ Savings		
	▶ d	Account number		
	74	Amount of line 72 you want **applied to your 2010 estimated tax** ▶	74		
Amount You Owe	75	**Amount you owe.** Subtract line 71 from line 60. For details on how to pay, see page 74 . ▶	75	
	76	Estimated tax penalty (see page 74)	76		

Third Party Designee

Do you want to allow another person to discuss this return with the IRS (see page 75)? ☐ **Yes.** Complete the following.   ☐ **No**

Designee's name ▶ _____ Phone no. ▶ _____ Personal identification number (PIN) ▶ ☐☐☐☐☐

Sign Here

Under penalties of perjury, I declare that I have examined this return and accompanying schedules and statements, and to the best of my knowledge and belief, they are true, correct, and complete. Declaration of preparer (other than taxpayer) is based on all information of which preparer has any knowledge.

Joint return? See page 15. Keep a copy for your records.

Your signature | Date | Your occupation | Daytime phone number

Spouse's signature. If a joint return, **both** must sign. | Date | Spouse's occupation

Paid Preparer's Use Only

Preparer's signature | Date | Check if self-employed ☐ | Preparer's SSN or PTIN

Firm's name (or yours if self-employed), address, and ZIP code | | EIN | Phone no.

Form **1040** (2009)

214

Form **1040A**

Department of the Treasury—Internal Revenue Service

U.S. Individual Income Tax Return (99) **2009** IRS Use Only—Do not write or staple in this space.

OMB No. 1545-0074

Label (See page 17.)

Use the IRS label.

Otherwise, please print or type.

Your first name and initial | Last name | Your social security number

If a joint return, spouse's first name and initial | Last name | Spouse's social security number

Home address (number and street). If you have a P.O. box, see page 17. | Apt. no.

▲ You **must** enter your SSN(s) above. ▲

City, town or post office, state, and ZIP code. If you have a foreign address, see page 17.

Checking a box below will not change your tax or refund.

Presidential Election Campaign ▶ Check here if you, or your spouse if filing jointly, want $3 to go to this fund (see page 17) ▶ ☐ You ☐ Spouse

Filing status
Check only one box.

1 ☐ Single
2 ☐ Married filing jointly (even if only one had income)
3 ☐ Married filing separately. Enter spouse's SSN above and full name here. ▶
4 ☐ Head of household (with qualifying person). (See page 18.) If the qualifying person is a child but not your dependent, enter this child's name here. ▶
5 ☐ Qualifying widow(er) with dependent child (see page 19)

Exemptions

6a ☐ **Yourself.** If someone can claim you as a dependent, **do not** check box 6a.
b ☐ **Spouse**

c **Dependents:**

(1) First name Last name	(2) Dependent's social security number	(3) Dependent's relationship to you	(4) ✔ if qualifying child for child tax credit (see page 20)
			☐
			☐
			☐
			☐
			☐
			☐

If more than six dependents, see page 20.

Boxes checked on 6a and 6b ___
No. of children on 6c who:
• lived with you ___
• did not live with you due to divorce or separation (see page 21) ___
Dependents on 6c not entered above ___
Add numbers on lines above ▶ ☐

d Total number of exemptions claimed.

Income

Attach Form(s) W-2 here. Also attach Form(s) 1099-R if tax was withheld.

If you did not get a W-2, see page 24.

Enclose, but do not attach, any payment. Also, please use Form 1040-V.

7 Wages, salaries, tips, etc. Attach Form(s) W-2. | 7
8a **Taxable** interest. Attach Schedule B if required. | 8a
b **Tax-exempt** interest. **Do not** include on line 8a. | 8b
9a Ordinary dividends. Attach Schedule B if required. | 9a
b Qualified dividends (see page 25). | 9b
10 Capital gain distributions (see page 25). | 10
11a IRA distributions. | 11a | **11b** Taxable amount (see page 25). | 11b
12a Pensions and annuities. | 12a | **12b** Taxable amount (see page 26). | 12b
13 Unemployment compensation in excess of $2,400 per recipient and Alaska Permanent Fund dividends (see page 28). | 13
14a Social security benefits. | 14a | **14b** Taxable amount (see page 28). | 14b
15 Add lines 7 through 14b (far right column). This is your **total income.** ▶ | 15

Adjusted gross income

16 Educator expenses (see page 30). | 16
17 IRA deduction (see page 30). | 17
18 Student loan interest deduction (see page 32). | 18
19 Tuition and fees deduction. Attach Form 8917. | 19
20 Add lines 16 through 19. These are your **total adjustments.** | 20
21 Subtract line 20 from line 15. This is your **adjusted gross income.** ▶ | 21

For Disclosure, Privacy Act, and Paperwork Reduction Act Notice, see page 87. Cat. No. 11327A Form **1040A** (2009)

Small Business Accounting Simplified

Tax, credits, and payments	**22**	Enter the amount from line 21 (adjusted gross income).	**22**	
	23a	Check if: { ☐ **You** were born before January 2, 1945, ☐ Blind } **Total boxes** ☐ **Spouse** was born before January 2, 1945, ☐ Blind } **checked ▶** 23a		
	b	If you are married filing separately and your spouse itemizes deductions, see page 34 and check here ▶ 23b ☐		

Standard Deduction for—

- People who checked any box on line 23a, 23b, or 24b or who can be claimed as a dependent, see page 34.
- All others:

Single or Married filing separately, $5,700

Married filing jointly or Qualifying widow(er), $11,400

Head of household, $8,350

24a	Enter your **standard deduction** (see left margin).	**24a**
b	If you are increasing your standard deduction by certain real estate taxes or new motor vehicle taxes, attach Schedule L and check here (see page 34) ▶ 24b ☐	
25	Subtract line 24a from line 22. If line 24a is more than line 22, enter -0-.	**25**
26	**Exemptions.** If line 22 is $125,100 or less and you did not provide housing to a Midwestern displaced individual, multiply $3,650 by the number on line 6d. Otherwise, see page 34.	**26**
27	Subtract line 26 from line 25. If line 26 is more than line 25, enter -0-. This is your **taxable income.** ▶	**27**
28	**Tax,** including any alternative minimum tax (see page 35).	**28**
29	Credit for child and dependent care expenses. Attach Form 2441. 29	
30	Credit for the elderly or the disabled. Attach Schedule R. 30	
31	Education credits from Form 8863, line 29. 31	
32	Retirement savings contributions credit. Attach Form 8880. 32	
33	Child tax credit (see page 38). 33	
34	Add lines 29 through 33. These are your **total credits.**	**34**
35	Subtract line 34 from line 28. If line 34 is more than line 28, enter -0-.	**35**
36	Advance earned income credit payments from Form(s) W-2, box 9.	**36**
37	Add lines 35 and 36. This is your **total tax.** ▶	**37**
38	Federal income tax withheld from Forms W-2 and 1099. 38	
39	2009 estimated tax payments and amount applied from 2008 return. 39	

If you have a qualifying child, attach Schedule EIC.

40	Making work pay and government retiree credits. Attach Schedule M. 40	
41a	**Earned income credit (EIC).** 41a	
b	Nontaxable combat pay election. 41b	
42	Additional child tax credit. Attach Form 8812. 42	
43	Refundable education credit from Form 8863, line 16. 43	
44	Add lines 38, 39, 40, 41a, 42, and 43. These are your **total payments.** ▶	**44**

Refund	**45**	If line 44 is more than line 37, subtract line 37 from line 44. This is the amount you **overpaid.**	**45**
Direct deposit? See page 64 and fill in 46b, 46c, and 46d or Form 8888.	**46a**	Amount of line 45 you want **refunded to you.** If Form 8888 is attached, check here ▶ ☐	**46a**
	▶ **b**	Routing number ☐☐☐☐☐☐☐☐☐ ▶ **c** Type: ☐ Checking ☐ Savings	
	▶ **d**	Account number ☐☐☐☐☐☐☐☐☐☐☐☐☐☐☐☐☐	
	47	Amount of line 45 you want **applied to your 2010 estimated tax.** 47	

Amount you owe	**48**	**Amount you owe.** Subtract line 44 from line 37. For details on how to pay, see page 66. ▶	**48**
	49	Estimated tax penalty (see page 66). 49	

Third party designee	Do you want to allow another person to discuss this return with the IRS (see page 67)? ☐ **Yes.** Complete the following. ☐ **No**
	Designee's name ▶ — Phone no. ▶ — Personal identification number (PIN) ▶ ☐☐☐☐☐

Sign here Joint return? See page 17. Keep a copy for your records.	Under penalties of perjury, I declare that I have examined this return and accompanying schedules and statements, and to the best of my knowledge and belief, they are true, correct, and accurately list all amounts and sources of income I received during the tax year. Declaration of preparer (other than the taxpayer) is based on all information of which the preparer has any knowledge.
	Your signature — Date — Your occupation — Daytime phone number —
	Spouse's signature. If a joint return, **both** must sign. — Date — Spouse's occupation —

Paid preparer's use only	Preparer's signature ▶	Date — Check if self-employed ☐	Preparer's SSN or PTIN —
	Firm's name (or yours if self-employed), address, and ZIP code ▶		EIN — Phone no. —

**SCHEDULE C
(Form 1040)**

Department of the Treasury
Internal Revenue Service (99)

Profit or Loss From Business
(Sole Proprietorship)

▶ **Partnerships, joint ventures, etc., generally must file Form 1065 or 1065-B.**

▶ **Attach to Form 1040, 1040NR, or 1041.** ▶ **See Instructions for Schedule C (Form 1040).**

OMB No. 1545-0074

2009

Attachment
Sequence No. **09**

Name of proprietor | Social security number (SSN)

| A | Principal business or profession, including product or service (see page C-2 of the instructions) | B Enter code from pages C-9, 10, & 11 ▶ |
| C | Business name. If no separate business name, leave blank. | D Employer ID number (EIN), if any |

E Business address (including suite or room no.) ▶ --
 City, town or post office, state, and ZIP code

F Accounting method: **(1)** ☐ Cash **(2)** ☐ Accrual **(3)** ☐ Other (specify) ▶ ------------------

G Did you "materially participate" in the operation of this business during 2009? If "No," see page C-3 for limit on losses   ☐ Yes ☐ No

H If you started or acquired this business during 2009, check here . . . . ▶ ☐

Part I   Income

1	Gross receipts or sales. **Caution.** See page C-4 and check the box if:		
	• This income was reported to you on Form W-2 and the "Statutory employee" box on that form was checked, or	⎫⎬⎭ ▶ ☐	
	• You are a member of a qualified joint venture reporting only rental real estate income not subject to self-employment tax. Also see page C-3 for limit on losses.		**1**
2	Returns and allowances		**2**
3	Subtract line 2 from line 1		**3**
4	Cost of goods sold (from line 42 on page 2)		**4**
5	**Gross profit.** Subtract line 4 from line 3		**5**
6	Other income, including federal and state gasoline or fuel tax credit or refund (see page C-4)		**6**
7	**Gross income.** Add lines 5 and 6 . . . . ▶		**7**

Part II   Expenses.   Enter expenses for business use of your home **only** on line 30.

8	Advertising	**8**		18	Office expense	**18**	
9	Car and truck expenses (see page C-4)	**9**		19	Pension and profit-sharing plans .	**19**	
				20	Rent or lease (see page C-6):		
10	Commissions and fees .	**10**		a	Vehicles, machinery, and equipment	**20a**	
11	Contract labor (see page C-4)	**11**		b	Other business property . . .	**20b**	
12	Depletion	**12**		21	Repairs and maintenance . .	**21**	
13	Depreciation and section 179 expense deduction (not included in Part III) (see page C-5)	**13**		22	Supplies (not included in Part III) .	**22**	
				23	Taxes and licenses	**23**	
				24	Travel, meals, and entertainment:		
				a	Travel	**24a**	
14	Employee benefit programs (other than on line 19) . .	**14**		b	Deductible meals and entertainment (see page C-6) . .	**24b**	
15	Insurance (other than health)	**15**		25	Utilities	**25**	
16	Interest:			26	Wages (less employment credits) .	**26**	
a	Mortgage (paid to banks, etc.)	**16a**		27	Other expenses (from line 48 on page 2)	**27**	
b	Other	**16b**					
17	Legal and professional services	**17**					

28	**Total expenses** before expenses for business use of home. Add lines 8 through 27 . . . . . ▶	**28**	
29	Tentative profit or (loss). Subtract line 28 from line 7	**29**	
30	Expenses for business use of your home. Attach **Form 8829**	**30**	
31	**Net profit or (loss).** Subtract line 30 from line 29.		
	• If a profit, enter on both **Form 1040, line 12,** and **Schedule SE, line 2,** or on **Form 1040NR, line 13** (if you checked the box on line 1, see page C-7). Estates and trusts, enter on **Form 1041, line 3.**	⎫⎬⎭	**31**
	• If a loss, you **must** go to line 32.		
32	If you have a loss, check the box that describes your investment in this activity (see page C-7).		
	• If you checked 32a, enter the loss on both **Form 1040, line 12,** and **Schedule SE, line 2,** or on **Form 1040NR, line 13** (if you checked the box on line 1, see the line 31 instructions on page C-7). Estates and trusts, enter on **Form 1041, line 3.**	⎫⎬⎬⎭	**32a** ☐ All investment is at risk. **32b** ☐ Some investment is not at risk.
	• If you checked 32b, you **must** attach **Form 6198.** Your loss may be limited.		

For Paperwork Reduction Act Notice, see page C-9 of the instructions.   Cat. No. 11334P   Schedule C (Form 1040) 2009

Small Business Accounting Simplified

Part III   **Cost of Goods Sold**   (see page C-8)

33   Method(s) used to value closing inventory: **a** ☐ Cost   **b** ☐ Lower of cost or market   **c** ☐ Other (attach explanation)

34   Was there any change in determining quantities, costs, or valuations between opening and closing inventory? If "Yes," attach explanation . . . . ☐ **Yes**   ☐ **No**

35	Inventory at beginning of year. If different from last year's closing inventory, attach explanation . . .	**35**
36	Purchases less cost of items withdrawn for personal use	**36**
37	Cost of labor. Do not include any amounts paid to yourself	**37**
38	Materials and supplies	**38**
39	Other costs	**39**
40	Add lines 35 through 39	**40**
41	Inventory at end of year	**41**
42	**Cost of goods sold.** Subtract line 41 from line 40. Enter the result here and on page 1, line 4 . . .	**42**

Part IV   **Information on Your Vehicle.** Complete this part **only** if you are claiming car or truck expenses on line 9 and are not required to file Form 4562 for this business. See the instructions for line 13 on page C-5 to find out if you must file Form 4562.

43   When did you place your vehicle in service for business purposes? (month, day, year)   ▶ _____ / _____ / _____

44   Of the total number of miles you drove your vehicle during 2009, enter the number of miles you used your vehicle for:

   a Business _____   **b** Commuting (see instructions) _____   **c** Other _____

45   Was your vehicle available for personal use during off-duty hours? . . . . ☐ **Yes**   ☐ **No**

46   Do you (or your spouse) have another vehicle available for personal use?. . . . . ☐ **Yes**   ☐ **No**

47a   Do you have evidence to support your deduction? . . . . ☐ **Yes**   ☐ **No**

   b If "Yes," is the evidence written? . . . . ☐ **Yes**   ☐ **No**

Part V   **Other Expenses.** List below business expenses not included on lines 8–26 or line 30.

_____	
_____	
_____	
_____	
_____	
_____	
_____	
_____	
_____	

48	**Total other expenses.** Enter here and on page 1, line 27	**48**

Schedule C (Form 1040) 2009

2009 Estimated Tax Worksheet
Keep for Your Records

1	Adjusted gross income you expect in 2009 (see instructions below)	**1**
2	• If you plan to itemize deductions, enter the estimated total of your itemized deductions. **Caution:** *If line 1 above is over $166,800 ($83,400 if married filing separately), your deduction may be reduced. See Pub. 505 for details.* • If you do not plan to itemize deductions, enter your standard deduction from page 1 or Pub. 505, Worksheet 2-3.	**2**
3	Subtract line 2 from line 1	**3**
4	Exemptions. Multiply $3,650 by the number of personal exemptions. **Caution:** *See Pub. 505 to figure the amount to enter if line 1 above is over: $250,200 if married filing jointly or qualifying widow(er); $208,500 if head of household; $166,800 if single; or $125,100 if married filing separately*	**4**
5	Subtract line 4 from line 3	**5**
6	**Tax.** Figure your tax on the amount on line 5 by using the **2009 Tax Rate Schedules** on page 5. **Caution:** *If you will have qualified dividends or a net capital gain, or expect to claim the foreign earned income exclusion or housing exclusion, see Pub. 505 to figure the tax*	**6**
7	Alternative minimum tax from **Form 6251**	**7**
8	Add lines 6 and 7. Add to this amount any other taxes you expect to include in the total on Form 1040, line 44, or Form 1040A, line 28	**8**
9	Credits (see instructions below). **Do not** include any income tax withholding on this line	**9**
10	Subtract line 9 from line 8. If zero or less, enter -0-	**10**
11	Self-employment tax (see instructions below). Estimate of 2009 net earnings from self-employment $_____ ; if **$106,800 or less,** multiply the amount by 15.3%; if **more than $106,800,** multiply the amount by 2.9%, add $13,243.20 to the result, and enter the total. **Caution:** *If you also have wages subject to social security tax or the 6.2% portion of tier 1 Railroad Retirement tax, see Pub. 505 to figure the amount to enter*	**11**
12	Other taxes (see instructions below)	**12**
13a	Add lines 10 through 12	**13a**
b	Earned income credit, additional child tax credit, and credits from **Forms 4136, 5405, 8801 (line 27),** and **8885**	**13b**
c	**Total 2009 estimated tax.** Subtract line 13b from line 13a. If zero or less, enter -0- . . . . ▶	**13c**
14a	Multiply line 13c by 90% (66⅔ % for farmers and fishermen) . . . . . [**14a**]	
b	Enter the tax shown on your 2008 tax return (110% of that amount if you are not a farmer or fisherman and the adjusted gross income shown on that return is more than $150,000 or, if married filing separately for 2009, more than $75,000) [**14b**]	
c	**Required annual payment to avoid a penalty.** Enter the **smaller** of line 14a or 14b . . . ▶	**14c**
	Caution: *Generally, if you do not prepay (through income tax withholding and estimated tax payments) at least the amount on line 14c, you may owe a penalty for not paying enough estimated tax. To avoid a penalty, make sure your estimate on line 13c is as accurate as possible. Even if you pay the required annual payment, you may still owe tax when you file your return. If you prefer, you can pay the amount shown on line 13c. For details, see Pub. 505.*	
15	Income tax withheld and estimated to be withheld during 2009 (including income tax withholding on pensions, annuities, certain deferred income, etc.)	**15**
16a	Subtract line 15 from line 14c . . . . [**16a**]	
	Is the result zero or less? ☐ **Yes.** Stop here. You are not required to make estimated tax payments. ☐ **No.** Go to line 16b.	
b	Subtract line 15 from line 13c . . . . [**16b**]	
	Is the result less than $1,000? ☐ **Yes.** Stop here. You are not required to make estimated tax payments. ☐ **No.** Go to line 17 to figure your required payment.	
17	If the first payment you are required to make is due April 15, 2009, enter ¼ of line 16a (minus any 2008 overpayment that you are applying to this installment) here, and on your estimated tax payment voucher(s) if you are paying by check or money order. **(Note:** *Household employers, see instructions below.)*	**17**

Instructions for the 2009 Estimated Tax Worksheet

Line 1. Adjusted gross income. Use your 2008 tax return and instructions as a guide to figuring the adjusted gross income you expect in 2009 (but be sure to consider the items listed under *What's New* that begins on page 1). For more details on figuring your adjusted gross income, see *Expected AGI—Line 1* in chapter 2 of Pub. 505. If you are self-employed, be sure to take into account the deduction for one-half of your self-employment tax (2008 Form 1040, line 27).

Line 9. Credits. See the 2008 Form 1040, lines 47 through 54, or Form 1040A, lines 29 through 33, and the related instructions.

Line 11. Self-employment tax. If you and your spouse make joint estimated tax payments and you both have self-employment income, figure the self-employment tax for each of you separately. Enter the total on line 11. When figuring your estimate of 2009 net earnings from self-employment, be sure to use only 92.35% (.9235) of your total net profit from self-employment.

Line 12. Other taxes. Use the instructions for the 2008 Form 1040 to determine if you expect to owe, for 2009, any of the taxes that would have been entered on your 2008 Form 1040, lines 59 (additional tax on early distributions only) and 60, and any write-ins on line 61, or any amount from Form 1040A, line 36. On line 12, enter the total of those taxes, subject to the following two exceptions.

Exception 1. Include household employment taxes from box b of Form 1040, line 60, on this line only if:

• You will have federal income tax withheld from wages, pensions, annuities, gambling winnings, or other income, or

• You would be required to make estimated tax payments (to avoid a penalty) even if you did not include household employment taxes when figuring your estimated tax.

If you meet one or both of the above, include in the amount on line 12 the total of your household employment taxes before subtracting advance EIC payments made to your employee(s).

Exception 2. Of the amounts for other taxes that may be entered on Form 1040, line 61, do not include on line 12: tax on recapture of a federal mortgage subsidy, uncollected employee social security and Medicare tax or RRTA tax on tips or group-term life insurance, tax on golden parachute payments, look-back interest due under section 167(g) or 460(b), or excise tax on insider stock compensation from an expatriated corporation. These taxes are not required to be paid until the due date of your income tax return (not including extensions).

Repayment of first-time homebuyer credit. If you claimed the first-time homebuyer credit for 2008 and the home ceased to be your main home in 2009, you generally must include on line 12 the entire credit you claimed for 2008. This includes situations where you sell the home or convert it to business or rental property. See Form 5405 for exceptions.

Line 17. If you are a household employer and you make advance EIC payments to your employee(s), reduce your required estimated tax payment for each period by the amount of advance EIC payments paid during the period.

-4-

219

Form **1040-SS**

Department of the Treasury
Internal Revenue Service

U.S. Self-Employment Tax Return (Including the Additional Child Tax Credit for Bona Fide Residents of Puerto Rico)
U.S. Virgin Islands, Guam, American Samoa, the Commonwealth of the Northern Mariana Islands (CNMI), or Puerto Rico. For the year Jan. 1–Dec. 31, 2008, or other tax year beginning   , 2008, and ending   , 20   .

OMB No. 1545-0090

2008

Please type or print

Your first name and initial	Last name	Your social security number
If a joint return, spouse's first name and initial	Last name	Spouse's social security number
Present home address (number, street, and apt. no., or rural route)		
City, town or post office, commonwealth or territory, and ZIP code		

Part I   Total Tax and Credits

1   Filing status. Check the box for your filing status (see page SS-4).
☐ Single
☐ Married filing jointly
☐ Married filing separately. Enter spouse's social security no. above and full name here. ▶ _____

2   Qualifying children. Complete **only** if you are a bona fide resident of Puerto Rico and you are claiming the additional child tax credit (see page SS-5).

(a) First name Last name	**(b)** Child's social security number	**(c)** Child's relationship to you

3 Self-employment tax from Part V, line 12	**3**	
4 Household employment taxes (see page SS-4). Attach Schedule H (Form 1040)	**4**	
5 **Total tax.** Add lines 3 and 4 (see page SS-4)	**5**	
6 2008 estimated tax payments (see page SS-4)	**6**	
7 Excess social security tax withheld (see page SS-5)	**7**	
8 Additional child tax credit from Part II, line 3	**8**	
9 Health coverage tax credit. Attach Form 8885	**9**	
10 **Total payments and credits.** Add lines 6 through 9	**10**	
11 If line 10 is more than line 5, subtract line 5 from line 10. This is the amount you **overpaid**	**11**	
12a Amount of line 11 to be **refunded to you.** If Form 8888 is attached, check here ▶ ☐	**12a**	

b Routing number ☐☐☐☐☐☐☐☐☐   ▶ **c** Type: ☐ Checking ☐ Savings

d Account number ☐☐☐☐☐☐☐☐☐☐☐☐☐☐☐☐☐

13 Amount of line 11 to be **applied to 2009 estimated tax** ▶	**13**	
14 **Amount you owe.** If line 5 is more than line 10, subtract line 10 from line 5. For details on how to pay, see page SS-1 ▶	**14**	

Third Party Designee

Do you want to allow another person to discuss this return with the IRS (see page SS-2)? ☐ **Yes.** Complete the following. ☐ **No**

Designee's name ▶	Phone no. ▶ ( )	Personal identification number (PIN) ▶ ☐☐☐☐☐

Sign Here

Joint return? See pg. SS-4.
Keep a copy for your records.

Under penalties of perjury, I declare that I have examined this return and accompanying schedules and statements, and to the best of my knowledge and belief, they are true, correct, and complete. Declaration of preparer (other than the taxpayer) is based on all information of which the preparer has any knowledge.

Your signature	Date	Daytime phone number ( )
Spouse's signature. If a joint return, **both** must sign.	Date	

Paid Preparer's Use Only

Preparer's signature ▶	Date	Check if self-employed ☐	Preparer's SSN or PTIN
Firm's name (or yours if self-employed), address, and ZIP code ▶		EIN	
		Phone no. ( )	

For Disclosure, Privacy Act, and Paperwork Reduction Act Notice, see page SS-8.   Cat. No. 17184B   Form **1040-SS** (2008)

Part II	Bona Fide Residents of Puerto Rico Claiming Additional Child Tax Credit—See page SS-5.

Caution. You must have three or more qualifying children to claim the additional child tax credit.

1	Income derived from sources within Puerto Rico	**1**	
2	Withheld social security and Medicare taxes from Forms 499R-2/W-2PR (attach copy of form(s)).	**2**	
3	**Additional child tax credit.** Use the worksheet on page SS-6 to figure the amount to enter here and in Part I, line 8	**3**	

Part III	Profit or Loss From Farming—See the instructions for Schedule F (Form 1040)

Name of proprietor	Social security number

Note. If you are filing a joint return and both you and your spouse had a profit or loss from a farming business, see *Joint returns* and *Husband-Wife Business* beginning on page SS-3 for more information.

Section A—Farm Income—Cash Method

Complete Sections A and B. (Accrual method taxpayers, complete Sections B and C, and Section A, line 11.)
Do not include sales of livestock held for draft, breeding, sport, or dairy purposes.

1	Sales of livestock and other items you bought for resale	**1**			
2	Cost or other basis of livestock and other items reported on line 1 .	**2**			
3	Subtract line 2 from line 1			**3**	
4	Sales of livestock, produce, grains, and other products you raised			**4**	
5a	Total cooperative distributions (Form(s) 1099-PATR).	**5a**	5b Taxable amount	**5b**	
6	Agricultural program payments received			**6**	
7	Commodity Credit Corporation loans reported under election (or forfeited).			**7**	
8	Crop insurance proceeds			**8**	
9	Custom hire (machine work) income			**9**	
10	Other income			**10**	
11	**Gross farm income.** Add amounts in the right column for lines 3 through 10. If accrual method taxpayer, enter the amount from Section C, line 50 . . . . ▶			**11**	

Section B—Farm Expenses—Cash and Accrual Method

Do not include personal or living expenses (such as taxes, insurance, or repairs on your home) that did not produce farm income. Reduce the amount of your farm expenses by any reimbursements before entering the expenses below.

12	Car and truck expenses (attach **Form 4562**) . . .	**12**		25	Pension and profit-sharing plans	**25**	
13	Chemicals	**13**		26	Rent or lease:		
14	Conservation expenses . .	**14**		a	Vehicles, machinery, and equipment	**26a**	
15	Custom hire (machine work)	**15**		b	Other (land, animals, etc.)	**26b**	
16	Depreciation and section 179 expense deduction not claimed elsewhere (attach **Form 4562** if required) . .	**16**		27	Repairs and maintenance	**27**	
				28	Seeds and plants purchased	**28**	
				29	Storage and warehousing	**29**	
17	Employee benefit programs other than on line 25 . . .	**17**		30	Supplies purchased . . .	**30**	
18	Feed purchased	**18**		31	Taxes	**31**	
19	Fertilizers and lime . . .	**19**		32	Utilities	**32**	
20	Freight and trucking . . .	**20**		33	Veterinary, breeding, and medicine	**33**	
21	Gasoline, fuel, and oil . .	**21**		34	Other expenses (specify):		
22	Insurance (other than health)	**22**		a	....	**34a**	
23	Interest:			b	....	**34b**	
a	Mortgage (paid to banks, etc.)	**23a**		c	....	**34c**	
b	Other	**23b**		d	....	**34d**	
24	Labor hired	**24**		e		**34e**	

35	**Total expenses.** Add lines 12 through 34e . . . . ▶	**35**	
36	**Net farm profit or (loss).** Subtract line 35 from line 11. Enter the result here and in Part V, line 1a	**36**	

Form **1040-SS** (2008)

Section C—Farm Income—Accrual Method

Do not include sales of livestock held for draft, breeding, sport, or dairy purposes on any of the lines below.

37	Sales of livestock, produce, grains, and other products during the year	37
38a	Total cooperative distributions (Form(s) 1099-PATR)	38a		38b	Taxable amount	38b
39	Agricultural program payments received	39
40	Commodity Credit Corporation loans reported under election (or forfeited).	40
41	Crop insurance proceeds	41
42	Custom hire (machine work) income	42
43	Other farm income (specify)	43
44	Add the amounts in the right column for lines 37 through 43	44
45	Inventory of livestock, produce, grains, and other products at the beginning of the year	45
46	Cost of livestock, produce, grains, and other products purchased during the year	46
47	Add lines 45 and 46	47
48	Inventory of livestock, produce, grains, and other products at the end of the year	48
49	Cost of livestock, produce, grains, and other products sold. Subtract line 48 from line 47*	49
50	**Gross farm income.** Subtract line 49 from line 44. Enter the result here and in Part III, line 11	50

*If you use the unit-livestock-price method or the farm-price method of valuing inventory and the amount on line 48 is larger than the amount on line 47, subtract line 47 from line 48. Enter the result on line 49. Add lines 44 and 49. Enter the total on line 50 and in Part III, line 11.

Part IV   Profit or Loss From Business (Sole Proprietorship)—See the instructions for Schedule C (Form 1040)

Name of proprietor   Social security number

Note. If you are filing a joint return and both you and your spouse had a profit or loss from a business, see *Joint returns* and *Husband-Wife Business* beginning on page SS-3 for more information.

Section A—Income

1	Gross receipts $ .... Less returns and allowances $ .... Balance ▶	1
2a	Inventory at beginning of year	2a
b	Purchases less cost of items withdrawn for personal use	2b
c	Cost of labor. Do not include any amounts paid to yourself	2c
d	Materials and supplies	2d
e	Other costs (attach statement)	2e
f	Add lines 2a through 2e	2f
g	Inventory at end of year	2g
h	Cost of goods sold. Subtract line 2g from line 2f	2h
3	**Gross profit.** Subtract line 2h from line 1	3
4	Other income	4
5	**Gross income.** Add lines 3 and 4 ▶	5

Section B—Expenses

6	Advertising	6	**18** Rent or lease:		
7	Car and truck expenses (attach **Form 4562**)	7	**a** Vehicles, machinery, and equipment	18a	
8	Commissions and fees	8	**b** Other business property	18b	
9	Contract labor	9	**19** Repairs and maintenance	19	
10	Depletion	10	**20** Supplies (not included in Section A)	20	
11	Depreciation and section 179 expense deduction (not included in Section A). (Attach **Form 4562** if required.)	11	**21** Taxes and licenses	21	
			22 Travel, meals, and entertainment:		
			a Travel	22a	
			b Deductible meals and entertainment	22b	
12	Employee benefit programs (other than on line 17)	12	**23** Utilities	23	
13	Insurance (other than health)	13	**24** Wages not included on line 2c	24	
14	Interest on business indebtedness	14	**25a** Other expenses (list type and amount):		
15	Legal and professional services	15			
16	Office expense	16			
17	Pension and profit-sharing plans	17	**25b** Total other expenses	25b	
26	**Total expenses.** Add lines 6 through 25b ▶			26	
27	**Net profit or (loss).** Subtract line 26 from line 5. Enter the result here and in Part V, line 2			27	

Form **1040-SS** (2008)

Self-Employment Tax—If you had **church employee income,** see page SS-3 before you begin.

b If you received social security retirement or disability benefits, enter the amount of Conservation Reserve Program payments included in Part III, line 6, plus your distributive share of these payments from farm partnerships . . . . **1b** (   )

c Wages subject to social security tax from Form 8919, line 10 (see page SS-7) **8c**

12 **Self-employment tax.** Add lines 10 and 11. Enter here and in Part I, line 3 . . . . **12**

Part VI

Note. If you are filing a joint return and both you and your spouse choose to use an optional method to figure net earnings, you must **each** complete and attach a **separate** Part VI.

Form **8829**	**Expenses for Business Use of Your Home**	OMB No. 1545-0074
	▶ File only with Schedule C (Form 1040). Use a separate Form 8829 for each home you used for business during the year.	**20**09
Department of the Treasury Internal Revenue Service (99)	▶ See separate instructions.	Attachment Sequence No. **66**

Name(s) of proprietor(s)	Your social security number

Part I   Part of Your Home Used for Business

1	Area used regularly and exclusively for business, regularly for daycare, or for storage of inventory or product samples (see instructions)	**1**	
2	Total area of home	**2**	
3	Divide line 1 by line 2. Enter the result as a percentage.	**3**	%
	For daycare facilities not used exclusively for business, go to line 4. All others go to line 7.		
4	Multiply days used for daycare during year by hours used per day	**4**	hr.
5	Total hours available for use during the year (365 days x 24 hours) (see instructions)	**5**	*8,760* hr.
6	Divide line 4 by line 5. Enter the result as a decimal amount . . .	**6**	.
7	Business percentage. For daycare facilities not used exclusively for business, multiply line 6 by line 3 (enter the result as a percentage). All others, enter the amount from line 3 . . . . . ▶	**7**	%

Part II   Figure Your Allowable Deduction

			(a) Direct expenses	(b) Indirect expenses		
8	Enter the amount from Schedule C, line 29, **plus** any net gain or (loss) derived from the business use of your home and shown on Schedule D or Form 4797. If more than one place of business, see instructions				**8**	
	See instructions for columns **(a)** and **(b)** before completing lines 9–21.					
9	Casualty losses (see instructions).	**9**				
10	Deductible mortgage interest (see instructions)	**10**				
11	Real estate taxes (see instructions)	**11**				
12	Add lines 9, 10, and 11	**12**				
13	Multiply line 12, column (b) by line 7			**13**		
14	Add line 12, column (a) and line 13				**14**	
15	Subtract line 14 from line 8. If zero or less, enter -0-				**15**	
16	Excess mortgage interest (see instructions) .	**16**				
17	Insurance	**17**				
18	Rent	**18**				
19	Repairs and maintenance	**19**				
20	Utilities	**20**				
21	Other expenses (see instructions).	**21**				
22	Add lines 16 through 21	**22**				
23	Multiply line 22, column (b) by line 7			**23**		
24	Carryover of operating expenses from 2008 Form 8829, line 42 . .			**24**		
25	Add line 22 column (a), line 23, and line 24.				**25**	
26	Allowable operating expenses. Enter the **smaller** of line 15 or line 25				**26**	
27	Limit on excess casualty losses and depreciation. Subtract line 26 from line 15				**27**	
28	Excess casualty losses (see instructions)			**28**		
29	Depreciation of your home from line 41 below			**29**		
30	Carryover of excess casualty losses and depreciation from 2008 Form 8829, line 43			**30**		
31	Add lines 28 through 30				**31**	
32	Allowable excess casualty losses and depreciation. Enter the **smaller** of line 27 or line 31 . .				**32**	
33	Add lines 14, 26, and 32.				**33**	
34	Casualty loss portion, if any, from lines 14 and 32. Carry amount to **Form 4684** (see instructions)				**34**	
35	**Allowable expenses for business use of your home.** Subtract line 34 from line 33. Enter here and on Schedule C, line 30. If your home was used for more than one business, see instructions ▶				**35**	

Part III   Depreciation of Your Home

36	Enter the **smaller** of your home's adjusted basis or its fair market value (see instructions) . .	**36**	
37	Value of land included on line 36	**37**	
38	Basis of building. Subtract line 37 from line 36	**38**	
39	Business basis of building. Multiply line 38 by line 7.	**39**	
40	Depreciation percentage (see instructions).	**40**	%
41	Depreciation allowable (see instructions). Multiply line 39 by line 40. Enter here and on line 29 above	**41**	

Part IV   Carryover of Unallowed Expenses to 2010

42	Operating expenses. Subtract line 26 from line 25. If less than zero, enter -0-	**42**	
43	Excess casualty losses and depreciation. Subtract line 32 from line 31. If less than zero, enter -0-	**43**	

For Paperwork Reduction Act Notice, see page 4 of separate instructions.   Cat. No. 13232M   Form **8829** (2009)

Form **1065**	**U.S. Return of Partnership Income**	OMB No. 1545-0099
Department of the Treasury Internal Revenue Service	For calendar year 2008, or tax year beginning .... , 2008, ending .... , 20...... . ▶ **See separate instructions.**	**20**0**8**

A Principal business activity	**Use the IRS label. Otherwise, print or type.**	Name of partnership	**D** Employer identification number
B Principal product or service		Number, street, and room or suite no. If a P.O. box, see the instructions.	**E** Date business started
C Business code number		City or town, state, and ZIP code	**F** Total assets (see the instructions) $

G Check applicable boxes: **(1)** ☐ Initial return **(2)** ☐ Final return **(3)** ☐ Name change **(4)** ☐ Address change **(5)** ☐ Amended return
(6) ☐ Technical termination - also check (1) or (2)

H Check accounting method: **(1)** ☐ Cash **(2)** ☐ Accrual **(3)** ☐ Other (specify) ▶ ------------------------------

I Number of Schedules K-1. Attach one for each person who was a partner at any time during the tax year ▶ ------------------

J Check if Schedule M-3 attached . . . . ☐

Caution. *Include **only** trade or business income and expenses on lines 1a through 22 below. See the instructions for more information.*

Income	**1a** Gross receipts or sales	**1a**		
	b Less returns and allowances	**1b**	**1c**	
	2 Cost of goods sold (Schedule A, line 8)		**2**	
	3 Gross profit. Subtract line 2 from line 1c		**3**	
	4 Ordinary income (loss) from other partnerships, estates, and trusts *(attach statement)*. . .		**4**	
	5 Net farm profit (loss) *(attach Schedule F (Form 1040))*		**5**	
	6 Net gain (loss) from Form 4797, Part II, line 17 *(attach Form 4797)* . . .		**6**	
	7 Other income (loss) *(attach statement)*		**7**	
	8 **Total income (loss).** Combine lines 3 through 7		**8**	
Deductions (see the instructions for limitations)	**9** Salaries and wages (other than to partners) (less employment credits)		**9**	
	10 Guaranteed payments to partners		**10**	
	11 Repairs and maintenance		**11**	
	12 Bad debts		**12**	
	13 Rent		**13**	
	14 Taxes and licenses		**14**	
	15 Interest		**15**	
	16a Depreciation *(if required, attach Form 4562)*	**16a**		
	b Less depreciation reported on Schedule A and elsewhere on return	**16b**	**16c**	
	17 Depletion (**Do not deduct oil and gas depletion.**)		**17**	
	18 Retirement plans, etc.		**18**	
	19 Employee benefit programs		**19**	
	20 Other deductions *(attach statement)*		**20**	
	21 **Total deductions.** Add the amounts shown in the far right column for lines 9 through 20 .		**21**	
	22 **Ordinary business income (loss).** Subtract line 21 from line 8		**22**	

Sign Here	Under penalties of perjury, I declare that I have examined this return, including accompanying schedules and statements, and to the best of my knowledge and belief, it is true, correct, and complete. Declaration of preparer (other than general partner or limited liability company member manager) is based on all information of which preparer has any knowledge.	
	▶ _____ ▶ _____ Signature of general partner or limited liability company member manager Date	May the IRS discuss this return with the preparer shown below (see instructions)? ☐ Yes ☐ No

Paid Preparer's Use Only	Preparer's signature	Date	Check if self-employed ▶ ☐	Preparer's SSN or PTIN
	Firm's name (or yours if self-employed), address, and ZIP code ▶		EIN ▶ Phone no. ( )	

For Privacy Act and Paperwork Reduction Act Notice, see separate instructions.   Cat. No. 11390Z   Form **1065** (2008)

Small Business Accounting Simplified

Schedule A   Cost of Goods Sold (see the instructions)

1	Inventory at beginning of year	**1**
2	Purchases less cost of items withdrawn for personal use	**2**
3	Cost of labor	**3**
4	Additional section 263A costs *(attach statement)*	**4**
5	Other costs *(attach statement)*	**5**
6	**Total.** Add lines 1 through 5	**6**
7	Inventory at end of year	**7**
8	**Cost of goods sold.** Subtract line 7 from line 6. Enter here and on page 1, line 2	**8**

9a Check all methods used for valuing closing inventory:

    (i) ☐ Cost as described in Regulations section 1.471-3

    (ii) ☐ Lower of cost or market as described in Regulations section 1.471-4

    (iii) ☐ Other (specify method used and attach explanation) ▶ .... ▶ ☐

  b Check this box if there was a writedown of "subnormal" goods as described in Regulations section 1.471-2(c) . . ▶ ☐

  c Check this box if the LIFO inventory method was adopted this tax year for any goods *(if checked, attach Form 970)* ▶ ☐

  d Do the rules of section 263A (for property produced or acquired for resale) apply to the partnership? . .   ☐ Yes ☐ No

  e Was there any change in determining quantities, cost, or valuations between opening and closing inventory?   ☐ Yes ☐ No

    If "Yes," attach explanation.

Schedule B   Other Information

		Yes	No
1	What type of entity is filing this return? Check the applicable box:		

  a ☐ Domestic general partnership   **b** ☐ Domestic limited partnership

  c ☐ Domestic limited liability company   **d** ☐ Domestic limited liability partnership

  e ☐ Foreign partnership   **f** ☐ Other ▶ ....

2   At any time during the tax year, was any partner in the partnership a disregarded entity, a partnership (including an entity treated as a partnership), a trust, an S corporation, an estate (other than an estate of a deceased partner), or a nominee or similar person? . . . .

3   At the end of the tax year:

  a Did any foreign or domestic corporation, partnership (including any entity treated as a partnership), or trust own, directly or indirectly, an interest of 50% or more in the profit, loss, or capital of the partnership? For rules of constructive ownership, see instructions. If "Yes," complete (i) through (v) below

(i) Name of Entity	(ii) Employer Identification Number (if any)	(iii) Type of Entity	(iv) Country of Organization	(v) Maximum Percentage Owned in Profit, Loss, or Capital

  b Did any individual or estate own, directly or indirectly, an interest of 50% or more in the profit, loss, or capital of the partnership? For rules of constructive ownership, see instructions. If "Yes," complete (i) through (iv) below

(i) Name of Individual or Estate	(ii) Social Security Number or Employer Identification Number (if any)	(iii) Country of Citizenship (see instructions)	(iv) Maximum Percentage Owned in Profit, Loss, or Capital

4   At the end of the tax year, did the partnership:

  a Own directly 20% or more, or own, directly or indirectly, 50% or more of the total voting power of all classes of stock entitled to vote of any foreign or domestic corporation? For rules of constructive ownership, see instructions. If "Yes," complete (i) through (iv) below . . . .

(i) Name of Corporation	(ii) Employer Identification Number (if any)	(iii) Country of Incorporation	(iv) Percentage Owned in Voting Stock

Form **1065** (2008)

Form 1065 (2008)   **Page 3**

b Own directly an interest of 20% or more, or own, directly or indirectly, an interest of 50% or more in the profit, loss, or capital in any foreign or domestic partnership (including an entity treated as a partnership) or in the beneficial interest of a trust? For rules of constructive ownership, see instructions. If "Yes," complete (i) through (v) below . | **Yes** | **No**

(i) Name of Entity	(ii) Employer Identification Number (if any)	(iii) Type of Entity	(iv) Country of Organization	(v) Maximum Percentage Owned in Profit, Loss, or Capital

5 Did the partnership file Form 8893, Election of Partnership Level Tax Treatment, or an election statement under section 6231(a)(1)(B)(ii) for partnership-level tax treatment, that is in effect for this tax year? See Form 8893 for more details . . . .

6 Does the partnership satisfy **all four** of the following conditions?

a The partnership's total receipts for the tax year were less than $250,000.

b The partnership's total assets at the end of the tax year were less than $1 million.

c Schedules K-1 are filed with the return and furnished to the partners on or before the due date (including extensions) for the partnership return.

d The partnership is not filing and is not required to file Schedule M-3 . . . .

    If "Yes," the partnership is not required to complete Schedules L, M-1, and M-2; Item F on page 1 of Form 1065; or Item L on Schedule K-1.

7 Is this partnership a publicly traded partnership as defined in section 469(k)(2)? . . . .

8 During the tax year, did the partnership have any debt that was cancelled, was forgiven, or had the terms modified so as to reduce the principal amount of the debt? . . . .

9 Has this partnership filed, or is it required to file, Form 8918, Material Advisor Disclosure Statement, to provide information on any reportable transaction? . . . .

10 At any time during calendar year 2008, did the partnership have an interest in or a signature or other authority over a financial account in a foreign country (such as a bank account, securities account, or other financial account)? See the instructions for exceptions and filing requirements for Form TD F 90-22.1, Report of Foreign Bank and Financial Accounts. If "Yes," enter the name of the foreign country. ▶ -

11 At any time during the tax year, did the partnership receive a distribution from, or was it the grantor of, or transferor to, a foreign trust? If "Yes," the partnership may have to file Form 3520, Annual Return To Report Transactions With Foreign Trusts and Receipt of Certain Foreign Gifts. See instructions . . . .

12a Is the partnership making, or had it previously made (and not revoked), a section 754 election? . . . . . See instructions for details regarding a section 754 election.

  b Did the partnership make for this tax year an optional basis adjustment under section 743(b) or 734(b)? If "Yes," attach a statement showing the computation and allocation of the basis adjustment. See instructions . . .

  c Is the partnership required to adjust the basis of partnership assets under section 743(b) or 734(b) because of a substantial built-in loss (as defined under section 743(d)) or substantial basis reduction (as defined under section 734(d))? If "Yes," attach a statement showing the computation and allocation of the basis adjustment. See instructions . . . . . .

13 Check this box if, during the current or prior tax year, the partnership distributed any property received in a like-kind exchange or contributed such property to another entity (including a disregarded entity) . ▶ ☐

14 At any time during the tax year, did the partnership distribute to any partner a tenancy-in-common or other undivided interest in partnership property? . . . .

15 If the partnership is required to file Form 8858, Information Return of U.S. Persons With Respect To Foreign Disregarded Entities, enter the number of Forms 8858 attached. See instructions ▶ - - - - - - - - - - - - - - - -

16 Does the partnership have any foreign partners? If "Yes," enter the number of Forms 8805, Foreign Partner's Information Statement of Section 1446 Withholding Tax, filed for this partnership. ▶ - - - - - - - - - - - - - - - -

17 Enter the number of Forms 8865, Return of U.S. Persons With Respect to Certain Foreign Partnerships, attached to this return. ▶ - - - - - - - - - - - - - - - -

Designation of Tax Matters Partner (see instructions)
Enter below the general partner designated as the tax matters partner (TMP) for the tax year of this return:

Name of designated TMP ▶		Identifying number of TMP ▶	
Address of designated TMP ▶			

Small Business Accounting Simplified

Schedule K	Partners' Distributive Share Items		Total amount	
Income (Loss)	**1** Ordinary business income (loss) (page 1, line 22)		**1**	
	2 Net rental real estate income (loss) *(attach Form 8825)*		**2**	
	3a Other gross rental income (loss)	3a		
	b Expenses from other rental activities *(attach statement)*. . . .	3b		
	c Other net rental income (loss). Subtract line 3b from line 3a . . .		**3c**	
	4 Guaranteed payments		**4**	
	5 Interest income		**5**	
	6 Dividends: **a** Ordinary dividends		**6a**	
	b Qualified dividends	6b		
	7 Royalties		**7**	
	8 Net short-term capital gain (loss) *(attach Schedule D (Form 1065))* . .		**8**	
	9a Net long-term capital gain (loss) *(attach Schedule D (Form 1065))*		**9a**	
	b Collectibles (28%) gain (loss)	9b		
	c Unrecaptured section 1250 gain *(attach statement)*	9c		
	10 Net section 1231 gain (loss) *(attach Form 4797)*		**10**	
	11 Other income (loss) *(see instructions)* Type ▶ _____		**11**	
Deductions	**12** Section 179 deduction *(attach Form 4562)*		**12**	
	13a Contributions		**13a**	
	b Investment interest expense		**13b**	
	c Section 59(e)(2) expenditures: **(1)** Type ▶ _____ **(2)** Amount ▶		**13c(2)**	
	d Other deductions *(see instructions)* Type ▶ _____		**13d**	
Self-Employ-ment	**14a** Net earnings (loss) from self-employment		**14a**	
	b Gross farming or fishing income		**14b**	
	c Gross nonfarm income		**14c**	
Credits	**15a** Low-income housing credit (section 42(j)(5))		**15a**	
	b Low-income housing credit (other)		**15b**	
	c Qualified rehabilitation expenditures (rental real estate) *(attach Form 3468)*. . .		**15c**	
	d Other rental real estate credits *(see instructions)* Type ▶ _____		**15d**	
	e Other rental credits *(see instructions)* Type ▶ _____		**15e**	
	f Other credits *(see instructions)* Type ▶ _____		**15f**	
Foreign Transactions	**16a** Name of country or U.S. possession ▶ _____			
	b Gross income from all sources		**16b**	
	c Gross income sourced at partner level		**16c**	
	Foreign gross income sourced at partnership level			
	d Passive category ▶ _____ **e** General category ▶ _____ **f** Other ▶		**16f**	
	Deductions allocated and apportioned at partner level			
	g Interest expense ▶ _____ **h** Other . . . . ▶		**16h**	
	Deductions allocated and apportioned at partnership level to foreign source income			
	i Passive category ▶ _____ **j** General category ▶ _____ **k** Other ▶		**16k**	
	l Total foreign taxes (check one): ▶ Paid ☐ Accrued ☐		**16l**	
	m Reduction in taxes available for credit *(attach statement)*		**16m**	
	n Other foreign tax information *(attach statement)*			
Alternative Minimum Tax (AMT) Items	**17a** Post-1986 depreciation adjustment		**17a**	
	b Adjusted gain or loss		**17b**	
	c Depletion (other than oil and gas)		**17c**	
	d Oil, gas, and geothermal properties—gross income		**17d**	
	e Oil, gas, and geothermal properties—deductions		**17e**	
	f Other AMT items *(attach statement)*		**17f**	
Other Information	**18a** Tax-exempt interest income		**18a**	
	b Other tax-exempt income		**18b**	
	c Nondeductible expenses		**18c**	
	19a Distributions of cash and marketable securities		**19a**	
	b Distributions of other property		**19b**	
	20a Investment income		**20a**	
	b Investment expenses		**20b**	
	c Other items and amounts *(attach statement)*			

Form **1065** (2008)

228

Form 1065 (2008)   Page **5**

Analysis of Net Income (Loss)

1   Net income (loss). Combine Schedule K, lines 1 through 11. From the result, subtract the sum of Schedule K, lines 12 through 13d, and 16l **1**

2 Analysis by partner type:	**(i)** Corporate	**(ii)** Individual (active)	**(iii)** Individual (passive)	**(iv)** Partnership	**(v)** Exempt organization	**(vi)** Nominee/Other
a General partners						
b Limited partners						

Schedule L   Balance Sheets per Books

	Assets	Beginning of tax year (a)	(b)	End of tax year (c)	(d)
1	Cash				
2a	Trade notes and accounts receivable				
b	Less allowance for bad debts				
3	Inventories				
4	U.S. government obligations				
5	Tax-exempt securities				
6	Other current assets (attach statement) . . .				
7	Mortgage and real estate loans				
8	Other investments (attach statement) . . .				
9a	Buildings and other depreciable assets. . . .				
b	Less accumulated depreciation				
10a	Depletable assets				
b	Less accumulated depletion				
11	Land (net of any amortization).				
12a	Intangible assets (amortizable only) . . .				
b	Less accumulated amortization				
13	Other assets (attach statement) . . .				
14	Total assets				
	Liabilities and Capital				
15	Accounts payable				
16	Mortgages, notes, bonds payable in less than 1 year .				
17	Other current liabilities (attach statement) . . .				
18	All nonrecourse loans				
19	Mortgages, notes, bonds payable in 1 year or more .				
20	Other liabilities (attach statement) . . .				
21	Partners' capital accounts				
22	Total liabilities and capital				

Schedule M-1   Reconciliation of Income (Loss) per Books With Income (Loss) per Return

Note. Schedule M-3 may be required instead of Schedule M-1 (see instructions).

1	Net income (loss) per books		**6** Income recorded on books this year not included on Schedule K, lines 1 through 11 (itemize):	
2	Income included on Schedule K, lines 1, 2, 3c, 5, 6a, 7, 8, 9a, 10, and 11, not recorded on books this year (itemize): _____		**a** Tax-exempt interest $ _____	
3	Guaranteed payments (other than health insurance)		**7** Deductions Included on Schedule K, lines 1 through 13d, and 16l, not charged against book income this year (itemize):	
4	Expenses recorded on books this year not included on Schedule K, lines 1 through 13d, and 16l (itemize):		**a** Depreciation $ _____	
a	Depreciation $ _____			
b	Travel and entertainment $ _____		**8** Add lines 6 and 7	
			9 Income (loss) (Analysis of Net Income (Loss), line 1). Subtract line 8 from line 5	
5	Add lines 1 through 4			

Schedule M-2   Analysis of Partners' Capital Accounts

1	Balance at beginning of year		**6** Distributions: **a** Cash	
2	Capital contributed: **a** Cash		**b** Property	
	b Property . . .		**7** Other decreases (itemize): _____	
3	Net income (loss) per books			
4	Other increases (itemize): _____			
			8 Add lines 6 and 7	
5	Add lines 1 through 4		**9** Balance at end of year. Subtract line 8 from line 5	

Form **1065** (2008)

651108

☐ Final K-1   ☐ Amended K-1   OMB No. 1545-0099

Schedule K-1
(Form 1065)

20**08**

Department of the Treasury
Internal Revenue Service

For calendar year 2008, or tax
year beginning _____ , 2008
ending _____ , 20____

**Partner's Share of Income, Deductions,
Credits, etc.**   ► **See back of form and separate instructions.**

Part I	Information About the Partnership

A Partnership's employer identification number

B Partnership's name, address, city, state, and ZIP code

C IRS Center where partnership filed return

D ☐ Check if this is a publicly traded partnership (PTP)

Part II	Information About the Partner

E Partner's identifying number

F Partner's name, address, city, state, and ZIP code

G ☐ General partner or LLC member-manager   ☐ Limited partner or other LLC member

H ☐ Domestic partner   ☐ Foreign partner

I What type of entity is this partner? _____

J Partner's share of profit, loss, and capital (see instructions):

	Beginning	Ending
Profit	_____ %	_____ %
Loss	_____ %	_____ %
Capital	_____ %	_____ %

K Partner's share of liabilities at year end:

Nonrecourse . . . . $ _____
Qualified nonrecourse financing . . $ _____
Recourse . . . . $ _____

L Partner's capital account analysis:

Beginning capital account . . . . . $ _____
Capital contributed during the year . $ _____
Current year increase (decrease) . . $ _____
Withdrawals & distributions . . . . $ (_____)
Ending capital account . . . . . $ _____

☐ Tax basis   ☐ GAAP   ☐ Section 704(b) book
☐ Other (explain)

Part III	Partner's Share of Current Year Income, Deductions, Credits, and Other Items

1	Ordinary business income (loss)	15	Credits
2	Net rental real estate income (loss)		
3	Other net rental income (loss)	16	Foreign transactions
4	Guaranteed payments		
5	Interest income		
6a	Ordinary dividends		
6b	Qualified dividends		
7	Royalties		
8	Net short-term capital gain (loss)		
9a	Net long-term capital gain (loss)	17	Alternative minimum tax (AMT) items
9b	Collectibles (28%) gain (loss)		
9c	Unrecaptured section 1250 gain		
10	Net section 1231 gain (loss)	18	Tax-exempt income and nondeductible expenses
11	Other income (loss)		
		19	Distributions
12	Section 179 deduction		
13	Other deductions	20	Other information
14	Self-employment earnings (loss)		

*See attached statement for additional information.

For IRS Use Only

For Paperwork Reduction Act Notice, see Instructions for Form 1065.   Cat. No. 11394R   Schedule K-1 (Form 1065) 2008

This list identifies the codes used on Schedule K-1 for all partners and provides summarized reporting information for partners who file Form 1040. For detailed reporting and filing information, see the separate Partner's Instructions for Schedule K-1 and the instructions for your income tax return.

1. Ordinary business income (loss). Determine whether the income (loss) is passive or nonpassive and enter on your return as follows.

	Report on
Passive loss	See the Partner's Instructions
Passive income	Schedule E, line 28, column (g)
Nonpassive loss	Schedule E, line 28, column (h)
Nonpassive income	Schedule E, line 28, column (j)

2. Net rental real estate income (loss)   See the Partner's Instructions

3. Other net rental income (loss)
Net income	Schedule E, line 28, column (g)
Net loss	See the Partner's Instructions

4. Guaranteed payments   Schedule E, line 28, column (j)
5. Interest income   Form 1040, line 8a
6a. Ordinary dividends   Form 1040, line 9a
6b. Qualified dividends   Form 1040, line 9b
7. Royalties   Schedule E, line 4
8. Net short-term capital gain (loss)   Schedule D, line 5, column (f)
9a. Net long-term capital gain (loss)   Schedule D, line 12, column (f)
9b. Collectibles (28%) gain (loss)   28% Rate Gain Worksheet, line 4 (Schedule D instructions)
9c. Unrecaptured section 1250 gain   See the Partner's Instructions
10. Net section 1231 gain (loss)   See the Partner's Instructions
11. Other income (loss)

Code	
A Other portfolio income (loss)	See the Partner's Instructions
B Involuntary conversions	See the Partner's Instructions
C Sec. 1256 contracts & straddles	Form 6781, line 1
D Mining exploration costs recapture	See Pub. 535
E Cancellation of debt	Form 1040, line 21 or Form 982
F Other income (loss)	See the Partner's Instructions

12. Section 179 deduction   See the Partner's Instructions
13. Other deductions

A Cash contributions (50%)	
B Cash contributions (30%)	
C Noncash contributions (50%)	
D Noncash contributions (30%)	See the Partner's Instructions
E Capital gain property to a 50% organization (30%)	
F Capital gain property (20%)	
G Contributions (100%)	
H Investment interest expense	Form 4952, line 1
I Deductions—royalty income	Schedule E, line 18
J Section 59(e)(2) expenditures	See the Partner's Instructions
K Deductions—portfolio (2% floor)	Schedule A, line 23
L Deductions—portfolio (other)	Schedule A, line 28
M Amounts paid for medical insurance	Schedule A, line 1 or Form 1040, line 29
N Educational assistance benefits	See the Partner's Instructions
O Dependent care benefits	Form 2441, line 14
P Preproductive period expenses	See the Partner's Instructions
Q Commercial revitalization deduction from rental real estate activities	See Form 8582 instructions
R Pensions and IRAs	See the Partner's Instructions
S Reforestation expense deduction	See the Partner's Instructions
T Domestic production activities information	See Form 8903 instructions
U Qualified production activities income	Form 8903, line 7
V Employer's Form W-2 wages	Form 8903, line 15
W Other deductions	See the Partner's Instructions

14. Self-employment earnings (loss)
Note. *If you have a section 179 deduction or any partner-level deductions, see the Partner's Instructions before completing Schedule SE.*

A Net earnings (loss) from self-employment	Schedule SE, Section A or B
B Gross farming or fishing income	See the Partner's Instructions
C Gross non-farm income	See the Partner's Instructions

15. Credits

A Low-income housing credit (section 42(j)(5)) from pre-2008 buildings	See the Partner's Instructions
B Low-income housing credit (other) from pre-2008 buildings	See the Partner's Instructions
C Low-income housing credit (section 42(j)(5)) from post-2007 buildings	Form 8586, line 11
D Low-income housing credit (other) from post-2007 buildings	Form 8586, line 11
E Qualified rehabilitation expenditures (rental real estate)	
F Other rental real estate credits	See the Partner's Instructions
G Other rental credits	
H Undistributed capital gains credit	Form 1040, line 68; check box a
I Alcohol and cellulosic biofuels credit	Form 6478, line 9

Code	*Report on*
J Work opportunity credit	Form 5884, line 3
K Disabled access credit	See the Partner's Instructions
L Empowerment zone and renewal community employment credit	Form 8844, line 3
M Credit for increasing research activities	See the Partner's Instructions
N Credit for employer social security and Medicare taxes	Form 8846, line 5
O Backup withholding	Form 1040, line 62
P Other credits	See the Partner's Instructions

16. Foreign transactions

A Name of country or U.S. possession	
B Gross income from all sources	Form 1116, Part I
C Gross income sourced at partner level	

Foreign gross income sourced at partnership level

D Passive category	
E General category	Form 1116, Part I
F Other	

Deductions allocated and apportioned at partner level

G Interest expense	Form 1116, Part I
H Other	Form 1116, Part I

Deductions allocated and apportioned at partnership level to foreign source income

I Passive category	
J General category	Form 1116, Part I
K Other	

Other information

L Total foreign taxes paid	Form 1116, Part II
M Total foreign taxes accrued	Form 1116, Part II
N Reduction in taxes available for credit	Form 1116, line 12
O Foreign trading gross receipts	Form 8873
P Extraterritorial income exclusion	Form 8873
Q Other foreign transactions	See the Partner's Instructions

17. Alternative minimum tax (AMT) items

A Post-1986 depreciation adjustment	
B Adjusted gain or loss	See the Partner's Instructions and the Instructions for Form 6251
C Depletion (other than oil & gas)	
D Oil, gas, & geothermal—gross income	
E Oil, gas, & geothermal—deductions	
F Other AMT items	

18. Tax-exempt income and nondeductible expenses

A Tax-exempt interest income	Form 1040, line 8b
B Other tax-exempt income	See the Partner's Instructions
C Nondeductible expenses	See the Partner's Instructions

19. Distributions

A Cash and marketable securities	
B Other property	See the Partner's Instructions
C Distribution subject to section 737	

20. Other information

A Investment income	Form 4952, line 4a
B Investment expenses	Form 4952, line 5
C Fuel tax credit information	Form 4136
D Qualified rehabilitation expenditures (other than rental real estate)	See the Partner's Instructions
E Basis of energy property	See the Partner's Instructions
F Recapture of low-income housing credit (section 42(j)(5))	Form 8611, line 8
G Recapture of low-income housing credit (other)	Form 8611, line 8
H Recapture of investment credit	See Form 4255
I Recapture of other credits	See the Partner's Instructions
J Look-back interest—completed long-term contracts	See Form 8697
K Look-back interest—income forecast method	See Form 8866
L Dispositions of property with section 179 deductions	
M Recapture of section 179 deduction	
N Interest expense for corporate partners	
O Section 453(l)(3) information	
P Section 453A(c) information	
Q Section 1260(b) information	See the Partner's Instructions
R Interest allocable to production expenditures	
S CCF nonqualified withdrawals	
T Depletion information—oil and gas	
U Amortization of reforestation costs	
V Unrelated business taxable income	
W Precontribution gain (loss)	
X Other information	

Form 1120
Department of the Treasury
Internal Revenue Service

U.S. Corporation Income Tax Return

For calendar year 2008 or tax year beginning _____ , 2008, ending _____ , 20 _____

▶ See separate instructions.

OMB No. 1545-0123

2008

A **Check if:**				B Employer identification number
1a Consolidated return (attach Form 851) ☐	Use IRS label. Otherwise, print or type.	Name		
b Life/nonlife consolidated return . . ☐		Number, street, and room or suite no. If a P.O. box, see instructions.		C Date incorporated
2 Personal holding co. (attach Sch. PH) . ☐				
3 Personal service corp. (see instructions) . ☐		City or town, state, and ZIP code		D Total assets (see instructions) $
4 Schedule M-3 attached ☐				

E Check if: **(1)** ☐ Initial return **(2)** ☐ Final return **(3)** ☐ Name change **(4)** ☐ Address change

Income	**1a** Gross receipts or sales		**b** Less returns and allowances	**c** Bal ▶	**1c**
	2 Cost of goods sold (Schedule A, line 8)				**2**
	3 Gross profit. Subtract line 2 from line 1c				**3**
	4 Dividends (Schedule C, line 19)				**4**
	5 Interest				**5**
	6 Gross rents				**6**
	7 Gross royalties				**7**
	8 Capital gain net income (attach Schedule D (Form 1120))				**8**
	9 Net gain or (loss) from Form 4797, Part II, line 17 (attach Form 4797) . .				**9**
	10 Other income (see instructions—attach schedule)				**10**
	11 **Total income.** Add lines 3 through 10 . . . . ▶				**11**
Deductions (See instructions for limitations on deductions.)	**12** Compensation of officers (Schedule E, line 4) . . . . ▶				**12**
	13 Salaries and wages (less employment credits)				**13**
	14 Repairs and maintenance				**14**
	15 Bad debts				**15**
	16 Rents				**16**
	17 Taxes and licenses				**17**
	18 Interest				**18**
	19 Charitable contributions				**19**
	20 Depreciation from Form 4562 not claimed on Schedule A or elsewhere on return (attach Form 4562) . . .				**20**
	21 Depletion				**21**
	22 Advertising				**22**
	23 Pension, profit-sharing, etc., plans				**23**
	24 Employee benefit programs				**24**
	25 Domestic production activities deduction (attach Form 8903)				**25**
	26 Other deductions (attach schedule)				**26**
	27 **Total deductions.** Add lines 12 through 26 . . . . ▶				**27**
	28 Taxable income before net operating loss deduction and special deductions. Subtract line 27 from line 11 . .				**28**
	29 **Less: a** Net operating loss deduction (see instructions)		**29a**		
	b Special deductions (Schedule C, line 20)		**29b**		**29c**
Tax, Refundable Credits, and Payments	**30** **Taxable income.** Subtract line 29c from line 28 (see instructions)				**30**
	31 **Total tax** (Schedule J, line 10)				**31**
	32a 2007 overpayment credited to 2008 . .	**32a**			
	b 2008 estimated tax payments	**32b**			
	c 2008 refund applied for on Form 4466 . .	**32c** (	) **d** Bal ▶	**32d**	
	e Tax deposited with Form 7004			**32e**	
	f Credits: **(1)** Form 2439		**(2)** Form 4136	**32f**	
	g Refundable credits from Form 3800, line 19c, and Form 8827, line 8c . .			**32h**	
	33 Estimated tax penalty (see instructions). Check if Form 2220 is attached . . . . . . ▶ ☐				**33**
	34 **Amount owed.** If line 32h is smaller than the total of lines 31 and 33, enter amount owed				**34**
	35 **Overpayment.** If line 32h is larger than the total of lines 31 and 33, enter amount overpaid				**35**
	36 Enter amount from line 35 you want: **Credited to 2009 estimated tax** ▶		Refunded ▶		**36**

Sign Here ▶

Under penalties of perjury, I declare that I have examined this return, including accompanying schedules and statements, and to the best of my knowledge and belief, it is true, correct, and complete. Declaration of preparer (other than taxpayer) is based on all information of which preparer has any knowledge.

▶ Signature of officer	Date	▶ Title

May the IRS discuss this return with the preparer shown below (see instructions)? ☐ Yes ☐ No

Paid Preparer's Use Only

Preparer's signature ▶		Date	Check if self-employed ☐	Preparer's SSN or PTIN
Firm's name (or yours if self-employed), address, and ZIP code ▶			EIN	
			Phone no.	

For Privacy Act and Paperwork Reduction Act Notice, see separate instructions.   Cat. No. 11450Q   Form **1120** (2008)

Schedule A　Cost of Goods Sold (see instructions)

1	Inventory at beginning of year	1
2	Purchases	2
3	Cost of labor	3
4	Additional section 263A costs (attach schedule)	4
5	Other costs (attach schedule)	5
6	**Total.** Add lines 1 through 5	6
7	Inventory at end of year	7
8	**Cost of goods sold.** Subtract line 7 from line 6. Enter here and on page 1, line 2	8

9a Check all methods used for valuing closing inventory:

　(i) ☐ Cost

　(ii) ☐ Lower of cost or market

　(iii) ☐ Other (Specify method used and attach explanation.) ▶ _____

b Check if there was a writedown of subnormal goods . . . . ▶ ☐

c Check if the LIFO inventory method was adopted this tax year for any goods (if checked, attach Form 970) . . . ▶ ☐

d If the LIFO inventory method was used for this tax year, enter percentage (or amounts) of closing inventory computed under LIFO **9d**

e If property is produced or acquired for resale, do the rules of section 263A apply to the corporation? . . . . . ☐ Yes　☐ No

f Was there any change in determining quantities, cost, or valuations between opening and closing inventory? If "Yes," attach explanation . . . . ☐ Yes　☐ No

Schedule C　Dividends and Special Deductions (see instructions)

		(a) Dividends received	(b) %	(c) Special deductions (a) × (b)
1	Dividends from less-than-20%-owned domestic corporations (other than debt-financed stock) . . .		70	
2	Dividends from 20%-or-more-owned domestic corporations (other than debt-financed stock) . . .		80	
3	Dividends on debt-financed stock of domestic and foreign corporations		see instructions	
4	Dividends on certain preferred stock of less-than-20%-owned public utilities		42	
5	Dividends on certain preferred stock of 20%-or-more-owned public utilities		48	
6	Dividends from less-than-20%-owned foreign corporations and certain FSCs		70	
7	Dividends from 20%-or-more-owned foreign corporations and certain FSCs		80	
8	Dividends from wholly owned foreign subsidiaries		100	
9	**Total.** Add lines 1 through 8. See instructions for limitation			
10	Dividends from domestic corporations received by a small business investment company operating under the Small Business Investment Act of 1958		100	
11	Dividends from affiliated group members		100	
12	Dividends from certain FSCs		100	
13	Dividends from foreign corporations not included on lines 3, 6, 7, 8, 11, or 12			
14	Income from controlled foreign corporations under subpart F (attach Form(s) 5471) . .			
15	Foreign dividend gross-up			
16	IC-DISC and former DISC dividends not included on lines 1, 2, or 3			
17	Other dividends			
18	Deduction for dividends paid on certain preferred stock of public utilities . . . . . ▶			
19	**Total dividends.** Add lines 1 through 17. Enter here and on page 1, line 4 . . . ▶			
20	**Total special deductions.** Add lines 9, 10, 11, 12, and 18. Enter here and on page 1, line 29b . . . . ▶			

Schedule E　Compensation of Officers (see instructions for page 1, line 12)

Note: *Complete Schedule E only if total receipts (line 1a plus lines 4 through 10 on page 1) are $500,000 or more.*

(a) Name of officer	(b) Social security number	(c) Percent of time devoted to business	Percent of corporation stock owned		(f) Amount of compensation
			(d) Common	(e) Preferred	
1		%	%	%	
		%	%	%	
		%	%	%	
		%	%	%	
		%	%	%	

2　Total compensation of officers . . . .

3　Compensation of officers claimed on Schedule A and elsewhere on return . . . .

4　Subtract line 3 from line 2. Enter the result here and on page 1, line 12 . . . .

Form **1120** (2008)

Small Business Accounting Simplified

Schedule J — Tax Computation (see instructions)

1	Check if the corporation is a member of a controlled group (attach Schedule O (Form 1120)) ▶ ☐	
2	Income tax. Check if a qualified personal service corporation (see instructions) ▶ ☐	**2**
3	Alternative minimum tax (attach Form 4626)	**3**
4	Add lines 2 and 3	**4**
5a	Foreign tax credit (attach Form 1118)	5a
b	Credit from Form 8834	5b
c	General business credit (attach Form 3800)	5c
d	Credit for prior year minimum tax (attach Form 8827)	5d
e	Bond credits from Form 8912	5e
6	**Total credits.** Add lines 5a through 5e	**6**
7	Subtract line 6 from line 4	**7**
8	Personal holding company tax (attach Schedule PH (Form 1120))	**8**
9	Other taxes. Check if from: ☐ Form 4255 ☐ Form 8611 ☐ Form 8697 ☐ Form 8866 ☐ Form 8902 ☐ Other (attach schedule)	**9**
10	**Total tax.** Add lines 7 through 9. Enter here and on page 1, line 31	**10**

Schedule K — Other Information (see instructions)

		Yes	No
1	Check accounting method: **a** ☐ Cash **b** ☐ Accrual **c** ☐ Other (specify) ▶ _____		
2	See the instructions and enter the:		
a	Business activity code no. ▶ _____		
b	Business activity ▶ _____		
c	Product or service ▶ _____		
3	Is the corporation a subsidiary in an affiliated group or a parent-subsidiary controlled group? If "Yes," enter name and EIN of the parent corporation ▶ _____		
4	At the end of the tax year:		
a	Did any foreign or domestic corporation, partnership (including any entity treated as a partnership), or trust own directly 20% or more, or own, directly or indirectly, 50% or more of the total voting power of all classes of the corporation's stock entitled to vote? For rules of constructive ownership, see instructions. If "Yes," complete (i) through (v).		

(i) Name of Entity	(ii) Employer Identification Number (if any)	(iii) Type of Entity	(iv) Country of Organization	(v) Percentage Owned in Voting Stock

		Yes	No
b	Did any individual or estate own directly 20% or more, or own, directly or indirectly, 50% or more of the total voting power of all classes of the corporation's stock entitled to vote? For rules of constructive ownership, see instructions. If "Yes," complete (i) through (iv).		

(i) Name of Individual or Estate	(ii) Identifying Number (if any)	(iii) Country of Citizenship (see instructions)	(iv) Percentage Owned in Voting Stock

Schedule K	Continued

5 At the end of the tax year, did the corporation:

				Yes	No

a Own directly 20% or more, or own, directly or indirectly, 50% or more of the total voting power of all classes of stock entitled to vote of any foreign or domestic corporation not included on **Form 851,** Affiliations Schedule? For rules of constructive ownership, see instructions . If "Yes," complete (i) through (iv).

(i) Name of Corporation	(ii) Employer Identification Number (if any)	(iii) Country of Incorporation	(iv) Percentage Owned in Voting Stock

b Own directly an interest of 20% or more, or own, directly or indirectly, an interest of 50% or more in any foreign or domestic partnership (including an entity treated as a partnership) or in the beneficial interest of a trust? For rules of constructive ownership, see instructions . If "Yes," complete (i) through (iv).

(i) Name of Entity	(ii) Employer Identification Number (if any)	(iii) Country of Organization	(iv) Maximum Percentage Owned in Profit, Loss, or Capital

6 During this tax year, did the corporation pay dividends (other than stock dividends and distributions in exchange for stock) in excess of the corporation's current and accumulated earnings and profits? (See sections 301 and 316.) . . . .

If "Yes," file **Form 5452,** Corporate Report of Nondividend Distributions.

If this is a consolidated return, answer here for the parent corporation and on Form 851 for each subsidiary.

7 At any time during the tax year, did one foreign person own, directly or indirectly, at least 25% of **(a)** the total voting power of all classes of the corporation's stock entitled to vote or **(b)** the total value of all classes of the corporation's stock? . . . . .

For rules of attribution, see section 318. If "Yes," enter:

(i) Percentage owned ▶ .... and **(ii)** Owner's country ▶ ....

(c) The corporation may have to file **Form 5472,** Information Return of a 25% Foreign-Owned U.S. Corporation or a Foreign Corporation Engaged in a U.S. Trade or Business. Enter the number of Forms 5472 attached ▶ ....

8 Check this box if the corporation issued publicly offered debt instruments with original issue discount . . . . . ▶ ☐

If checked, the corporation may have to file **Form 8281,** Information Return for Publicly Offered Original Issue Discount Instruments.

9 Enter the amount of tax-exempt interest received or accrued during the tax year ▶ $ ....

10 Enter the number of shareholders at the end of the tax year (if 100 or fewer) ▶ ....

11 If the corporation has an NOL for the tax year and is electing to forego the carryback period, check here . . . . . . ▶ ☐

If the corporation is filing a consolidated return, the statement required by Regulations section 1.1502-21(b)(3) must be attached or the election will not be valid.

12 Enter the available NOL carryover from prior tax years (do not reduce it by any deduction on line 29a.) ▶ $ ....

13 Are the corporation's total receipts (line 1a plus lines 4 through 10 on page 1) for the tax year **and** its total assets at the end of the tax year less than $250,000? . . . .

If "Yes," the corporation is not required to complete Schedules L, M-1, and M-2 on page 5. Instead, enter the total amount of cash distributions and the book value of property distributions (other than cash) made during the tax year. ▶ $ ....

Form **1120** (2008)

Small Business Accounting Simplified

Schedule L — Balance Sheets per Books

		Beginning of tax year		End of tax year	
Assets		(a)	(b)	(c)	(d)
1	Cash				
2a	Trade notes and accounts receivable				
b	Less allowance for bad debts	( )		( )	
3	Inventories				
4	U.S. government obligations				
5	Tax-exempt securities (see instructions) . . .				
6	Other current assets (attach schedule) . . .				
7	Loans to shareholders				
8	Mortgage and real estate loans				
9	Other investments (attach schedule) . . .				
10a	Buildings and other depreciable assets . . .				
b	Less accumulated depreciation	( )		( )	
11a	Depletable assets				
b	Less accumulated depletion	( )		( )	
12	Land (net of any amortization)				
13a	Intangible assets (amortizable only)				
b	Less accumulated amortization	( )		( )	
14	Other assets (attach schedule)				
15	Total assets				
Liabilities and Shareholders' Equity					
16	Accounts payable				
17	Mortgages, notes, bonds payable in less than 1 year				
18	Other current liabilities (attach schedule) . . .				
19	Loans from shareholders				
20	Mortgages, notes, bonds payable in 1 year or more				
21	Other liabilities (attach schedule)				
22	Capital stock: **a** Preferred stock				
	b Common stock				
23	Additional paid-in capital				
24	Retained earnings—Appropriated (attach schedule)				
25	Retained earnings—Unappropriated				
26	Adjustments to shareholders' equity (attach schedule)				
27	Less cost of treasury stock		( )		( )
28	Total liabilities and shareholders' equity . . .				

Schedule M-1 — Reconciliation of Income (Loss) per Books With Income per Return

Note: Schedule M-3 required instead of Schedule M-1 if total assets are $10 million or more—see instructions

1	Net income (loss) per books		
2	Federal income tax per books		
3	Excess of capital losses over capital gains . .		
4	Income subject to tax not recorded on books this year (itemize): _____		
	_____		
5	Expenses recorded on books this year not deducted on this return (itemize):		
a	Depreciation . . . . $ _____		
b	Charitable contributions . $ _____		
c	Travel and entertainment . $ _____		
	_____		
6	Add lines 1 through 5		

7	Income recorded on books this year not included on this return (itemize):		
	Tax-exempt interest $ _____		
	_____		
	_____		
8	Deductions on this return not charged against book income this year (itemize):		
a	Depreciation . . . $ _____		
b	Charitable contributions $ _____		
	_____		
9	Add lines 7 and 8		
10	Income (page 1, line 28)—line 6 less line 9		

Schedule M-2 — Analysis of Unappropriated Retained Earnings per Books (Line 25, Schedule L)

1	Balance at beginning of year		
2	Net income (loss) per books		
3	Other increases (itemize): _____		
	_____		
	_____		
4	Add lines 1, 2, and 3		

5	Distributions: **a** Cash		
	b Stock		
	c Property . . .		
6	Other decreases (itemize): _____		
7	Add lines 5 and 6		
8	Balance at end of year (line 4 less line 7)		

Form **1120** (2008)

Form **1120S**	**U.S. Income Tax Return for an S Corporation**	OMB No. 1545-0130
Department of the Treasury Internal Revenue Service	► Do not file this form unless the corporation has filed or is attaching Form 2553 to elect to be an S corporation. ► See separate instructions.	**20**08

For calendar year 2008 or tax year beginning _____ **, 2008, ending** _____ **, 20** ___

A S election effective date	**Use IRS label. Other-wise, print or type.** Name	**D** Employer identification number
B Business activity code number *(see instructions)*	Number, street, and room or suite no. If a P.O. box, see instructions.	**E** Date incorporated
C Check if Sch. M-3 attached ☐	City or town, state, and ZIP code	**F** Total assets *(see instructions)* $

G Is the corporation electing to be an S corporation beginning with this tax year? ☐ Yes ☐ No   If "Yes," attach Form 2553 if not already filed

H Check if: **(1)** ☐ Final return **(2)** ☐ Name change **(3)** ☐ Address change **(4)** ☐ Amended return **(5)** ☐ S election termination or revocation

I Enter the number of shareholders who were shareholders during any part of the tax year . . . . ►

Caution. *Include **only** trade or business income and expenses on lines 1a through 21. See the instructions for more information.*

Income

1a	Gross receipts or sales _____ **b** Less returns and allowances _____	**c** Bal ►	**1c**
2	Cost of goods sold (Schedule A, line 8)		**2**
3	Gross profit. Subtract line 2 from line 1c		**3**
4	Net gain (loss) from Form 4797, Part II, line 17 *(attach Form 4797)* . . .		**4**
5	Other income (loss) *(see instructions—attach statement)*		**5**
6	**Total income (loss).** Add lines 3 through 5. . . . . ►		**6**

Deductions *(see instructions for limitations)*

7	Compensation of officers	**7**
8	Salaries and wages (less employment credits)	**8**
9	Repairs and maintenance	**9**
10	Bad debts	**10**
11	Rents	**11**
12	Taxes and licenses	**12**
13	Interest	**13**
14	Depreciation not claimed on Schedule A or elsewhere on return *(attach Form 4562)* .	**14**
15	Depletion **(Do not deduct oil and gas depletion.)**	**15**
16	Advertising	**16**
17	Pension, profit-sharing, etc., plans	**17**
18	Employee benefit programs	**18**
19	Other deductions *(attach statement)*	**19**
20	**Total deductions.** Add lines 7 through 19 . . . . ►	**20**
21	**Ordinary business income (loss).** Subtract line 20 from line 6 . .	**21**

Tax and Payments

22a	Excess net passive income or LIFO recapture tax *(see instructions)*	**22a**	
b	Tax from Schedule D (Form 1120S)	**22b**	
c	Add lines 22a and 22b *(see instructions for additional taxes)* . .		**22c**
23a	2008 estimated tax payments and 2007 overpayment credited to 2008	**23a**	
b	Tax deposited with Form 7004	**23b**	
c	Credit for federal tax paid on fuels *(attach Form 4136)* . . .	**23c**	
d	Add lines 23a through 23c		**23d**
24	Estimated tax penalty *(see instructions)*. Check if Form 2220 is attached . . . . ► ☐		**24**
25	**Amount owed.** If line 23d is smaller than the total of lines 22c and 24, enter amount owed . .		**25**
26	**Overpayment.** If line 23d is larger than the total of lines 22c and 24, enter amount overpaid . .		**26**
27	Enter amount from line 26 **Credited to 2009 estimated tax** ► _____ **Refunded** ►		**27**

Sign Here

Under penalties of perjury, I declare that I have examined this return, including accompanying schedules and statements, and to the best of my knowledge and belief, it is true, correct, and complete. Declaration of preparer (other than taxpayer) is based on all information of which preparer has any knowledge.

Signature of officer	Date	Title	May the IRS discuss this return with the preparer shown below (see instructions)? ☐ **Yes** ☐ **No**

Paid Preparer's Use Only

Preparer's signature ►	Date	Check if self-employed ☐	Preparer's SSN or PTIN
Firm's name (or yours if self-employed), address, and ZIP code ►		EIN Phone no. ( )	

For Privacy Act and Paperwork Reduction Act Notice, see separate instructions.   Cat. No. 11510H   Form **1120S** (2008)

Small Business Accounting Simplified

Schedule A   Cost of Goods Sold (see instructions)

1	Inventory at beginning of year	**1**
2	Purchases	**2**
3	Cost of labor	**3**
4	Additional section 263A costs *(attach statement)*	**4**
5	Other costs *(attach statement)*	**5**
6	**Total.** Add lines 1 through 5	**6**
7	Inventory at end of year	**7**
8	**Cost of goods sold.** Subtract line 7 from line 6. Enter here and on page 1, line 2	**8**

9a   Check all methods used for valuing closing inventory: *(i)* ☐   Cost as described in Regulations section 1.471-3

    (ii) ☐   Lower of cost or market as described in Regulations section 1.471-4

    (iii) ☐   Other (Specify method used and attach explanation.) ▶ ....

   b   Check if there was a writedown of subnormal goods as described in Regulations section 1.471-2(c) . . . . ▶ ☐

   c   Check if the LIFO inventory method was adopted this tax year for any goods (if checked, attach Form 970) . . . . . . ▶ ☐

   d   If the LIFO inventory method was used for this tax year, enter percentage (or amounts) of closing inventory computed under LIFO   **9d**

   e   If property is produced or acquired for resale, do the rules of section 263A apply to the corporation? . . . . ☐ Yes   ☐ No

   f   Was there any change in determining quantities, cost, or valuations between opening and closing inventory? . . ☐ Yes   ☐ No
     If "Yes," attach explanation.

Schedule B   Other Information (see instructions)

		Yes	No

1   Check accounting method: **a** ☐ Cash   **b** ☐ Accrual   **c** ☐ Other (specify) ▶............................

2   See the instructions and enter the:

   a Business activity ▶ ....   **b** Product or service ▶ ....

3   At the end of the tax year, did the corporation own, directly or indirectly, 50% or more of the voting stock of a domestic corporation? (For rules of attribution, see section 267(c).) If "Yes," attach a statement showing: **(a)** name and employer identification number (EIN), **(b)** percentage owned, and **(c)** if 100% owned, was a QSub election made? . . . .

4   Has this corporation filed, or is it required to file, a return under section 6111 to provide information on any reportable transaction? . . . .

5   Check this box if the corporation issued publicly offered debt instruments with original issue discount . . ▶ ☐
    If checked, the corporation may have to file **Form 8281,** Information Return for Publicly Offered Original Issue Discount Instruments.

6   If the corporation: **(a)** was a C corporation before it elected to be an S corporation **or** the corporation acquired an asset with a basis determined by reference to its basis (or the basis of any other property) in the hands of a C corporation **and (b)** has net unrealized built-in gain (defined in section 1374(d)(1)) in excess of the net recognized built-in gain from prior years, enter the net unrealized built-in gain reduced by net recognized built-in gain from prior years . . . . ▶ $ ....

7   Enter the accumulated earnings and profits of the corporation at the end of the tax year. $ _____

8   Are the corporation's total receipts *(see instructions)* for the tax year **and** its total assets at the end of the tax year less than $250,000? If "Yes," the corporation is not required to complete Schedules L and M-1 . . . .

Schedule K   Shareholders' Pro Rata Share Items

				Total amount

Income (Loss)

1	Ordinary business income (loss) (page 1, line 21)		**1**	
2	Net rental real estate income (loss) *(attach Form 8825)*		**2**	
3a	Other gross rental income (loss)	**3a**		
b	Expenses from other rental activities *(attach statement)* . .	**3b**		
c	Other net rental income (loss). Subtract line 3b from line 3a		**3c**	
4	Interest income		**4**	
5	Dividends: **a** Ordinary dividends		**5a**	
	b Qualified dividends	**5b**		
6	Royalties		**6**	
7	Net short-term capital gain (loss) *(attach Schedule D (Form 1120S))*		**7**	
8a	Net long-term capital gain (loss) *(attach Schedule D (Form 1120S))*		**8a**	
b	Collectibles (28%) gain (loss)	**8b**		
c	Unrecaptured section 1250 gain *(attach statement)* . . .	**8c**		
9	Net section 1231 gain (loss) *(attach Form 4797)*		**9**	
10	Other income (loss) *(see instructions)* . . . Type ▶		**10**	

Form 1120S (2008)   Page **3**

	Shareholders' Pro Rata Share Items (continued)		Total amount	
Deductions	**11** Section 179 deduction *(attach Form 4562)*	**11**		
	12a Contributions	**12a**		
	b Investment interest expense	**12b**		
	c Section 59(e)(2) expenditures **(1)** Type ▶_____ **(2)** Amount ▶	**12c(2)**		
	d Other deductions *(see instructions)* . . . Type ▶	**12d**		
Credits	**13a** Low-income housing credit (section 42(j)(5))	**13a**		
	b Low-income housing credit (other)	**13b**		
	c Qualified rehabilitation expenditures (rental real estate) *(attach Form 3468)*	**13c**		
	d Other rental real estate credits *(see instructions)* Type ▶_____	**13d**		
	e Other rental credits *(see instructions)* . . . Type ▶_____	**13e**		
	f Alcohol and cellulosic biofuel fuels credit *(attach Form 6478)*	**13f**		
	g Other credits *(see instructions)* . . . . . Type ▶	**13g**		
Foreign Transactions	**14a** Name of country or U.S. possession ▶_____			
	b Gross income from all sources	**14b**		
	c Gross income sourced at shareholder level	**14c**		
	Foreign gross income sourced at corporate level			
	d Passive category	**14d**		
	e General category	**14e**		
	f Other *(attach statement)*	**14f**		
	Deductions allocated and apportioned at shareholder level			
	g Interest expense	**14g**		
	h Other	**14h**		
	Deductions allocated and apportioned at corporate level to foreign source income			
	i Passive category	**14i**		
	j General category	**14j**		
	k Other *(attach statement)*	**14k**		
	Other information			
	l Total foreign taxes (check one): ▶ ☐ Paid ☐ Accrued	**14l**		
	m Reduction in taxes available for credit *(attach statement)*	**14m**		
	n Other foreign tax information *(attach statement)*			
Alternative Minimum Tax (AMT) Items	**15a** Post-1986 depreciation adjustment	**15a**		
	b Adjusted gain or loss	**15b**		
	c Depletion (other than oil and gas)	**15c**		
	d Oil, gas, and geothermal properties—gross income	**15d**		
	e Oil, gas, and geothermal properties—deductions	**15e**		
	f Other AMT items *(attach statement)*	**15f**		
Items Affecting Shareholder Basis	**16a** Tax-exempt interest income	**16a**		
	b Other tax-exempt income	**16b**		
	c Nondeductible expenses	**16c**		
	d Property distributions	**16d**		
	e Repayment of loans from shareholders	**16e**		
Other Information	**17a** Investment income	**17a**		
	b Investment expenses	**17b**		
	c Dividend distributions paid from accumulated earnings and profits	**17c**		
	d Other items and amounts *(attach statement)*			
Reconciliation	**18** **Income/loss reconciliation.** Combine the amounts on lines 1 through 10 in the far right column. From the result, subtract the sum of the amounts on lines 11 through 12d and 14l	**18**		

Form **1120S** (2008)

Small Business Accounting Simplified

Schedule L — Balance Sheets per Books

	Beginning of tax year		End of tax year	
Assets	(a)	(b)	(c)	(d)
1 Cash				
2a Trade notes and accounts receivable				
b Less allowance for bad debts	( )		( )	
3 Inventories				
4 U.S. government obligations				
5 Tax-exempt securities (see instructions)				
6 Other current assets (attach statement)				
7 Loans to shareholders				
8 Mortgage and real estate loans				
9 Other investments (attach statement)				
10a Buildings and other depreciable assets				
b Less accumulated depreciation	( )		( )	
11a Depletable assets				
b Less accumulated depletion	( )		( )	
12 Land (net of any amortization)				
13a Intangible assets (amortizable only)				
b Less accumulated amortization	( )		( )	
14 Other assets (attach statement)				
15 Total assets				
Liabilities and Shareholders' Equity				
16 Accounts payable				
17 Mortgages, notes, bonds payable in less than 1 year				
18 Other current liabilities (attach statement)				
19 Loans from shareholders				
20 Mortgages, notes, bonds payable in 1 year or more				
21 Other liabilities (attach statement)				
22 Capital stock				
23 Additional paid-in capital				
24 Retained earnings				
25 Adjustments to shareholders' equity (attach statement)				
26 Less cost of treasury stock		( )		( )
27 Total liabilities and shareholders' equity				

Schedule M-1 — Reconciliation of Income (Loss) per Books With Income (Loss) per Return

Note: Schedule M-3 required instead of Schedule M-1 if total assets are $10 million or more—see instructions

1 Net income (loss) per books		5 Income recorded on books this year not included on Schedule K, lines 1 through 10 (itemize):	
2 Income included on Schedule K, lines 1, 2, 3c, 4, 5a, 6, 7, 8a, 9, and 10, not recorded on books this year (itemize): _____		a Tax-exempt interest $ _____	
3 Expenses recorded on books this year not included on Schedule K, lines 1 through 12 and 14l (itemize):		6 Deductions included on Schedule K, lines 1 through 12 and 14l, not charged against book income this year (itemize):	
a Depreciation $ _____		a Depreciation $ _____	
b Travel and entertainment $ _____			
		7 Add lines 5 and 6	
4 Add lines 1 through 3		8 Income (loss) (Schedule K, line 18). Line 4 less line 7	

Schedule M-2 — Analysis of Accumulated Adjustments Account, Other Adjustments Account, and Shareholders' Undistributed Taxable Income Previously Taxed (see instructions)

	(a) Accumulated adjustments account	(b) Other adjustments account	(c) Shareholders' undistributed taxable income previously taxed
1 Balance at beginning of tax year			
2 Ordinary income from page 1, line 21			
3 Other additions			
4 Loss from page 1, line 21	( )		
5 Other reductions	( )	( )	
6 Combine lines 1 through 5			
7 Distributions other than dividend distributions			
8 Balance at end of tax year. Subtract line 7 from line 6			

Form **1120S** (2008)

Form 1120-W
(WORKSHEET)
Department of the Treasury
Internal Revenue Service

Estimated Tax for Corporations

For calendar year 2009, or tax year beginning .... , 2009, and ending .... , 20 .....

(Keep for the corporation's records—Do not send to the Internal Revenue Service.)

OMB No. 1545-0975

2009

Part I	**Estimated Tax Computation**

1 Taxable income expected for the tax year **1**

Qualified personal service corporations (defined in the instructions), skip lines 2 through 13 and go to line 14. Members of a controlled group, see instructions.

2 Enter the **smaller** of line 1 or $50,000 . . . . **2**

3 Multiply line 2 by 15% **3**

4 Subtract line 2 from line 1 . . . . **4**

5 Enter the **smaller** of line 4 or $25,000 . . . . . . **5**

6 Multiply line 5 by 25% **6**

7 Subtract line 5 from line 4 . . . . **7**

8 Enter the **smaller** of line 7 or $9,925,000 . . . . . **8**

9 Multiply line 8 by 34% **9**

10 Subtract line 8 from line 7 . . . . **10**

11 Multiply line 10 by 35% **11**

12 If line 1 is greater than $100,000, enter the **smaller** of **(a)** 5% of the excess over $100,000 or **(b)** $11,750. Otherwise, enter -0- **12**

13 If line 1 is greater than $15 million, enter the **smaller** of **(a)** 3% of the excess over $15 million or **(b)** $100,000. Otherwise, enter -0- **13**

14 Add lines 3, 6, 9, and 11 through 13. (Qualified personal service corporations, multiply line 1 by 35%.) **14**

15 Alternative tax. If the corporation has qualified timber gain, complete Part II and enter the amount from line 37 here. Otherwise, skip lines 15 and 16 and go to line 17 . . . . **15**

16 Enter smaller of line 14 or line 15 . . . . **16**

17 Alternative minimum tax (see instructions) **17**

18 **Total.** If the corporation has qualified timber gain, add lines 16 and 17. Otherwise, add lines 14 and 17 **18**

19 Tax credits (see instructions) **19**

20 Subtract line 19 from line 18 . . . . **20**

21 Other taxes (see instructions) **21**

22 **Total tax.** Add lines 20 and 21 . . . . **22**

23 Credit for federal tax paid on fuels (see instructions) **23**

24 Subtract line 23 from line 22. **Note:** *If the result is less than $500, the corporation is not required to make estimated tax payments* **24**

25a Enter the tax shown on the corporation's 2008 tax return (see instructions). **Caution:** *If the tax is zero or the tax year was for less than 12 months, skip this line and enter the amount from line 24 on line 25b* **25a**

b Enter the **smaller** of line 24 or line 25a. If the corporation is required to skip line 25a, enter the amount from line 24 . . . . **25b**

		(a)	(b)	(c)	(d)
26	**Installment due dates** (see instructions) . . . . . ▶ **26**				
27	**Required installments.** Enter 25% of line 25b in columns **(a)** through **(d)** unless the corporation uses the annualized income installment method or adjusted seasonal installment method or is a "large corporation" (see instructions) **27**				

For Paperwork Reduction Act Notice, see instructions.   Cat. No. 11525G   Form **1120-W** (2009)

Small Business Accounting Simplified

Part II | **Alternative Tax for Corporations with Qualified Timber Gain.** *Complete Part II **only** if the corporation has qualified timber gain under section 1201(b). Regulated investment companies (RICs), see instructions.*

28	Enter qualified timber gain (as defined in section 1201(b)(2))	**28**
29	Enter net capital gain	**29**
30	Enter the smallest of: (a) the amount on line 28; (b) the amount on line 29; or (c) the amount on Part I, line 1	**30**
31	Multiply line 30 by 15%	**31**
32	Subtract line 29 from Part I, line 1	**32**
33	Enter the tax on line 32 using the same steps used to figure the tax on page 1, Part I, line 14	**33**
34	Add lines 30 and 32	**34**
35	Subtract line 34 from Part I, line 1. If zero or less, enter -0-	**35**
36	Multiply line 35 by 35%	**36**
37	Add lines 31, 33, and 36. Enter here and on Part I, line 15	**37**

Form **1120-W** (2009)

242

Schedule A   Adjusted Seasonal Installment Method and Annualized Income Installment Method
(see instructions)

Part I   **Adjusted Seasonal Installment Method**
(Use this method only if the base period percentage for any 6 consecutive months is at least 70%.)

		(a)	(b)	(c)	(d)
1	Enter taxable income for the following periods:	First 3 months	First 5 months	First 8 months	First 11 months
a	Tax year beginning in 2006. **1a**				
b	Tax year beginning in 2007. **1b**				
c	Tax year beginning in 2008. **1c**				
2	Enter taxable income for each period for the tax year beginning in 2009 (see instructions for the treatment of extraordinary items). **2**				
3	Enter taxable income for the following periods:	First 4 months	First 6 months	First 9 months	Entire year
a	Tax year beginning in 2006. **3a**				
b	Tax year beginning in 2007. **3b**				
c	Tax year beginning in 2008. **3c**				
4	Divide the amount in each column on line 1a by the amount in column (d) on line 3a. **4**				
5	Divide the amount in each column on line 1b by the amount in column (d) on line 3b. **5**				
6	Divide the amount in each column on line 1c by the amount in column (d) on line 3c. **6**				
7	Add lines 4 through 6. **7**				
8	Divide line 7 by 3.0. **8**				
9a	Divide line 2 by line 8. **9a**				
b	Extraordinary items (see instructions). **9b**				
c	Add lines 9a and 9b. **9c**				
10	Figure the tax on the amount on line 9c by following the same steps used to figure the tax on page 1 of Form 1120-W. **10**				
11a	Divide the amount in columns (a) through (c) on line 3a by the amount in column (d) on line 3a. **11a**				
b	Divide the amount in columns (a) through (c) on line 3b by the amount in column (d) on line 3b. **11b**				
c	Divide the amount in columns (a) through (c) on line 3c by the amount in column (d) on line 3c. **11c**				
12	Add lines 11a through 11c. **12**				
13	Divide line 12 by 3.0. **13**				
14	Multiply the amount in columns (a) through (c) of line 10 by the amount in the corresponding column of line 13. In column (d), enter the amount from line 10, column (d). **14**				
15	Enter any alternative minimum tax for each payment period (see instructions). **15**				
16	Enter any other taxes for each payment period (see instructions). **16**				
17	Add lines 14 through 16. **17**				
18	For each period, enter the same type of credits as allowed on page 1, Part I, lines 19 and 23 (see instructions). **18**				
19	Subtract line 18 from line 17. If zero or less, enter -0-. **19**				

Form **1120-W** (2009)

Part II Annualized Income Installment Method

			(a)	(b)	(c)	(d)
			First ____ months	First ____ months	First ____ months	First ____ months
20	Annualization periods (see instructions).	20				
21	Enter taxable income for each annualization period (see instructions for the treatment of extraordinary items).	21				
22	Annualization amounts (see instructions).	22				
23a	Annualized taxable income. Multiply line 21 by line 22.	23a				
b	Extraordinary items (see instructions).	23b				
c	Add lines 23a and 23b.	23c				
24	Figure the tax on the amount in each column on line 23c by following the same steps used to figure the tax on page 1 of Form 1120-W.	24				
25	Enter any alternative minimum tax for each annualization period (see instructions).	25				
26	Enter any other taxes for each annualization period (see instructions).	26				
27	Total tax. Add lines 24 through 26.	27				
28	For each annualization period, enter the same type of credits as allowed on page 1, Part I, lines 19 and 23 (see instructions).	28				
29	Total tax after credits. Subtract line 28 from line 27. If zero or less, enter -0-.	29				
30	Applicable percentage.	30	25%	50%	75%	100%
31	Multiply line 29 by line 30.	31				

Part III Required Installments

			1st installment	2nd installment	3rd installment	4th installment
	Note: *Complete lines 32 through 38 of one column before completing the next column.*					
32	If only Part I or Part II is completed, enter the amount in each column from line 19 **or** line 31. If both parts are completed, enter the **smaller** of the amounts in each column from line 19 or line 31.	32				
33	Add the amounts in all preceding columns of line 38 (see instructions).	33				
34	**Adjusted seasonal or annualized income installments.** Subtract line 33 from line 32. If zero or less, enter -0-.	34				
35	Enter 25% of page 1, Part I, line 25b in each column. (**Note:** *"Large corporations," see the instructions for page 1, Part I, line 27 for the amount to enter.*)	35				
36	Subtract line 38 of the preceding column from line 37 of the preceding column.	36				
37	Add lines 35 and 36.	37				
38	**Required installments.** Enter the **smaller** of line 34 or line 37 here and on page 1, Part I, line 27 (see instructions).	38				

Form **1120-W** (2009)

Form 2553
(Rev. December 2007)
Department of the Treasury
Internal Revenue Service

Election by a Small Business Corporation
(Under section 1362 of the Internal Revenue Code)
► See Parts II and III on page 3 and the separate instructions.
► The corporation can fax this form to the IRS (see separate instructions).

OMB No. 1545-0146

Note. This election to be an S corporation can be accepted only if all the tests are met under **Who May Elect** on page 1 of the instructions; all shareholders have signed the consent statement; an officer has signed below; and the exact name and address of the corporation and other required form information are provided.

Part I **Election Information**

Type or Print

Name (see instructions)	**A** Employer identification number
Number, street, and room or suite no. (If a P.O. box, see instructions.)	**B** Date incorporated
City or town, state, and ZIP code	**C** State of incorporation

D Check the applicable box(es) if the corporation, after applying for the EIN shown in **A** above, changed its ☐ name or ☐ address

E Election is to be effective for tax year beginning (month, day, year) (see instructions) . . . . . ► ___/___/___

Caution. A corporation (entity) making the election for its first tax year in existence will usually enter the beginning date of a short tax year that begins on a date other than January 1.

F Selected tax year:
(1) ☐ Calendar year
(2) ☐ Fiscal year ending (month and day) ► _____
(3) ☐ 52-53-week year ending with reference to the month of December
(4) ☐ 52-53-week year ending with reference to the month of ► _____

If box (2) or (4) is checked, complete Part II

G If more than 100 shareholders are listed for item J (see page 2), check this box if treating members of a family as one shareholder results in no more than 100 shareholders (see test 2 under **Who May Elect** in the instructions) ► ☐

H Name and title of officer or legal representative who the IRS may call for more information | **I** Telephone number of officer or legal representative
( )

If this S corporation election is being filed with Form 1120S, I declare that I had reasonable cause for not filing Form 2553 timely, and if this election is made by an entity eligible to elect to be treated as a corporation, I declare that I also had reasonable cause for not filing an entity classification election timely. See below for my explanation of the reasons the election or elections were not made on time (see instructions).

Sign Here

Under penalties of perjury, I declare that I have examined this election, including accompanying schedules and statements, and to the best of my knowledge and belief, it is true, correct, and complete.

► _____   _____   _____
Signature of officer   Title   Date

For Paperwork Reduction Act Notice, see separate instructions.   Cat. No. 18629R   Form **2553** (Rev. 12-2007)

245

Small Business Accounting Simplified

Part I　Election Information (continued)

J Name and address of each shareholder or former shareholder required to consent to the election. (See the instructions for column K.)	K Shareholders' Consent Statement. Under penalties of perjury, we declare that we consent to the election of the above-named corporation to be an S corporation under section 1362(a) and that we have examined this consent statement, including accompanying schedules and statements, and to the best of our knowledge and belief, it is true, correct, and complete. We understand our consent is binding and may not be withdrawn after the corporation has made a valid election. (Sign and date below.)		L Stock owned or percentage of ownership (see instructions)		M Social security number or employer identification number (see instructions)	N Shareholder's tax year ends (month and day)
	Signature	Date	Number of shares or percentage of ownership	Date(s) acquired		

Form **2553** (Rev. 12-2007)

246

Form 2553 (Rev. 12-2007)   Page **3**

| **Part II** | **Selection of Fiscal Tax Year** (see instructions) |

Note. All corporations using this part must complete item O and item P, Q, or R.

O   Check the applicable box to indicate whether the corporation is:

   1. ☐   A new corporation **adopting** the tax year entered in item F, Part I.

   2. ☐   An existing corporation **retaining** the tax year entered in item F, Part I.

   3. ☐   An existing corporation **changing** to the tax year entered in item F, Part I.

P   Complete item P if the corporation is using the automatic approval provisions of Rev. Proc. 2006-46, 2006-45 I.R.B. 859, to request **(1)** a natural business year (as defined in section 5.07 of Rev. Proc. 2006-46) or **(2)** a year that satisfies the ownership tax year test (as defined in section 5.08 of Rev. Proc. 2006-46). Check the applicable box below to indicate the representation statement the corporation is making.

   1. Natural Business Year ► ☐   I represent that the corporation is adopting, retaining, or changing to a tax year that qualifies as its natural business year (as defined in section 5.07 of Rev. Proc. 2006-46) and has attached a statement showing separately for each month the gross receipts for the most recent 47 months (see instructions). I also represent that the corporation is not precluded by section 4.02 of Rev. Proc. 2006-46 from obtaining automatic approval of such adoption, retention, or change in tax year.

   2. Ownership Tax Year ► ☐   I represent that shareholders (as described in section 5.08 of Rev. Proc. 2006-46) holding more than half of the shares of the stock (as of the first day of the tax year to which the request relates) of the corporation have the same tax year or are concurrently changing to the tax year that the corporation adopts, retains, or changes to per item F, Part I, and that such tax year satisfies the requirement of section 4.01(3) of Rev. Proc. 2006-46. I also represent that the corporation is not precluded by section 4.02 of Rev. Proc. 2006-46 from obtaining automatic approval of such adoption, retention, or change in tax year.

Note. If you do not use item P and the corporation wants a fiscal tax year, complete either item Q or R below. Item Q is used to request a fiscal tax year based on a business purpose and to make a back-up section 444 election. Item R is used to make a regular section 444 election.

Q   Business Purpose—To request a fiscal tax year based on a business purpose, check box Q1. See instructions for details including payment of a user fee. You may also check box Q2 and/or box Q3.

   1. Check here ► ☐   if the fiscal year entered in item F, Part I, is requested under the prior approval provisions of Rev. Proc. 2002-39, 2002-22 I.R.B. 1046. Attach to Form 2553 a statement describing the relevant facts and circumstances and, if applicable, the gross receipts from sales and services necessary to establish a business purpose. See the instructions for details regarding the gross receipts from sales and services. If the IRS proposes to disapprove the requested fiscal year, do you want a conference with the IRS National Office?

   ☐ Yes   ☐ No

   2. Check here ► ☐   to show that the corporation intends to make a back-up section 444 election in the event the corporation's business purpose request is not approved by the IRS. (See instructions for more information.)

   3. Check here ► ☐   to show that the corporation agrees to adopt or change to a tax year ending December 31 if necessary for the IRS to accept this election for S corporation status in the event (1) the corporation's business purpose request is not approved and the corporation makes a back-up section 444 election, but is ultimately not qualified to make a section 444 election, or (2) the corporation's business purpose request is not approved and the corporation did not make a back-up section 444 election.

R   Section 444 Election—To make a section 444 election, check box R1. You may also check box R2.

   1. Check here ► ☐   to show that the corporation will make, if qualified, a section 444 election to have the fiscal tax year shown in item F, Part I. To make the election, you must complete **Form 8716**, Election To Have a Tax Year Other Than a Required Tax Year, and either attach it to Form 2553 or file it separately.

   2. Check here ► ☐   to show that the corporation agrees to adopt or change to a tax year ending December 31 if necessary for the IRS to accept this election for S corporation status in the event the corporation is ultimately not qualified to make a section 444 election.

| **Part III** | **Qualified Subchapter S Trust (QSST) Election Under Section 1361(d)(2)*** |

Income beneficiary's name and address	Social security number
Trust's name and address	Employer identification number

Date on which stock of the corporation was transferred to the trust (month, day, year) . . . . ►   /   /

In order for the trust named above to be a QSST and thus a qualifying shareholder of the S corporation for which this Form 2553 is filed, I hereby make the election under section 1361(d)(2). Under penalties of perjury, I certify that the trust meets the definitional requirements of section 1361(d)(3) and that all other information provided in Part III is true, correct, and complete.

_____   _____

Signature of income beneficiary or signature and title of legal representative or other qualified person making the election   Date

*Use Part III to make the QSST election only if stock of the corporation has been transferred to the trust on or before the date on which the corporation makes its election to be an S corporation. The QSST election must be made and filed separately if stock of the corporation is transferred to the trust **after** the date on which the corporation makes the S election.

♲ Printed on recycled paper   Form **2553** (Rev. 12-2007)

Form **8832**
(Rev. March 2007)
Department of the Treasury
Internal Revenue Service

Entity Classification Election

OMB No. 1545-1516

Type or Print

Name of eligible entity making election

Employer identification number

Number, street, and room or suite no. If a P.O. box, see instructions.

City or town, state, and ZIP code. If a foreign address, enter city, province or state, postal code and country. Follow the country's practice for entering the postal code.

▶ Check if: ☐ Address change

1 Type of election (see instructions):

a ☐ Initial classification by a newly-formed entity. Skip lines 2a and 2b and go to line 3.
b ☐ Change in current classification. Go to line 2a.

2a Has the eligible entity previously filed an entity election that had an effective date within the last 60 months?

☐ **Yes.** Go to line 2b.
☐ **No.** Skip line 2b and go to line 3.

2b Was the eligible entity's prior election for initial classification by a newly formed entity effective on the date of formation?

☐ **Yes.** Go to line 3.
☐ **No.** Stop here. You generally are not currently eligible to make the election (see instructions).

3 Does the eligible entity have more than one owner?

☐ **Yes.** You can elect to be classified as a partnership or an association taxable as a corporation. Skip line 4 and go to line 5.
☐ **No.** You can elect to be classified as an association taxable as a corporation or disregarded as a separate entity. Go to line 4.

4 If the eligible entity has only one owner, provide the following information:

a Name of owner ▶ --
b Identifying number of owner ▶ ---

5 If the eligible entity is owned by one or more affiliated corporations that file a consolidated return, provide the name and employer identification number of the parent corporation:

a Name of parent corporation ▶ --
b Employer identification number ▶ ---

For Paperwork Reduction Act Notice, see instructions.   Cat. No. 22598R   Form **8832** (Rev. 3-2007)

6   Type of entity (see instructions):

a ☐ A domestic eligible entity electing to be classified as an association taxable as a corporation.
b ☐ A domestic eligible entity electing to be classified as a partnership.
c ☐ A domestic eligible entity with a single owner electing to be disregarded as a separate entity.
d ☐ A foreign eligible entity electing to be classified as an association taxable as a corporation.
e ☐ A foreign eligible entity electing to be classified as a partnership.
f ☐ A foreign eligible entity with a single owner electing to be disregarded as a separate entity.

7   If the eligible entity is created or organized in a foreign jurisdiction, provide the foreign country of
organization ▶ . . . .

8   Election is to be effective beginning (month, day, year) (see instructions) . . . . ▶ ___/___/___

9   Name and title of contact person whom the IRS may call for more information | **10** Contact person's telephone number

(   )

Consent Statement and Signature(s) (see instructions)

Under penalties of perjury, I (we) declare that I (we) consent to the election of the above-named entity to be classified as indicated above, and that I (we) have examined this consent statement, and to the best of my (our) knowledge and belief, it is true, correct, and complete. If I am an officer, manager, or member signing for all members of the entity, I further declare that I am authorized to execute this consent statement on their behalf.

Signature(s)	Date	Title

Form **8832** (Rev. 3-2007)

Small Business Accounting Simplified

Form **940 for 2008:** **Employer's Annual Federal Unemployment (FUTA) Tax Return**   850108
Department of the Treasury — Internal Revenue Service

OMB No. 1545-0028

(EIN)
Employer identification number [ ][ ] — [ ][ ][ ][ ][ ][ ]

Name (not your trade name)

Trade name (if any)

Address
Number   Street   Suite or room number

City   State   ZIP code

Type of Return
(Check all that apply.)

- a. Amended
- b. Successor employer
- c. No payments to employees in 2008
- d. Final: Business closed or stopped paying wages

Read the separate instructions before you fill out this form. Please type or print within the boxes.

Part 1: Tell us about your return. If any line does NOT apply, leave it blank.

1   If you were required to pay your state unemployment tax in ...

   1a One state only, write the state abbreviation 1a

   - OR -

   1b More than one state (You are a multi-state employer) . . . . 1b ☐ Check here. Fill out Schedule A.

2   If you paid wages in a state that is subject to CREDIT REDUCTION . . . . 2 ☐ Check here. Fill out Schedule A (Form 940), Part 2.

Part 2: Determine your FUTA tax before adjustments for 2008. If any line does NOT apply, leave it blank.

3   Total payments to all employees   3   .

4   Payments exempt from FUTA tax 4   .

   Check all that apply: 4a ☐ Fringe benefits   4c ☐ Retirement/Pension   4e ☐ Other
                          4b ☐ Group-term life insurance 4d ☐ Dependent care

5   Total of payments made to each employee in excess of $7,000 5   .

6   Subtotal (line 4 + line 5 = line 6)   6   .

7   Total taxable FUTA wages (line 3 – line 6 = line 7)   7   .

8   FUTA tax before adjustments (line 7 × .008 = line 8)   8   .

Part 3: Determine your adjustments. If any line does NOT apply, leave it blank.

9   If ALL of the taxable FUTA wages you paid were excluded from state unemployment tax, multiply line 7 by .054 (line 7 × .054 = line 9). Then go to line 12   9   .

10 If SOME of the taxable FUTA wages you paid were excluded from state unemployment tax, OR you paid ANY state unemployment tax late (after the due date for filing Form 940), fill out the worksheet in the instructions. Enter the amount from line 7 of the worksheet onto line 10 .   10   .

   Skip line 11 for 2008 and go to line 12.

11 If credit reduction applies, enter the amount from line 3 of Schedule A (Form 940) 11   .

Part 4: Determine your FUTA tax and balance due or overpayment for 2008. If any line does NOT apply, leave it blank.

12 Total FUTA tax after adjustments (lines 8 + 9 + 10 + 11 = line 12)   12   .

13 FUTA tax deposited for the year, including any payment applied from a prior year .   13   .

14 Balance due (If line 12 is more than line 13, enter the difference on line 14.)
   - If line 14 is more than $500, you must deposit your tax.
   - If line 14 is $500 or less, you may pay with this return. For more information on how to pay, see the separate instructions   14   .

15 Overpayment (If line 13 is more than line 12, enter the difference on line 15 and check a box below.)   15   .

Check one: ☐ Apply to next return.
           ☐ Send a refund.

▶ You **MUST** fill out both pages of this form and **SIGN** it.

Next ➡

For Privacy Act and Paperwork Reduction Act Notice, see the back of Form 940-V, Payment Voucher.   Cat. No. 11234O   Form **940** (2008)

250

850208

Name (not your trade name)	Employer identification number (EIN)

Part 5: Report your FUTA tax liability by quarter only if line 12 is more than $500. If not, go to Part 6.

16   Report the amount of your FUTA tax liability for each quarter; do NOT enter the amount you deposited. If you had no liability for a quarter, leave the line blank.

16a   **1st quarter** (January 1 – March 31) . . . . **16a** [.   ]

16b   **2nd quarter** (April 1 – June 30) . . . . **16b** [.   ]

16c   **3rd quarter** (July 1 – September 30) . . . . **16c** [.   ]

16d   **4th quarter** (October 1 – December 31) . . . . **16d** [.   ]

17   **Total tax liability for the year** (lines 16a + 16b + 16c + 16d = line 17) **17** [.   ]   **Total must equal line 12.**

Part 6: May we speak with your third-party designee?

Do you want to allow an employee, a paid tax preparer, or another person to discuss this return with the IRS? See the instructions for details.

☐   **Yes.**   Designee's name and phone number [   ]   ( ) –

Select a 5-digit Personal Identification Number (PIN) to use when talking to IRS [ ] [ ] [ ] [ ] [ ]

☐   **No.**

Part 7: Sign here. You MUST fill out both pages of this form and SIGN it.

Under penalties of perjury, I declare that I have examined this return, including accompanying schedules and statements, and to the best of my knowledge and belief, it is true, correct, and complete, and that no part of any payment made to a state unemployment fund claimed as a credit was, or is to be, deducted from the payments made to employees. Declaration of preparer (other than taxpayer) is based on all information of which preparer has any knowledge.

✗ **Sign your name here** [   ]

Print your name here [   ]

Print your title here [   ]

Date   [/   /   ]

Best daytime phone ( ) –

Paid preparer's use only   Check if you are self-employed . . . ☐

Preparer's name	[ ]	Preparer's SSN/PTIN	[ ]
Preparer's signature	[ ]	Date	[/ /]
Firm's name (or yours if self-employed)	[ ]	EIN	[ ]
Address	[ ]	Phone	( ) –
City	[ ] State [ ]	ZIP code	[ ]

Form **940** (2008)

Form 940-V,
Payment Voucher

What Is Form 940-V?

Form 940-V is a transmittal form for your check or money order. Using Form 940-V allows us to process your payment more accurately and efficiently. If you have any balance due of $500 or less on your 2008 Form 940, fill out Form 940-V and send it with your check or money order.

Note. If your balance is more than $500, see *When Must You Deposit Your FUTA Tax?* in the Instructions for Form 940.

How Do You Fill Out Form 940-V?

Type or print clearly.

Box 1. Enter your employer identification number (EIN). Do not enter your social security number (SSN).

Box 2. Enter the amount of your payment. Be sure to put dollars and cents in the appropriate spaces.

Box 3. Enter your business name and complete address exactly as they appear on your Form 940.

How Should You Prepare Your Payment?

- Make your check or money order payable to the *United States Treasury*. Do not send cash.
- On the memo line of your check or money order, write:
  — your EIN,
  — Form 940, and
  — 2008.
- Carefully detach Form 940-V along the dotted line.
- Do not staple your payment to the voucher.
- Mail your 2008 Form 940, your payment, and Form 940-V in the envelope that came with your 2008 Form 940 instruction booklet. If you do not have that envelope, use the table in the Instructions for Form 940 to find the mailing address.

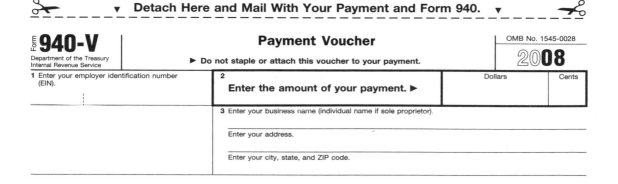

✂ ▼ **Detach Here and Mail With Your Payment and Form 940.** ▼ ✂

Form **940-V**	**Payment Voucher**	OMB No. 1545-0028
Department of the Treasury Internal Revenue Service	▶ Do not staple or attach this voucher to your payment.	20**08**

1 Enter your employer identification number (EIN).	2 Enter the amount of your payment. ▶		Dollars	Cents

3 Enter your business name (individual name if sole proprietor).

Enter your address.

Enter your city, state, and ZIP code.

State Unemployment Tax Agencies

Alabama	(334) 242-8830	www.dir.alabama.gov
Alaska	(888) 448-3527	www.labor.state.ak.us/estax/
Arizona	(602) 771-6601	www.azdes.gov/esa/uitax/uithome.asp
Arkansas	(501) 682-3798	www.state.ar.us/esd
California	(888) 745-3886	www.edd.cahwnet.gov
Colorado	(800) 480-8299	www.coworkforce.com
Connecticut	(860) 263-6550	www.ctdol.state.ct.us
Delaware	(302) 761-8484	www.delawareworks.com
District of Columbia	(202) 698-7550	www.dcnetworks.org
Florida	(800) 482-8293	dor.myflorida.com/dor/uc
Georgia	(404) 232-3301	www.dol.state.ga.us
Hawaii	(808) 586-8913	www.hawaii.gov/labor
Idaho	(800) 448-2977	www.labor.state.id.us
Illinois	(800) 247-4984	www.ides.state.il.us
Indiana	(317) 232-7436	www.in.gov/dwd
Iowa	(515) 281-5339	www.iowaworkforce.org/ui
Kansas	(785) 296-5027	www.dol.ks.gov
Kentucky	(502) 564-2272	www.oet.ky.gov
Louisiana	(225) 342-2944	www.laworks.net/homepage.asp
Maine	(207) 621-5120	www.state.me.us/labor
Maryland	(800) 492-5524	www.dllr.state.md.us
Massachusetts	(617) 626-5050	www.detma.org
Michigan	(313) 456-2180	www.michigan.gov/uia
Minnesota	(651) 296-6141	www.uimn.org/tax
Mississippi	(866) 806-0272	www.mdes.ms.gov
Missouri	(573) 751-3340	www.dolir.mo.gov
Montana	(406) 444-3834	www.uid.dli.mt.gov
Nebraska	(402) 471-9940	www.dol.nebraska.gov
Nevada	(775) 684-6300	https://uitax.nvdetr.org
New Hampshire	(603) 228-4033	www.nhes.state.nh.us
New Jersey	(609) 633-6400	lwd.dol.state.nj.us
New Mexico	(505) 841-8576	www.dws.state.nm.us
New York	(518) 457-4179	www.labor.state.ny.us
North Carolina	(919) 733-7396	www.ncesc.com
North Dakota	(701) 328-2814	www.jobsnd.com
Ohio	(614) 466-2319	www.jfs.ohio.gov
Oklahoma	(405) 557-7143	www.ok.gov/oesc_web
Oregon	(503) 947-1488	www.oregon.gov/employ/tax
Pennsylvania	(717) 787-7679	www.dli.state.pa.us
Puerto Rico	(787) 754-5818	
Rhode Island	(401) 574-8700	www.uitax.ri.gov
South Carolina	(803) 737-3075	www.sces.org/ui
South Dakota	(605) 626-2312	www.state.sd.us
Tennessee	(615) 741-2486	www.state.tn.us/labor-wfd/esdiv.html
Texas	(512) 463-2700	www.twc.state.tx.us
Utah	(801) 526-9400	www.jobs.utah.gov
Vermont	(802) 828-4252	www.labor.vermont.gov
Virgin Islands	(340) 776-1440	www.vidol.gov
Virginia	(804) 371-7159	www.VaEmploy.com
Washington	(360) 902-9360	www.esd.wa.gov/uitax/index.php
West Virginia	(304) 558-2676	www.wvbep.org/bep/uc/
Wisconsin	(608) 261-6700	www.dwd.state.wi.us
Wyoming	(307) 235-3217	wydoe.state.wy.us

Small Business Accounting Simplified

Form 941 for 2009: Employer's QUARTERLY Federal Tax Return

(Rev. April 2009)   Department of the Treasury — Internal Revenue Service

950109

OMB No. 1545-0029

(EIN)
Employer identification number ☐☐☐ — ☐☐☐☐☐☐☐

Name *(not your trade name)*

Trade name *(if any)*

Address

Number   Street   Suite or room number

City   State   ZIP code

Report for this Quarter of 2009
(Check one.)

☐ **1:** January, February, March

☐ **2:** April, May, June

☐ **3:** July, August, September

☐ **4:** October, November, December

Read the separate instructions before you complete Form 941. Type or print within the boxes.

Part 1: Answer these questions for this quarter.

1 Number of employees who received wages, tips, or other compensation for the pay period including: *Mar. 12* (Quarter 1), *June 12* (Quarter 2), *Sept. 12* (Quarter 3), *Dec. 12* (Quarter 4) **1**

2 Wages, tips, and other compensation **2**

3 Income tax withheld from wages, tips, and other compensation **3**

4 If no wages, tips, and other compensation are subject to social security or Medicare tax ☐ Check and go to line 6.

5 Taxable social security and Medicare wages and tips:

Column 1   *Column 2*

5a Taxable social security wages [   ] × .124 = [   ]

5b Taxable social security tips [   ] × .124 = [   ]

5c Taxable Medicare wages & tips [   ] × .029 = [   ]

5d Total social security and Medicare taxes (*Column 2,* lines 5a + 5b + 5c = line 5d) . **5d**

6 **Total taxes before adjustments** (lines 3 + 5d = line 6) **6**

7 CURRENT QUARTER'S ADJUSTMENTS, for example, a fractions of cents adjustment. See the instructions.

7a Current quarter's fractions of cents . . . .

7b Current quarter's sick pay . . . .

7c Current quarter's adjustments for tips and group-term life insurance

7d **TOTAL ADJUSTMENTS.** Combine all amounts on lines 7a through 7c **7d**

8 **Total taxes after adjustments.** Combine lines 6 and 7d **8**

9 Advance earned income credit (EIC) payments made to employees **9**

10 **Total taxes after adjustment for advance EIC** (line 8 – line 9 = line 10) **10**

11 Total deposits for this quarter, including overpayment applied from a prior quarter and overpayment applied from Form 941-X or Form 944-X **11**

12a COBRA premium assistance payments (see instructions) . . . . . .

12b Number of individuals provided COBRA premium assistance reported on line 12a . . . .

13 Add lines 11 and 12a **13**

14 **Balance due.** If line 10 is more than line 13, write the difference here **14**
For information on how to pay, see the instructions.

15 **Overpayment.** If line 13 is more than line 10, write the difference here

☐ Apply to next return.
Check one ☐ Send a refund.

▶ You **MUST** complete both pages of Form 941 and **SIGN** it.

Next ➡

For Privacy Act and Paperwork Reduction Act Notice, see the back of the Payment Voucher.   Cat. No. 17001Z   Form **941** (Rev. 4-2009)

950209

Name *(not your trade name)*	Employer identification number (EIN)

Part 2: Tell us about your deposit schedule and tax liability for this quarter.

If you are unsure about whether you are a monthly schedule depositor or a semiweekly schedule depositor, see *Pub. 15 (Circular E)*, section 11.

16 [ ][ ] **Write the state abbreviation for the state where you made your deposits** OR **write "MU" if you made your deposits in** *multiple* **states.**

17 Check one: [ ] **Line 10 is less than $2,500.** Go to Part 3.

[ ] **You were a monthly schedule depositor for the entire quarter. Enter your tax liability for each month.** Then go to Part 3.

Tax liability: Month 1 [.]

Month 2 [.]

Month 3 [.]

Total liability for quarter [.] **Total must equal line 10.**

[ ] **You were a semiweekly schedule depositor for any part of this quarter.** Complete *Schedule B (Form 941): Report of Tax Liability for Semiweekly Schedule Depositors*, and attach it to Form 941.

Part 3: Tell us about your business. If a question does NOT apply to your business, leave it blank.

18 If your business has closed or you stopped paying wages . . . . [ ] Check here, and

enter the final date you paid wages [/ /] .

19 If you are a seasonal employer and you do not have to file a return for every quarter of the year . . [ ] Check here.

Part 4: May we speak with your third-party designee?

Do you want to allow an employee, a paid tax preparer, or another person to discuss this return with the IRS? See the instructions for details.

[ ] **Yes.** Designee's name and phone number [   ] ( ) –

Select a 5-digit Personal Identification Number (PIN) to use when talking to the IRS. [ ][ ][ ][ ][ ]

[ ] **No.**

Part 5: Sign here. You MUST complete both pages of Form 941 and SIGN it.

Under penalties of perjury, I declare that I have examined this return, including accompanying schedules and statements, and to the best of my knowledge and belief, it is true, correct, and complete. Declaration of preparer (other than taxpayer) is based on all information of which preparer has any knowledge.

X **Sign your name here** [   ]

Print your name here [   ]

Print your title here [   ]

Date [/ /]

Best daytime phone ( ) –

Paid preparer's use only

Check if you are self-employed . . . . [ ]

Preparer's name		Preparer's SSN/PTIN	
Preparer's signature		Date	/ /
Firm's name (or yours if self-employed)		EIN	
Address		Phone	( ) –
City		State	ZIP code

Page **2**

Form **941** (Rev. 4-2009)

255

Form 941-V,
Payment Voucher

Purpose of Form

Complete Form 941-V, Payment Voucher, if you are making a payment with Form 941, Employer's QUARTERLY Federal Tax Return. We will use the completed voucher to credit your payment more promptly and accurately, and to improve our service to you.

If you have your return prepared by a third party and make a payment with that return, please provide this payment voucher to the return preparer.

Making Payments With Form 941

To avoid a penalty, make your payment with Form 941 **only if:**

● Your net taxes for the quarter (line 10 on Form 941) are less than $2,500 and you are paying in full with a timely filed return or

● You are a monthly schedule depositor making a payment in accordance with the Accuracy of Deposits Rule. See section 11 of Pub. 15 (Circular E), Employer's Tax Guide, for details. In this case, the amount of your payment may be $2,500 or more.

Otherwise, you must deposit your payment at an authorized financial institution or by using the Electronic Federal Tax Payment System (EFTPS). See section 11 of Pub. 15 (Circular E) for deposit instructions. Do not use Form 941-V to make federal tax deposits.

Caution. *Use Form 941-V when making any payment with Form 941. However, if you pay an amount with Form 941 that should have been deposited, you may be subject to a penalty. See* Deposit Penalties *in section 11 of Pub. 15 (Circular E).*

Specific Instructions

Box 1—Employer identification number (EIN). If you do not have an EIN, apply for one on Form SS-4, Application for Employer Identification Number, and write "Applied For" and the date you applied in this entry space.

Box 2—Amount paid. Enter the amount paid with Form 941.

Box 3—Tax period. Darken the capsule identifying the quarter for which the payment is made. Darken only one capsule.

Box 4—Name and address. Enter your name and address as shown on Form 941.

● Enclose your check or money order made payable to the "United States Treasury." Be sure to enter your EIN, "Form 941," and the tax period on your check or money order. Do not send cash. Do not staple Form 941-V or your payment to Form 941 (or to each other).

● Detach Form 941-V and send it with your payment and Form 941 to the address in the Instructions for Form 941.

Note. You must also complete the entity information above Part 1 on Form 941.

✂ - - - - - - ▼ **Detach Here and Mail With Your Payment and Form 941.** ▼ - - - - - ✂

Form **941-V** Department of the Treasury Internal Revenue Service	**Payment Voucher** ▶ Do not staple this voucher or your payment to Form 941.	OMB No. 1545-0029 20**09**

1 Enter your employer identification number (EIN).	2 **Enter the amount of your payment.** ▶		Dollars	Cents

3 Tax period		4 Enter your business name (individual name if sole proprietor).

⬭ 1st Quarter	⬭ 3rd Quarter	Enter your address.
⬭ 2nd Quarter	⬭ 4th Quarter	Enter your city, state, and ZIP code.

Do Not Staple 6969

Form **1096**
Department of the Treasury
Internal Revenue Service

**Annual Summary and Transmittal of
U.S. Information Returns**

OMB No. 1545-0108

20**08**

FILER'S name

Street address (including room or suite number)

City, state, and ZIP code

Name of person to contact	Telephone number ( )	**For Official Use Only**
Email address	Fax number ( )	

1 Employer identification number	2 Social security number	3 Total number of forms	4 Federal income tax withheld $	5 Total amount reported with this Form 1096 $

6 Enter an "X" in only one box below to indicate the type of form being filed. | 7 If this is your **final return**, enter an "X" here . . . ▶ ☐

W-2G 32	1098 81	1098-C 78	1098-E 84	1098-T 83	1099-A 80	1099-B 79	1099-C 85	1099-CAP 73	1099-DIV 91	1099-G 86	1099-H 71	1099-INT 92	1099-LTC 93
☐	☐	☐	☐	☐	☐	☐	☐	☐	☐	☐	☐	☐	☐

1099-MISC 95	1099-OID 96	1099-PATR 97	1099-Q 31	1099-R 98	1099-S 75	1099-SA 94	5498 28	5498-ESA 72	5498-SA 27
☐	☐	☐	☐	☐	☐	☐	☐	☐	☐

Return this entire page to the Internal Revenue Service. Photocopies are not acceptable.

9595   ☐ VOID   ☐ CORRECTED

PAYER'S name, street address, city, state, ZIP code, and telephone no.	1 Rents $	OMB No. 1545-0115	**Miscellaneous Income**
	2 Royalties $	20**09** Form **1099-MISC**	
	3 Other income $	4 Federal income tax withheld $	**Copy A** **For Internal Revenue Service Center**
PAYER'S federal identification number RECIPIENT'S identification number	5 Fishing boat proceeds $	6 Medical and health care payments $	**File with Form 1096.**
RECIPIENT'S name	7 Nonemployee compensation $	8 Substitute payments in lieu of dividends or interest $	For Privacy Act and Paperwork Reduction Act
Street address (including apt. no.)	9 Payer made direct sales of $5,000 or more of consumer products to a buyer (recipient) for resale ▶ ☐	10 Crop insurance proceeds $	Notice, see the **2009 General Instructions for Forms 1099,**
City, state, and ZIP code	11	12	**1098, 3921, 3922, 5498, and**
Account number (see instructions) 2nd TIN not. ☐	13 Excess golden parachute payments $	14 Gross proceeds paid to an attorney $	**W-2G.**
15a Section 409A deferrals $	15b Section 409A income $	16 State tax withheld $	17 State/Payer's state no.	18 State income $

Form **1099-MISC**   Cat. No. 14425J   Department of the Treasury - Internal Revenue Service

Do Not Cut or Separate Forms on This Page — Do Not Cut or Separate Forms on This Page

Small Business Accounting Simplified

22222 Void ☐	**a** Employee's social security number	**For Official Use Only** ▶ OMB No. 1545-0008	

b Employer identification number (EIN)	**1** Wages, tips, other compensation	**2** Federal income tax withheld
c Employer's name, address, and ZIP code	**3** Social security wages	**4** Social security tax withheld
	5 Medicare wages and tips	**6** Medicare tax withheld
	7 Social security tips	**8** Allocated tips
d Control number	**9** Advance EIC payment	**10** Dependent care benefits

e Employee's first name and initial	Last name	Suff.	**11** Nonqualified plans	**12a** See instructions for box 12	
			13 Statutory employee ☐ Retirement plan ☐ Third-party sick pay ☐	**12b**	
			14 Other	**12c**	
				12d	
f Employee's address and ZIP code					

15 State	Employer's state ID number	**16** State wages, tips, etc.	**17** State income tax	**18** Local wages, tips, etc.	**19** Local income tax	**20** Locality name

Form **W-2** Wage and Tax Statement   **2009**   Department of the Treasury—Internal Revenue Service

Copy A For Social Security Administration — Send this entire page with Form W-3 to the Social Security Administration; photocopies are **not** acceptable.

For Privacy Act and Paperwork Reduction Act Notice, see back of Copy D.

Cat. No. 10134D

Do Not Cut, Fold, or Staple Forms on This Page — Do Not Cut, Fold, or Staple Forms on This Page

DO NOT STAPLE

33333	**a** Control number	**For Official Use Only** ▶ OMB No. 1545-0008	

b Kind of Payer	941 ☐ Military ☐ 943 ☐ 944 ☐ CT-1 ☐ Hshld. emp. ☐ Medicare govt. emp. ☐ Third-party sick pay ☐	**1** Wages, tips, other compensation	**2** Federal income tax withheld
		3 Social security wages	**4** Social security tax withheld
c Total number of Forms W-2	**d** Establishment number	**5** Medicare wages and tips	**6** Medicare tax withheld
e Employer identification number (EIN)		**7** Social security tips	**8** Allocated tips
f Employer's name		**9** Advance EIC payments	**10** Dependent care benefits
		11 Nonqualified plans	**12** Deferred compensation
		13 For third-party sick pay use only	
		14 Income tax withheld by payer of third-party sick pay	
g Employer's address and ZIP code			
h Other EIN used this year			

15 State	Employer's state ID number	**16** State wages, tips, etc.	**17** State income tax
		18 Local wages, tips, etc.	**19** Local income tax
Contact person		Telephone number ( )	For Official Use Only
Email address		Fax number ( )	

Under penalties of perjury, I declare that I have examined this return and accompanying documents, and, to the best of my knowledge and belief, they are true, correct, and complete.

Signature ▶ _____   Title ▶ _____   Date ▶ _____

Form **W-3** Transmittal of Wage and Tax Statements   **2009**   Department of the Treasury Internal Revenue Service

Form W-4 (2009)

Purpose. Complete Form W-4 so that your employer can withhold the correct federal income tax from your pay. Consider completing a new Form W-4 each year and when your personal or financial situation changes.

Exemption from withholding. If you are exempt, complete **only** lines 1, 2, 3, 4, and 7 and sign the form to validate it. Your exemption for 2009 expires February 16, 2010. See Pub. 505, Tax Withholding and Estimated Tax.

Note. You cannot claim exemption from withholding if (a) your income exceeds $950 and includes more than $300 of unearned income (for example, interest and dividends) and (b) another person can claim you as a dependent on their tax return.

Basic instructions. If you are not exempt, complete the **Personal Allowances Worksheet** below. The worksheets on page 2 further adjust your withholding allowances based on itemized deductions, certain credits, adjustments to income, or two-earner/multiple job situations.

Complete all worksheets that apply. However, you may claim fewer (or zero) allowances. For regular wages, withholding must be based on allowances you claimed and may not be a flat amount or percentage of wages.

Head of household. Generally, you may claim head of household filing status on your tax return only if you are unmarried and pay more than 50% of the costs of keeping up a home for yourself and your dependent(s) or other qualifying individuals. See Pub. 501, Exemptions, Standard Deduction, and Filing Information, for information.

Tax credits. You can take projected tax credits into account in figuring your allowable number of withholding allowances. Credits for child or dependent care expenses and the child tax credit may be claimed using the **Personal Allowances Worksheet** below. See Pub. 919, How Do I Adjust My Tax Withholding, for information on converting your other credits into withholding allowances.

Nonwage income. If you have a large amount of nonwage income, such as interest or

dividends, consider making estimated tax payments using Form 1040-ES, Estimated Tax for Individuals. Otherwise, you may owe additional tax. If you have pension or annuity income, see Pub. 919 to find out if you should adjust your withholding on Form W-4 or W-4P.

Two earners or multiple jobs. If you have a working spouse or more than one job, figure the total number of allowances you are entitled to claim on all jobs using worksheets from only one Form W-4. Your withholding usually will be most accurate when all allowances are claimed on the Form W-4 for the highest paying job and zero allowances are claimed on the others. See Pub. 919 for details.

Nonresident alien. If you are a nonresident alien, see the Instructions for Form 8233 before completing this Form W-4.

Check your withholding. After your Form W-4 takes effect, use Pub. 919 to see how the amount you are having withheld compares to your projected total tax for 2009. See Pub. 919, especially if your earnings exceed $130,000 (Single) or $180,000 (Married).

Personal Allowances Worksheet (Keep for your records.)

A	Enter "1" for **yourself** if no one else can claim you as a dependent	**A** _____
B	Enter "1" if: { ● You are single and have only one job; or ● You are married, have only one job, and your spouse does not work; or ● Your wages from a second job or your spouse's wages (or the total of both) are $1,500 or less. } . .	**B** _____
C	Enter "1" for your **spouse**. But, you may choose to enter "-0-" if you are married and have either a working spouse or more than one job. (Entering "-0-" may help you avoid having too little tax withheld.) . . .	**C** _____
D	Enter number of **dependents** (other than your spouse or yourself) you will claim on your tax return	**D** _____
E	Enter "1" if you will file as **head of household** on your tax return (see conditions under **Head of household** above) .	**E** _____
F	Enter "1" if you have at least $1,800 of **child or dependent care expenses** for which you plan to claim a credit . .	**F** _____
	(**Note. Do not** include child support payments. See Pub. 503, Child and Dependent Care Expenses, for details.)	
G	**Child Tax Credit** (including additional child tax credit). See Pub. 972, Child Tax Credit, for more information.	
	● If your total income will be less than $61,000 ($90,000 if married), enter "2" for each eligible child; then **less** "1" if you have three or more eligible children.	
	● If your total income will be between $61,000 and $84,000 ($90,000 and $119,000 if married), enter "1" for each eligible child plus "1" **additional** if you have six or more eligible children.	**G** _____
H	Add lines A through G and enter total here. (**Note.** This may be different from the number of exemptions you claim on your tax return.) ▶	**H** _____

For accuracy, complete all worksheets that apply.	{	● If you plan to **itemize or claim adjustments to income** and want to reduce your withholding, see the **Deductions and Adjustments Worksheet** on page 2. ● If you have **more than one job** or are **married and you and your spouse both work** and the combined earnings from all jobs exceed $40,000 ($25,000 if married), see the **Two-Earners/Multiple Jobs Worksheet** on page 2 to avoid having too little tax withheld. ● If **neither** of the above situations applies, **stop here** and enter the number from line H on line 5 of Form W-4 below.

- - - - - - - - - - - Cut here and give Form W-4 to your employer. Keep the top part for your records. - - - - - - - - - -

Form **W-4** Department of the Treasury Internal Revenue Service	**Employee's Withholding Allowance Certificate** ▶ Whether you are entitled to claim a certain number of allowances or exemption from withholding is subject to review by the IRS. Your employer may be required to send a copy of this form to the IRS.	OMB No. 1545-0074 20**09**

1 Type or print your first name and middle initial.	Last name	**2 Your social security number**

Home address (number and street or rural route)	**3** ☐ Single ☐ Married ☐ Married, but withhold at higher Single rate. **Note.** If married, but legally separated, or spouse is a nonresident alien, check the "Single" box.
City or town, state, and ZIP code	**4** If your last name differs from that shown on your social security card, check here. You must call 1-800-772-1213 for a replacement card. ▶ ☐

5	Total number of allowances you are claiming (from line **H** above **or** from the applicable worksheet on page 2)	**5** _____
6	Additional amount, if any, you want withheld from each paycheck	**6** $ _____
7	I claim exemption from withholding for 2009, and I certify that I meet **both** of the following conditions for exemption. ● Last year I had a right to a refund of **all** federal income tax withheld because I had **no** tax liability **and** ● This year I expect a refund of **all** federal income tax withheld because I expect to have **no** tax liability. If you meet both conditions, write "Exempt" here . . . . ▶ **7**	

Under penalties of perjury, I declare that I have examined this certificate and to the best of my knowledge and belief, it is true, correct, and complete.

Employee's signature
(Form is not valid unless you sign it.) ▶ _____ Date ▶ _____

8 Employer's name and address (Employer: Complete lines 8 and 10 only if sending to the IRS.)	**9** Office code (optional)	**10** Employer identification number (EIN)

For Privacy Act and Paperwork Reduction Act Notice, see page 2.   Cat. No. 10220Q   Form **W-4** (2009)

Deductions and Adjustments Worksheet

Note. Use this worksheet *only* if you plan to itemize deductions, claim certain credits, adjustments to income, or an additional standard deduction

1	Enter an estimate of your 2009 itemized deductions. These include qualifying home mortgage interest, charitable contributions, state and local taxes, medical expenses in excess of 7.5% of your income, and miscellaneous deductions. (For 2009, you may have to reduce your itemized deductions if your income is over $166,800 ($83,400 if married filing separately). See *Worksheet 2* in Pub. 919 for details.) . .	1 $ _____

2 Enter: $\left\{ \begin{array}{l} \$11,400 \text{ if married filing jointly or qualifying widow(er)} \\ \$ 8,350 \text{ if head of household} \\ \$ 5,700 \text{ if single or married filing separately} \end{array} \right\}$ . . . .   **2** $ _____

3 **Subtract** line 2 from line 1. If zero or less, enter "-0-" . . . .   **3** $ _____
4 Enter an estimate of your 2009 adjustments to income and any additional standard deduction. (Pub. 919) . . . .   **4** $ _____
5 **Add** lines 3 and 4 and enter the total. (Include any amount for credits from *Worksheet 8* in Pub. 919.) . .   **5** $ _____
6 Enter an estimate of your 2009 nonwage income (such as dividends or interest) . . . .   **6** $ _____
7 **Subtract** line 6 from line 5. If zero or less, enter "-0-" . . . .   **7** $ _____
8 **Divide** the amount on line 7 by $3,500 and enter the result here. Drop any fraction . . . . . .   **8** _____
9 Enter the number from the **Personal Allowances Worksheet,** line H, page 1 . . . . . .   **9** _____
10 **Add** lines 8 and 9 and enter the total here. If you plan to use the **Two-Earners/Multiple Jobs Worksheet,** also enter this total on line 1 below. Otherwise, **stop here** and enter this total on Form W-4, line 5, page 1   **10** _____

Two-Earners/Multiple Jobs Worksheet (See *Two earners or multiple jobs* on page 1.)

Note. Use this worksheet *only* if the instructions under line H on page 1 direct you to.

1 Enter the number from line H, page 1 (or from line 10 above if you used the **Deductions and Adjustments Worksheet**)   **1** _____

2 Find the number in **Table 1** below that applies to the **LOWEST** paying job and enter it here. **However,** if you are married filing jointly and wages from the highest paying job are $50,000 or less, do not enter more than "3." . . . .   **2** _____

3 If line 1 is **more than or equal to** line 2, subtract line 2 from line 1. Enter the result here (if zero, enter "-0-") and on Form W-4, line 5, page 1. **Do not** use the rest of this worksheet . . . . .   **3** _____

Note. If line 1 is *less than* line 2, enter "-0-" on Form W-4, line 5, page 1. Complete lines 4–9 below to calculate the additional withholding amount necessary to avoid a year-end tax bill.

4 Enter the number from line 2 of this worksheet . . . .   **4** _____
5 Enter the number from line 1 of this worksheet . . . .   **5** _____
6 **Subtract** line 5 from line 4 . . . .   **6** _____
7 Find the amount in **Table 2** below that applies to the **HIGHEST** paying job and enter it here . . . . .   **7** $ _____
8 **Multiply** line 7 by line 6 and enter the result here. This is the additional annual withholding needed . .   **8** $ _____
9 Divide line 8 by the number of pay periods remaining in 2009. For example, divide by 26 if you are paid every two weeks and you complete this form in December 2008. Enter the result here and on Form W-4, line 6, page 1. This is the additional amount to be withheld from each paycheck . . . .   **9** $ _____

Table 1

Married Filing Jointly		**All Others**	
If wages from **LOWEST** paying job are—	Enter on line 2 above	If wages from **LOWEST** paying job are—	Enter on line 2 above
$0 - $4,500	0	$0 - $6,000	0
4,501 - 9,000	1	6,001 - 12,000	1
9,001 - 18,000	2	12,001 - 19,000	2
18,001 - 22,000	3	19,001 - 26,000	3
22,001 - 26,000	4	26,001 - 35,000	4
26,001 - 32,000	5	35,001 - 50,000	5
32,001 - 38,000	6	50,001 - 65,000	6
38,001 - 46,000	7	65,001 - 80,000	7
46,001 - 55,000	8	80,001 - 90,000	8
55,001 - 60,000	9	90,001 - 120,000	9
60,001 - 65,000	10	120,001 and over	10
65,001 - 75,000	11		
75,001 - 95,000	12		
95,001 - 105,000	13		
105,001 - 120,000	14		
120,001 and over	15		

Table 2

Married Filing Jointly		**All Others**	
If wages from **HIGHEST** paying job are—	Enter on line 7 above	If wages from **HIGHEST** paying job are—	Enter on line 7 above
$0 - $65,000	$550	$0 - $35,000	$550
65,001 - 120,000	910	35,001 - 90,000	910
120,001 - 185,000	1,020	90,001 - 165,000	1,020
185,001 - 330,000	1,200	165,001 - 370,000	1,200
330,001 and over	1,280	370,001 and over	1,280

AMOUNT OF DEPOSIT (Do NOT type, please print.)

DOLLARS · CENTS

MONTH TAX YEAR ENDS →

Darken only one TYPE OF TAX		Darken only one TAX PERIOD
941	945	1st Quarter
1120	1042	2nd Quarter
943	990-T	3rd Quarter
720	990-PF	4th Quarter
CT-1	944	
940		86

EMPLOYER IDENTIFICATION NUMBER →

BANK NAME/ DATE STAMP

IRS USE ONLY

Name _____

Address _____

City _____

State _____ ZIP _____

Telephone number ( )

FOR BANK USE IN MICR ENCODING

Federal Tax Deposit Coupon
Form 8109-B (Rev. 12-2006)

↑ **SEPARATE ALONG THIS LINE AND SUBMIT TO DEPOSITARY WITH PAYMENT** ↑ OMB NO. 1545-0257

What's new. The oval for Form 990-C has been deleted. Form 990-C has been replaced by Form 1120-C, U.S. Income Tax Return for Cooperative Associations. Filers of Form 1120-C must use the 1120 oval when completing Form 8109-B.

The type of tax ovals for the 1120, 1042, and 944 have been moved on the coupon. Read the type of tax to the right of the oval before you darken the oval.

Note. Except for the name, address, and telephone number, entries must be made in pencil. Use soft lead (for example, a #2 pencil) so that the entries can be read more accurately by optical scanning equipment. The name, address, and telephone number may be completed other than by hand. You cannot use photocopies of the coupons to make your deposits. Do not staple, tape, or fold the coupons.

The IRS encourages you to make federal tax deposits using the Electronic Federal Tax Payment System (EFTPS). For more information on EFTPS, go to *www.eftps.gov* or call 1-800-555-4477.

Purpose of form. Use Form 8109-B to make a tax deposit only in the following two situations.

1. You have not yet received your resupply of preprinted deposit coupons (Form 8109).

2. You are a new entity and have already been assigned an employer identification number (EIN), but you have not received your initial supply of preprinted deposit coupons (Form 8109). If you have not received your EIN, see *Exceptions* below.

Note. If you do not receive your resupply of deposit coupons, a deposit is due or you do not receive your initial supply within 5–6 weeks of receipt of your EIN, call 1-800-829-4933.

How to complete the form. Enter your name as shown on your return or other IRS correspondence, address, and EIN in the spaces provided. Do not make a name or address change on this form (see Form 8822, Change of Address). If you are required to file a Form 1120, 1120-C, 990-PF (with net investment income), 990-T, or 2438, enter the month in which your tax year ends in the MONTH TAX YEAR ENDS boxes. For example, if your tax year ends in January, enter 01; if it ends in December, enter 12. Make your entries for EIN and MONTH TAX YEAR ENDS (if applicable) as shown in Amount of deposit below.

Exceptions. If you have applied for an EIN, have not received it, and a deposit must be made, do not use Form 8109-B. Instead, send your payment to the IRS address where you file your return. Make your check or money order payable to the United States Treasury and show on it your name (as shown on Form SS-4, Application for Employer Identification Number), address, kind of tax, period covered, and date you applied for an EIN. Do not use Form 8109-B to deposit delinquent taxes assessed by the IRS. Pay those taxes directly to the IRS. See Pub. 15 (Circular E), Employer's Tax Guide, for information.

Amount of deposit. Enter the amount of the deposit in the space provided. Enter the amount legibly, forming the characters as shown below:

Hand print money amounts without using dollar signs, commas, a decimal point, or leading zeros. If the deposit is for whole dollars only, enter "00" in the CENTS boxes. For example, a deposit of $7,635.22 would be entered like this:

DOLLARS · CENTS

Caution. *Darken only one space for TYPE OF TAX and only one space for TAX PERIOD. Darken the space to the left of the applicable form and tax period. Darkening the wrong space or multiple spaces may delay proper crediting to your account. See below for an explanation of Types of Tax and Marking the Proper Tax Period.*

Types of Tax

Form 941 Employer's QUARTERLY Federal Tax Return (includes Forms 941-M, 941-PR, and 941-SS)

Form 943 Employer's Annual Tax Return for Agricultural Employees

Form 944 Employer's ANNUAL Federal Tax Return (includes Forms 944-PR, 944(SP), and 944-SS)

Form 945 Annual Return of Withheld Federal Income Tax

Form 720 Quarterly Federal Excise Tax Return

Form CT-1 Employer's Annual Railroad Retirement Tax Return

Form 940 Employer's Annual Federal Unemployment (FUTA) Tax Return (includes Form 940-PR)

Form 1120 U.S. Corporation Income Tax Return (includes Form 1120 series of returns, such as new Form 1120-C, and Form 2438)

Form 990-T Exempt Organization Business Income Tax Return

Form 990-PF Return of Private Foundation or Section 4947(a)(1) Nonexempt Charitable Trust Treated as a Private Foundation

Form 1042 Annual Withholding Tax Return for U.S. Source Income of Foreign Persons

Marking the Proper Tax Period

Payroll taxes and withholding. For Forms 941, 940, 943, 944, 945, CT-1, and 1042, if your liability was incurred during:

● January 1 through March 31, darken the 1st quarter space;
● April 1 through June 30, darken the 2nd quarter space;
● July 1 through September 30, darken the 3rd quarter space; and
● October 1 through December 31, darken the 4th quarter space.

Note. If the liability was incurred during one quarter and deposited in another quarter, darken the space for the quarter in which the tax liability was incurred. For example, if the liability was incurred in March and deposited in April, darken the 1st quarter space.

Excise taxes. For Form 720, follow the instructions above for Forms 941, 940, etc. For Form 990-PF, with net investment income, follow the instructions on page 2 for Form 1120, 990-T, and 2438.

Department of the Treasury
Internal Revenue Service

Form **8109-B** (Rev. 12-2006)
Cat. No. 61042S

Glossary

Account: A separate record of an asset, liability, income, or expense of a business.

Accounting: The process for recording, summarizing, and interpreting business financial records.

Accounting method: The method of recording income and expenses for a business; can be either *accrual method* or *cash method*.

Accounting period: A specific time period covered by the financial statements of a business.

Accounting system: Specific system of recordkeeping used to set up accounting records of a business; see also *single-entry* or *double-entry*.

Accounts payable: Money owed by a business to another for goods or services purchased on credit. Money that the business intends to pay to another.

Accounts receivable: Money owed to the business by another for goods or services sold on credit. Money that the business expects to receive.

Accrual method: Accounting method in which all income and expenses are counted when earned or incurred regardless of when the actual cash is received or paid.

Accrued expenses: Expenses that have been incurred but have not yet been paid.

Accrued income: Income that has been earned but has not yet been received.

ACRS: Accelerated Cost Recovery System. Generally, a method of depreciation used for assets purchased between 1980 and 1987.

Aging: The method used to determine how long accounts receivable have been owed to a business.

Assets: Everything that a business owns, including amounts of money that are owed to the business.

Balance sheet: The business financial statement that depicts the financial status of the business on a specific date by summarizing the assets and liabilities of the business.

Balance sheet equation: Assets equals liabilities plus equity or "Equity equals Assets minus liabilities."

Bookkeeping: The actual process of recording the figures in accounting records.

C-corporation: A business entity owned by shareholders that is not an *S-corporation*.

Capital expenses: An expense for the purchase of a fixed asset; an asset with a useful life of over one year. Generally, must be depreciated rather than deducted as a business expense.

Cash: All currency, coins, and checks that a business has on hand or in a bank account.

Cash method: Accounting method in which income and expenses are not counted until the actual cash is received or paid.

Chart of accounts: A listing of the types and numbers of the various accounts that a business uses for its accounting records.

Check register: Running record of checks written, deposits, and other transactions for bank account.

Corporation: A business entity owned by shareholders; may be a *C-* or an *S-type corporation*.

Cost of Goods Sold: The amount that a business has paid for the inventory that it has sold during a specific period. Calculated by adding beginning inventory and additions to inventory and then deducting the ending inventory value.

Credit: In double-entry accounting, an increase in liability or income accounts or a decrease in asset or expense accounts.

Current assets: Cash and any other assets that can be converted to cash or consumed by the business within one year.

Current liabilities: Debts of a business that must be paid within one year.

Current ratio: A method of determining the liquidity of a business. Calculated by dividing current assets by current liabilities.

Debit: In double-entry accounting, a decrease in liability or income accounts or an increase in asset or expense accounts.

Debt: The amount that a business owes to another. Also known as *liability*.

Debt ratio: A method of determining the indebtedness of a business. Calculated by dividing total liabilities by total assets.

Dividends: In a corporation, a proportionate share of the net profits of a business that the board of directors has determined should be paid out to shareholders, rather than held as *retained earnings*.

Double-entry accounting: An accounting system under which each transaction is recorded twice: as a credit and as a debit. A very difficult system of accounting to learn and understand.

Expenses: The costs to a business of producing its income.

Equity: Any debt that a business owes. It is *owner's equity* if owed to the business owners and *liabilities* if owed to others.

FICA: Federal Insurance Contributions Act. Taxes withheld from employees and paid by employers for Social Security and Medicare.

FIFO: First-in, first-out method of accounting for inventory. The inventory value is based on the cost of the latest items purchased.

Financial statements: Reports that summarize the finances of a business; generally a *profit and loss statement* and a *balance sheet*.

Fiscal year: A 12-month accounting period used by a business.

Fiscal year reporting: For income tax purposes, reporting business taxes for any 12-month period that does not end on December 31st of each year.

Fixed assets: Assets of a business that will not be sold or consumed within one year. Generally, fixed assets (other than land) must be depreciated.

FUTA: Federal Unemployment Tax Act. Federal business unemployment taxes.

General journal: In double-entry accounting, used to record all transactions of a business in chronological order. Transactions are then posted (or transferred) to appropriate accounts in general ledger.

General ledger: In double-entry accounting, the central listing of all accounts of a business.

Gross profit: Gross sales minus the cost of goods sold.

Gross sales: The total amount received for goods and services during an accounting period.

Gross wages: Total amount of an employee's compensation before deduction of any taxes or benefits.

Income statement: Financial statement that shows the income and expenses for a business.

Initial capital: The money or property that an owner or owners contribute to starting a business.

Intangible personal property: Generally, property not attached to land and which you cannot hold or touch (for example: copyrights, business goodwill, etc.).

Inventory: Goods that are held by a business for sale to customers.

Invoice: A bill for the sale of goods or services that is sent to the buyer.

Ledgers: Accounting books for a business. Generally, refers to entire set of accounts for a business.

LIFO: Last-in, first-out method of valuing inventory. Total value is based on the cost of the earliest items purchased.

Limited Liability Company: A type of business entity which provides protection from liability for its owner/members.

Liquidity: Ability of a company to convert its assets to cash and meet its obligations with that cash.

Long-term assets: The assets of a business that will be held for over one year. Those assets of a business that are subject to depreciation (except for land).

Long-term liabilities: The debts of a business that will not be due for over one year.

MACRS: Modified Accelerated Cost Recovery System. A method of depreciation for use with assets purchased after January 1, 1987.

Net income: The amount of money that a business has after deducting the cost of goods sold and the cost of all expenses. Also referred to as *net profit*.

Net loss: The amount by which a business has expenses and costs of goods sold greater than income.

Net sales: The value of sales after deducting the cost of goods sold from gross sales.

Net wages: The amount of compensation that an employee will actually be paid after the deductions for taxes and benefits.

Net worth: The value of the owner's share in a business. The value of a business determined by deducting the debts of a business from the assets of a business. Also referred to as *owner's equity*.

Operating margin: Net sales divided by gross sales. The actual profit on goods sold, before deductions for expenses.

Operating statement: Financial statement that shows the income and expenses for a business.

Owner's equity: The value of an owner's share in a business. Also referred to as *capital*.

Partnership: An unincorporated business entity that is owned by two or more persons

Payee: Person or business to whom a payment is made.

Payor: Person or business that makes a payment.

Personal property: All business property other than land and buildings that are attached to the land.

Petty cash fund: A cash fund that is used to pay for minor expenses that cannot be paid by check. Petty cash is not to be used for handling sales revenue. Considered part of cash on hand.

Petty cash register: The sheet for recording petty cash transactions.

Physical inventory: The actual process of counting and valuing the inventory on hand at the end of an accounting period.

Posting: In double-entry accounting, the process of transferring data from journals to ledgers.

Plant assets: Long-term assets of a business. Those business assets that are subject to depreciation (other than land).

Prepaid expenses: Expenses that are paid for before they are used (insurance, rent, etc.).

Profit and loss statement: Financial statement that shows the income and expenses for a business.

Retail price: The price for which a product is sold to the public.

Retained earnings: In a corporation, the portion of the annual profits of a business that are kept and reinvested in the business, rather than paid to shareholders in the form of *dividends*.

Real property: Land and any buildings or improvements that are attached to the land.

Reconciliation: Process of bringing a bank statement into agreement with business check register.

Revenue: Income that a business brings in from the sale of goods or services, or through investments.

S-corporation: A type of business corporation in which all of the expenses and profits are passed through to its shareholders to be taxed in the manner of partnerships.

Salary: Fixed weekly, monthly, or annual compensation for an employee.

Sales: Money brought into a business from the sale of goods or services.

Salvage value: The value of an asset after it has been fully depreciated.

Single-entry accounting: A business recordkeeping system that generally tracks only income and expense accounts. Used generally by small businesses; it is much easier to use and understand than *double-entry accounting*.

Shareholder's equity: In a corporation, the owner's equity of a business divided by the number of outstanding shares.

Sole proprietorship: An unincorporated business entity in which one person owns entire company.

Supplies: Materials used in conducting the day-to-day affairs of a business (as opposed to raw materials used in manufacturing).

Tangible personal property: Property not attached to land that you can hold and touch (for example: machinery, furniture, equipment).

Taxes payable: Total of all taxes due but not yet paid.

Trial balance: In double-entry accounting, a listing of all the balances in the general ledger in order to show that debits and credits balance.

Wages: Hourly compensation paid to employees. As opposed to *salary*.

Wages payable: Total of all wages and salaries due to employees but not yet paid out.

Wholesale price: The cost to a business of goods purchased for later sale to the public.

Working capital: The money available for immediate business operations. Current assets minus current liabilities.

Index

Nova Publishing Company
Small Business and Consumer Legal Books and Software

Legal Toolkit Series

Estate Planning Toolkit	ISBN 13: 978-1-892949-44-8	Book w/CD	$39.95
Business Start-Up Toolkit	ISBN 13: 978-1-892949-43-1	Book w/CD	$39.95
Legal Forms Toolkit	ISBN 13: 978-1-892949-48-6	Book w/CD	$39.95
No-Fault Divorce Toolkit	ISBN 13: 978-1-892949-35-6	Book w/CD	$39.95
Personal Bankruptcy Toolkit	ISBN 13: 978-1-892949-42-4	Book w/CD	$29.95
Will and Living Will Toolkit	ISBN 13: 978-1-892949-47-9	Book w/CD	$29.95

Law Made Simple Series

Advance Health Care Directives	ISBN 13: 978-1-892949-23-3	Book w/CD	$24.95
Living Trusts Simplified	ISBN 0-935755-51-9	Book w/CD	$28.95
Personal Legal Forms Simplified (3rd Edition)	ISBN 0-935755-97-7	Book w/CD	$28.95
Powers of Attorney Simplified	ISBN 13: 978-1-892949-40-0	Book w/CD	$24.95

Small Business Made Simple Series

Corporation: Small Business Start-up Kit (2nd Edition)	ISBN 1-892949-06-7	Book w/CD	$29.95
Employer Legal Forms	ISBN 13: 978-1-892949-26-4	Book w/CD	$24.95
Landlord Legal Forms	ISBN 13: 978-1-892949-24-0	Book w/CD	$24.95
Limited Liability Company: Start-up Kit (3rd Edition)	ISBN 13: 978-1-892949-37-0	Book w/CD	$29.95
Partnership: Start-up Kit (2nd Edition)	ISBN 1-892949-07-5	Book w/CD	$29.95
Real Estate Forms Simplified (2nd Edition)	ISBN 13: 978-1-892949-49-3	Book w/CD	$29.95
S-Corporation: Small Business Start-up Kit (3rd Edition)	ISBN 13: 978-1-892949-36-3	Book w/CD	$29.95
Small Business Accounting Simplified (5th Edition)	ISBN 13: 978-1-892949-50-9	Book w/CD	$29.95
Small Business Bookkeeping System Simplified	ISBN 0-935755-74-8	Book only	$14.95
Small Business Legal Forms Simplified (4th Edition)	ISBN 0-935755-98-5	Book w/CD	$29.95
Small Business Payroll System Simplified	ISBN 0-935755-55-1	Book only	$14.95
Sole Proprietorship: Start-up Kit (2nd Edition)	ISBN 1-892949-08-3	Book w/CD	$29.95

Legal Self-Help Series

Divorce Yourself: The National Divorce Kit (6th Edition)	ISBN 1-892949-12-1	Book w/CD	$39.95
Prepare Your Own Will: The National Will Kit (6th Edition)	ISBN 1-892949-15-6	Book w/CD	$29.95

National Legal Kits

Simplified Divorce Kit (3rd Edition)	ISBN 13: 978-1-892949-39-4	Book w/CD	$19.95
Simplified Family Legal Forms Kit (2nd Edition)	ISBN 13: 978-1-892949-41-7	Bookw/CD	$19.95
Simplified Incorporation Kit	ISBN 1-892949-33-4	Book w/CD	$19.95
Simplified Limited Liability Company Kit	ISBN 1-892949-32-6	Book w/CD	$19.95
Simplified Living Will Kit (2nd Edition)	ISBN 13: 978-1-892949-45-5	Book w/CD	$19.95
Simplified S-Corporation Kit	ISBN 1-892949-31-8	Book w/CD	$19.95
Simplified Will Kit (3rd Edition)	ISBN 1-892949-38-5	Book w/CD	$19.95

Ordering Information

Distributed by:
National Book Network
4501 Forbes Blvd. Suite 200
Lanham MD 20706

Shipping: $4.50 for first & $.75 for additionall
Phone orders with Visa/MC: (800) 462-6420
Fax orders with Visa/MC: (800) 338-4550
Internet: www.novapublishing.com
Free shipping on all internet orders (within in the U.S.)